COMPUTERS AND PEOPLE

(A series of publications intended to inform members of the general public about aspects of computers and their use which may be of interest to them.)

Computers and the Year 2000

Although partly about the future this book is primarily concerned with the action needed today. The applications of computer techniques are increasingly shaping our lives and the way that this process takes place is dependent on decisions made today.

This is not a technical book but should be of interest to all concerned about our future. It deals with the general background and the worlds of government, industry and human values. Despite its non-technical nature, it is not intended exclusively for the layman but also for the computer professional.

Other titles in the series:

Working with Computers: a guide to jobs and careers

Privacy, Computers and You

Factfinder 12: Computer Courses

THE NATIONAL COMPUTING CENTRE LIMITED

The National Computing Centre Limited is a non-profit organisation financed by industry, commerce and government. It is dedicated to promoting the wider and more effective use of computers throughout the economy. In realising its objectives the Centre

gives *information* and *advice*

provides *education* and *training*

promotes *standards* and *codes of practice*

co-operates with, and *co-ordinates* the work of, other organisations concerned with computers and their use.

Any interested company, organisation, or individual can benefit from the work of the centre by subscribing as a member. Throughout the country facilities are provided for members to participate in working parties, study groups and discussions and to influence NCC policy. A regular Journal — 'NCC Interface' — keeps members informed of new developments and NCC activities. Special facilities are offered for courses, training material, publications and software packages.

For further details, get in touch with the Centre at Quay House, Quay Street Manchester M3 3HU. Telephone: 061-832 9731

or at one of the following regional offices

Belfast	1st Floor 117 Lisburn Road BT9 7BP	Glasgow	Claremont House North Claremont Street C3
Telephone: 0232 665997		Telephone: 041-332 0117	
Birmingham	Prudential Buildings St. Philip's Place Colmore Row B32 PL	London	Audrey House Ely Place EC1
Telephone: 021-236 7149		Telephone: 01-242 1044	
Bristol	Royal Exchange Building 6th Floor, 41 Corn Street BS1 1HG		
Telephone: Bristol 27077			

COMPUTERS AND PEOPLE

Computers
and the Year 2000

edited by
Lord AVEBURY
RON COVERSON
JOHN HUMPHRIES
BRIAN MEEK

PUBLISHED BY NCC PUBLICATIONS

US Library of Congress Catalogue No: **72-97124**

I SBN 85012 074 8

This book is set in Times Roman Series
by Wright's (Sandbach) Limited,
Sandbach, Cheshire, England

Foreword

It is very rare indeed for a book to be published upon a comparatively new technology, and one that is inevitably bound to bring about a profound change in the lives of people and the world in which we live, and for it to be equally intelligible and interesting both to the layman and the technocrat.

That this book achieves that desirable objective is because those who have contributed to its pages have been concerned to deal not with the technology of the computer itself but with the impact of the use of the computer upon the lives of people and indeed their very existence.

If the world is to disappear in a nuclear catastrophe, it will be a computer that will have worked out the day and the time and the place.

If the lives of people are to be saved by those whose condition means hospitalization in intensive care units, the computer will play a major role in so doing.

The computer may also be the means of circumventing the horrors of a nuclear explosion, just as it may well be the instrument by which road, rail and air accidents may be prevented.

Its application as a tool of management can help to bring greater rewards for human effort.

Indeed there is no field of human activity in which the computer cannot play a part.

Because of the fantastic speed of change, the computer will be called upon to perform in an ever increasing degree.

Because of that, this book performs the useful service of widening our own horizons of knowledge upon a subject which to so many people is a mystery.

As these pages unfold, the curtains are quietly drawn back to reveal the computer for what it is, a unique piece of equipment with which we are going to live for the rest of our lives.

ROBENS OF WOLDINGHAM

Contents

Preface

This book has had its origins in a conference on "Computers and the Year 2000" held in London in 1971. The conference was organised by Ron Coverson on behalf of the Liberal Computer Study Group and sponsored by the Science and Technology Panel of the Liberal Party. Some parts of this book are based on papers written for this conference (details are given in the "Acknowledgements" which follow) but these have been completely rewritten and much of the content is new. It must be made clear that despite its sponsorship this was a non-political conference, and that presentation of papers at the conference or subsequent authorship of parts of this book by no means implies that the person concerned necessarily supports or is sympathetic towards the Liberal Party. We hope that the fact of its publication by the National Computing Centre is sufficient indication of the absence of party political bias. It should also be stressed that every contributor is writing in his personal capacity and not as a representative of the organisation which employs him.

Multi-author works inevitably suffer to some extent from unevenness of content and style. In order to minimise this unevenness the authors have agreed to a quite exceptional degree of editing of their original drafts, even to the extent on occasion of substantial changes of content or approach. The editors would like to thank them for their co-operation in this, and hope that it will be agreed that the main objective, to make the book as far as possible readable as a continuous narrative, has been achieved. The Editors, of course, accept complete responsibility for the remaining shortcomings.

A note on the sharing of editorial duties is in order. John Humphries has acted in a consultant capacity from the National Computing Centre, as well as guiding the volume through the production stages. Ron Coverson conceived the original idea and defined the scope and approach of the original conference and therefore the book also; he recruited most of the authors and commissioned the papers on which a number of chapters are based, and, since the conference, has been mainly involved with content

Lord Avebury has been mainly concerned with the political aspects of computer development. Brian Meek has been mainly responsible for co-ordination, and for continuity of argument and style. However, these divisions have not been rigid and each of the four editors has made some contribution to each of these various aspects.

Considerable numbers of people not listed as contributors or mentioned in the acknowledgements have helped to bring this book into existence, notably those who participated in the original conference, and members of staff of the National Computing Centre. These are too numerous to mention individually; however, our special thanks must go to Miss Pamela Thompson of the Computer Unit, Queen Elizabeth College, London University, who dealt with the very substantial amount of correspondence and other secretarial work involved in the editorial process.

Lord AVEBURY
RON COVERSON
JOHN HUMPHRIES
BRIAN MEEK

September 1972

Full list of Contributors

Introduction: BRIAN MEEK

Part One

Chapter 1: Dr. STANLEY GILL
Chapter 2: CHARLES ROSS
Chapter 3: Prof. F. H. GEORGE

Part Two

Chapter 4: ROGER FORD
Chapter 5: JOHN HARGREAVES, BRIAN MEEK,
LAWRY FREEDMAN (see Note 1)
Chapter 6: Prof. JOHN ANDERSON
Chapter 7: BRIAN MEEK
Chapter 8: K. H. M. NOBLE (see Note 2)

Part Three

Chapter 9: Prof. I. M. KHABAZA, R. C. COLVILL (see Note 3)
Chapter 10: COLIN HORN
Chapter 11: E. J. FISHER
Chapter 12: PHILIP VINCE
Chapter 13: BRIAN M. MURPHY
Chapter 14: BRIAN MEEK

Part Four

Chapter 15: BRIAN MEEK
Chapter 16: ALAN MAYNE
Chapter 17: BRIAN MEEK, PHILIP VINCE
Chapter 18: CLIVE PAYNE
Chapter 19: ROGER FORD
Chapter 20: L. E. MALLETT

Part Five

Chapter 21: Lord AVEBURY
Chapter 22: BRIAN MEEK

Notes

1. Chapter 5 was written by Brian Meek largely on the basis of a conference paper (see Preface) by John Hargreaves, but drawing on another conference paper by Lawry Freedman on "Computers and the arms race".

2. Brian Meek is responsible for the form of Chapter 8 as it appears in the text; K. H. M. Noble wrote the original draft, but due to mischance did not receive the edited version in time to revise the text.

3. Professor Khabaza and Mr. Colvill both wrote conference papers, on "Multiaccess" and "Printing and publishing" respectively. Both were used in the preparation of Chapter 9.

Biographical notes

Prof. JOHN ANDERSON is Professor of Medicine at King's College Hospital Medical School, London.

Lord AVEBURY is Chairman of Digico Ltd.; as Eric Lubbock he was M.P. for Orpington from 1962 to 1970.

R. C. COLVILL is a marketing staff professional with a leading international computer manufacturer.

RON COVERSON is an applications programmer, a member of Abbey National Building Society's Systems and Methods Department.

E. J. FISHER is a senior systems analyst with British Aircraft Corporation Ltd.

ROGER FORD is a management consultant with twelve years' experience in the computer industry, particularly in real-time information handling.

LAWRY FREEDMAN is a postgraduate student of politics at the University of York.

Prof. F. H. GEORGE is head of the Department of Cybernetics at Brunel University and Chairman of the Bureau of Information Science, and has written many books, the best-known of which is *The Brain as a Computer*.

Dr. STANLEY GILL is a software consultant and formerly Professor of Computer Science at Imperial College London; he was President of the British Computer Society 1967-68.

JOHN HARGREAVES is Director of Public Affairs for IBM United Kingdom Ltd., with broad responsibility for the political and social impact of technology on society.

COLIN HORN is a professional banker in one of the London Clearing Banks who for ten years has been engaged on organisational work and the development of data processing.

Prof. I. M. KHABAZA is Director of the Computer Centre and head of the Department of Computer Science and Statistics at Queen Mary College, London.

L. E. MALLETT is a barrister working in the legal department of ICL, and a member of the British Computer Society Committee on Privacy and Public Welfare which gave written and oral evidence to the Younger Committee.

ALAN MAYNE works at the Research Group in Traffic Studies, University College, London, and is also co-chairman of SPUR (Study Panel for Unified Research).

BRIAN MEEK is Director of the Computer Unit at Queen Elizabeth College, London.

BRIAN M. MURPHY, Controller of Public Affairs at ICL, came late to computers after service as a regular soldier; he has specialised in the effects of computers upon society and in government computer policy in Britain and Europe.

K. H. M. NOBLE, a senior consultant with Computer Analysts and Programmers Ltd. at the time Chapter 8 was written, is now a departmental manager at ICL.

CLIVE PAYNE is Director of the Research Services Unit at Nuffield College, Oxford.

CHARLES ROSS is a director of five independent companies in the computing software and services industries and is a member of the Council of the British Computer Society and the Real Time Club.

PHILIP VINCE is Systems Engineering Manager at IBM United Kingdom Ltd.

Acknowledgements

Chapters 1, 4, 5, 6, 7, 9, 10, 11, 12, 13, 15, 16 and 20 are all based in whole or in part on working papers or presentations at the conference mentioned in the preface.

We are grateful to J. M. MacLeod of C.A.P. Ltd. for his assistance with Chapter 8.

The closing paragraphs of Chapter 15 are substantially based on part of the pamphlet "Computers in a world of change" by John Hargreaves; we are grateful to Mr. Hargreaves for his permission to use it in this way.

The authors of Chapter 17 drew on a conference paper by Alan Mayne; the comment about domestic equipment was made at the conference by Mrs. Marilyn Coverson.

We are grateful to numerous authors for supplying items for the bibliography.

Introduction:
Thirty Years

This is a book about the future — the immediate future, extending over about the next thirty years. Thus it is concerned with the whole period between the present and the year 2000 of its title, rather than with that year in particular. Specifically, it is a book about those aspects of that period which will be affected by computers or computer techniques. It is not the first such book, nor is it likely to be the last; and, since the number of these books is already considerable, it is appropriate to begin by explaining the particular approach we have adopted, for comparison with past and future attempts to deal with the same subject.

Firstly, although this book is about computers, and has been written by people specialising in or concerned with computers, it is not a technical book. A general understanding of what computers are and what they do is assumed, but no more than can be obtained by watching television documentaries or reading newspaper articles about computers; technical terms have been kept to the minimum necessary to avoid tedious repetition or circumlocution, and to be on the safe side a glossary of computer terminology used in the text has been appended. On the other hand, it is not just a "general interest" text, to be read as background information or out of casual curiosity as one might read a book about what a foreign country is like or how telephones work or the way the chemical industry operates. This book is intended to provoke thought, and preferably also action; it is therefore, despite its non-technical nature, not intended exclusively for the layman, but also for the computer professional.

Secondly, despite its concern with the future, the main purpose of the book is not to make predictions, though some predictive element is unavoidable. It is not an exercise in crystal-gazing or (to use a currently fashionable neologism) futurology — which, if the difference is of any importance, is crystal-gazing with a substratum of scientific method.

There are two principal reasons for this, which it is perhaps as well to make clear.

The less important reason is the sheer difficulty of making predictions. This is so much a truism as to be in itself meaningless; most prediction is difficult, but this has not noticeably inhibited people from attempting it, even on some occasions with success. But prediction in this area is especially difficult, and here in turn two main factors are involved. One is the nature of the modern world. A hundred years ago, someone looking forward to the end of his century may well have had great difficulty in predicting what would happen, but at least would have been reasonably certain that the world would still be in existence roughly as he knew it, that food would be produced, raw materials exploited and so on, even if he thought that the political organisation of the world might have altered dramatically, or that some scientific advance might have transformed the way that people lived.

But in the twentieth century we are no longer so fortunate. If the world does manage to avoid the nuclear catastrophe, or at least postpone it to the twenty-first century, it may still fail to avoid an environmental-cum-population catastrophe; and a look at the world's leaders, both major and minor, inevitably leads any intelligent person to view the chances of escaping either disaster, let alone both, with profound pessimism. Even without these factors, the sheer complexity of the modern world tends to defeat the would-be forecaster, particularly if economic factors are involved; economics is demonstrably an area of human affairs where enormous academic effort has failed almost totally to reduce it to any kind of rationality, even to allow reliable short-term predictions, and as far as long-term predictions are concerned it must approximate very closely to that ultimate scholastic democracy wherein the uninformed hunch stands as good a chance of being right as the expert assessment.

The other factor which makes prediction particularly difficult is related to the complexity mentioned above, namely the sheer pace of technological advance, especially in the field which mainly concerns us. Since this is adequately brought out in Part One, which surveys the technical and historical background to the subsequent discussion, there is no need to discuss this in detail immediately; however, the point should be made that a high proportion of the advances in computer techniques which the main body of the work discusses are ones which have been developed already, ones which are currently being developed, or at least ones which are currently projected and which there is little reason to doubt are technically feasible. Thus the book is based for the most part on what the authors believe will be possible, rather than on what might be possible; indeed, if the primary purpose of the book had been to predict, it could have been argued that the predictions would be based firmly on current knowledge, though it might have been necessary to admit that in consequence they could err greatly on the conservative side.

This brings us to the second and more important reason why this is not principally a book of forecasts. Although we are concerned with computer techniques, and what these techniques are capable of, the way in which they are exploited will depend not only on such technical factors, but on human decisions, conscious or unconscious, about whether and to what extent and in what manner to put them to use. In a predictive exercise, this just adds to the difficulties; in a multi-author book like this one it might be possible to reach agreement on technical forecasts, but much harder to do so on how the techniques ought to be exploited (except in terms so general as to be valueless, e.g. "for the benefit of mankind"), and virtually impossible to do so on what is likely in actuality to happen. More to the point, discussion of the issues, the possible decisions and the likely outcomes itself tends to alter the situation, and hence to affect the decisions themselves. The observer is not, in matters like these, external to the scene he is observing, and the act of observation changes what is observed; in the hazardous world of political prediction (for it is politics, in the widest sense, we are talking about) there are many examples of self-fulfilling prophecies — or, for that matter, self-defeating ones.

But however the authors of this book are divided on other issues (and we have not made any special effort to discover what differences there are), they are united on this: that applications of computer techniques will come more and more to shape our lives, for good or ill; that the way this process will occur is not inevitable, but will be significantly dependent on human decisions; and that the possible consequences of these decisions are so far-reaching that every effort must be made to foresee the problems that will arise, so that these decisions will be taken consciously and in good time — not by accident, because the problem was not noticed until it was too late, or in a panic, because the problem was ignored until the eleventh hour. The purpose of this book, therefore, is to try to identify places where problems may arise, in particular those where important choices with potentially significant consequences will be open. As mentioned above, an element of prediction is unavoidable; but the primary aim is to detect where and how the future might be influenced. The emphasis is not on the predictions as such, but on the need for decisions to be made consciously; we are concerned with possibilities, not estimates of probabilities.

What worries us most is that decisions may be made by default. The job of detecting the problems is one largely for the computer professional, and there are many examples in the past of professionals not looking far enough forward into the consequences of an innovation, or of their making only glib and superficial estimates of its effects. It is therefore worth while to impress upon them both the need to look ahead, and to inform those whose job it is to make the decisions (who will often not be computer people) of what their options are and of how important the choice of the best course of action may be. However, the final responsibility will rest with those decisionmakers, and again there are plenty of examples (particularly where technical innovation is concerned) of decisions not being taken in time, either because the problem was not recognised, or because it was recognised but it was considered that "for the time being no action is called for but the situation should be kept under review." All too often such an attitude is no more than a rationalisation of the hope that the problem either will go away altogether or at least, when it becomes too urgent to put off any longer, will turn out to be the responsibility not of that decisionmaker but of someone else. The trouble with the "pragmatic" approach of "keeping one's options open" — which is little more than this kind of indecision raised to the level of a guiding principle — is that, by the time the decision is finally taken, most of the options have been closed by the chance of circumstance or the decisions of others.

Hence it is to the decisionmakers, and the computer professionals who will advise them, that this book is mainly addressed. The timescale has been chosen because it seems as far as one can reasonably expect to look ahead even in the most general terms; the year 2000 is a convenient and evocative peg on which to hang the discussion, but no more than that, and we have made no attempt to apply it as a rigid deadline any more than we wish to claim the precision that the use of 2000 rather than 1999 or 2001 might imply. It has also been chosen because, in our view, thirty or so years is about the period over which most of the major decisions affecting the large-scale exploitation of computers will have to be taken. By the year 2000 we expect that the pattern will largely be set, because so much capital will have been invested, and so many customs will have become established. And, if this still seems plenty of time, it should not be forgotten that virtually all with an important part to play are already alive today, most will at least be at school, many are already working, and some are already in responsible positions and capable of influencing events. Even those in top positions today, who will be retired long before many of the things we shall describe actually come about, have some role to play, if only by the way that they groom their eventual successors.

So to our theme. In Part One we shall describe the background — the computer scene as it has developed so far, and the basic matters of technical capability. (Incidentally, we shall show how some decisions *have already been* taken which will significantly affect future developments, and how easy it is to "decide by default".) Parts Two and Three consider the worlds of government and of non-governmental organisation respectively. Part Four looks at the possible impact on human beings and their lives — both the way the decisions as to computer exploitation could affect them, and the decisions open to them as individuals. Finally, in Part Five we return to the general theme, sum up, and try to draw together some conclusions about the kinds of problems that the decisionmakers of the remaining years of this century will have to face.

1 The background

1   Setting the scene

One might sum up the present image of computers in the minds of the British public thus:

> "Computers are clever but unreliable devices, prone to printing incorrect bills and sending them to the wrong addresses, but nevertheless they are a good thing because they increase productivity, and it is therefore right and proper that the British Government has rescued the British Computer Industry from imminent domination by foreign firms."

There is also in the United Kingdom a private view, not often expressed but tenaciously held by a significant proportion of top civil servants and businessmen:

> "Computers are the expensive toys of an arrogant and self-centred band of young people who are trying to get power for themselves by using their technical knowledge to confuse their elders and betters."

Both of these views contain a grain of truth, but both also betray an appalling ignorance of the real nature of computers. This gap between the facts about computers and the widely held views of them is perhaps the most alarming aspect of the present situation, and while it would be impolite to suggest that similar attitudes are necessarily so entrenched in other countries, lack of understanding of computers and their potentialities is certainly widespread. There is little sign at the moment, at least in the United Kingdom, that it is getting any better, and it probably accounts in large measure for that country's failure to grasp the opportunities which it has had.

The instinctive mandarin reaction there has been to give the subject as little attention as possible and to hope that it goes away. But this reaction has been self-defeating. The net result is simply that the arrogant young technologists who finally succeed in raping the Establishment are American rather than British.

In a book concerned with decision-making about the exploitation of computers, it is worth looking in some detail at that failure — probably the biggest failure in the short history of computing to date, and a perfect example of decision by default. To do this, we must go back to the beginning of computing as we know it today.

The Golden Age of computing was the quinquennium from 1945 to 1950. There had been important developments before this: the work of Babbage in the second quarter of the nineteenth century, the gradual development of mechanical desk calculators from that time onwards, the introduction of punched cards at the end of the century, and several others. But it was in 1945 that the first true electronic computer was built: the ENIAC (Electronic Numerical Integrator and Calculator) at the Moore School of Electrical Engineering in Philadelphia, USA, a product of the wartime boom in electronics and of the urgent load of computing for defence purposes.

The ENIAC was completed and worked early in 1946 (surprisingly, because with 18,000 tubes it was far larger than any other electronic device in existence) but, in design, it was already obsolete. It was the electronic equivalent of the mechanical decimal-wheel type of calculator, and the circuits that simulated the revolving wheels and so performed the operations of addition and subtraction were also the machine's only means of retaining or "remembering" numbers. It was already realised that for effective high speed computing a large internal "memory" was essential, and that the way to provide this was through a special unit designed for this purpose.

Immediately after the Second World War teams set to work in several countries, especially the USA and the UK, to produce these "memory units" or "stores". Two types were in vogue: the mercury delay line (adopted by Cambridge University and the National Physical Laboratory) and the electrostatic store (developed at the Telecommunications Research Establishment and the University of Manchester). F. C. Williams, working with T. Kilburn at Manchester, made the first successful electrostatic store which became known throughout the world as the "Williams memory" and was adopted by IBM on some of its early machines.

The availability of stores provided designers with a neat solution to another problem that also confronted them: the problem of instructing the machine what operations to perform. ENIAC had required a vast array of plugged connections to be set up for each job, so arranged that each unit would be triggered into action at the right moment by a pulse from another unit that had just operated. With a store, all this plugging could be replaced by coded instructions loaded in the store. The extra convenience and flexibility thus obtained added immensely to the power and versatility of the electronic computer. From that time onwards, almost all electronic computers were of the "stored program" type (with the exception of analogue-type machines used in some scientific and technical applications, and the very small desk-top machines developed in the last decade for personal use).

The first two stored program machines in the world to operate were those at the Universities of Manchester and Cambridge, in England, which were working early in 1949. The Manchester machine led to the successful Ferranti "Mark I" series, the second of which became the first electronic computer to be exported; it was installed at the University of Toronto in 1952. The Cambridge machine, the EDSAC, became the first to be put to regular use; it was here that the principles of programming were explored in practice for the first time, and Cambridge became a centre of pilgrimage for computer scientists from all over the world between 1949 and 1953. It was on the EDSAC that J. Lyons & Co. based their own machine LEO ("Lyons' Electronic Office") which they built themselves in 1951, and which proved the practicability of electronic data processing in business a decade ahead of its general acceptance.

Meanwhile, in the United States similar developments followed swiftly. A machine called the Univac was being built in 1949 by the Eckert-Mauchly Computer Corporation, founded by J. P. Eckert and J. W. Mauchly who had worked together in the ENIAC team. The design of the Univac was bold and daring: it was oriented plainly towards business data processing, at a time when electronic computing was still a scientific novelty. The project was supported by a contract from the Bureau of Census, but, nevertheless, it ran into financial difficulties. Early in 1950 Remington-Rand came into the picture; it sent one of its directors, General Leslie Groves (the man who had previously headed Project Manhattan to develop the first atomic bomb) on a tour of British computer centres. His report led to the Univac becoming a Remington-Rand machine, and gave his company a lead in electronic computing over its nearest American rival, IBM, which was still only dabbling in electronics.

Nevertheless, at this point of time, Britain had a small but clear lead over the USA.

The significance of electronics lay simply in its enormous speed. There were difficulties in exploiting it fully, but the speed advantage was so great that even if it were only partly realised the consequences were bound to be far-reaching. These consequences stemmed largely from the reduction in costs. Although electronic computers were expensive, the cost of a single arithmetical operation fell dramatically to less than a hundredth of what it had previously been, with prospects of further reductions as the new technology improved. The speed also created potential benefits by enabling computed results to be obtained earlier and thus (in many instances) to be more valuable.

These consequences were clearly destined to affect everything that involved computing, and also a lot of things that potentially involved computing but where this had hitherto been ruled out by the cost or time required. For example, wherever a critical decision could be improved with the aid of more thorough calculations, or even perhaps with any calculation at all in place of sheer guesswork, then these calculations became economically much more feasible. In the fields of engineering design and business planning especially, it became suddenly attractive to conduct much more extensive analyses before committing large sums to new ventures.

In fact the new technology was, essentially, a massive leap forward in man's ability to handle information. As such it was to be compared with those earlier inventions for information handling, printing and tele-communications. These in their turn had brought profound changes in human society. Computers would do the same, except that whereas the earlier inventions were concerned solely with copying and transmitting information, computers actually derived new information from old.

The history of the last twenty years has borne out this diagnosis. Investment in computers has increased at a rate surpassing that exhibited by any other industry. In the United Kingdom, this investment increased a thousandfold between 1954 and 1969. For a short early period it increased at 100% per annum; for most of the sixties the rate was 40% and even now, after some recession, it seems likely to remain at 20% for several more years.

Computers are now in regular use for routine business data processing. Their power is also being put to use in countless new kinds of application: in reservation systems, as aids to managers, to operate databanks, to control traffic, as nerve centres in factory automation, to assist the medical profession, and so on endlessly. Computing already costs the United Kingdom several hundreds of millions of pounds each year, and it is becoming a major item in the national economy. The manufacture of computers will soon be the world's third largest industry.

Technical developments are still moving fast. In the equipment itself, or "hardware", the microcircuits are much cheaper, more reliable and more compact than seemed possible only a few years ago; new displays and printing devices are appearing; new communication systems are being developed, and also larger and larger stores and bigger and faster computers, as well as pocket-size minicomputers.

In the techniques of programming computers, progress is slower. The pace of new applications is now set more by the programming than by advances in the available hardware. But there is progress, leading us steadily towards a more systematic and manageable way of composing large programs. These points will be discussed in more detail in the next chapter.

There is also steady progress in another area, that of so-called "artificial intelligence". Though this is so far little more than an academic study, its ultimate goal, if achieved, would be more than an academic matter, for it is no less than the programming of a computer to exercise, for practical purposes, a degree of intelligence comparable with that of a human. Its present successes are extremely limited in scope, but some are quite impressive in their own way, such as the automatic construction of proofs of theorems. If, however, an intelligence of human calibre is achieved (not aesthetically, perhaps, but at least in terms of logical power) then this must be the ultimate technological jackpot. Once achieved, the replication of this intelligence would be easy, and all manner of human tasks would rapidly become mechanisable. Success in human affairs would depend less on the competence of managers than on that of computers; indeed, they would no longer be truly "human" affairs. The last critical point would have been passed when the artificial intelligence surpassed that of its own designers; further "progress" would then no longer be limited by human abilities, and it is doubtful whether it could remain for long subject to human control.

All this is at present entirely fanciful, and seems as far away as the atomic bomb seemed in, say, 1920. In other words, it just conceivably might happen within our thirty years' timescale; hence, although the book as a whole is necessarily constructed on the basis of techniques currently in use or being developed, it would be wrong to ignore the possibility altogether, the remoteness of the critical possibility being balanced by its importance if achieved. Chapter 3, therefore, is devoted to a more detailed introduction to artificial intelligence, so that this potential can be borne in mind throughout the subsequent discussion. Though much of the analysis of the impact of computers in different fields of human activity will not be directly related to it, but to conventional computer techniques, we shall from time to time note places where the impact of artificial intelligence might be of particular importance.

However, having discussed briefly where we are today and how we got there, we can now see where the British decisionmakers made their decisions by default. Let us return to the year 1949, when only two faltering stored-program computers existed, and the United Kingdom was the Mecca of the computing world. Contact was close amongst the hundred or two people working on computers at that time, and news spread rapidly. Within a year or two, dozens of computer-building projects had started.

Most of them were in the USA. For some reason, interest in computers in the UK grew much more slowly. While the generously funded "Whirlwind" project got underway at MIT, destined to lead to massive computer systems for air defence, the potential users in Britain hung back. Computer manufacture in Britain became a fascinating sideline for electrical firms, rather than a serious business for the business equipment industry. By 1953 it was clear that the USA was taking the lead, even though IBM itself had not yet seriously entered the computer stakes.

Throughout the rest of the 1950s, no concern was felt in the UK about falling behind. Far from looking to the year 2000, no-one seemed to be looking more than eighteen months ahead. The proud motto of one firm was: "In the long run we're all dead" — and, sure enough, in the long run they very nearly were. Perhaps the computer manufacturing industry would have been more enterprising if its domestic customers and the government had been more forthcoming, but at this stage the computer industry was tiny compared with atomic energy and aircraft, on which the country was spending vast public sums, and it was simply ignored. The National Research Development Corporation gave financial backing, but this amounted to little more than oiling the wheels. A few bodies gave small research funds. A few government agencies placed orders, but not many, and never with the idea of helping the British industry. Atomic energy research, always the biggest user of computing, and in America a big sponsor of computer developments, in Britain was slow to accept its commitment to computing. In 1956 Ferranti Ltd. asked the Atomic Weapons Research Establishment for £250,000 towards the cost of developing a new scientific computer. The AWRE declined, though within a couple of years it was forced to sign a rental agreement with IBM involving much greater sums, because it was then too late for British industry to meet its needs. Also in 1956, at a Royal Society meeting held to plan the collection of scientific data during the International Geophysical Year, it was agreed that no provision should be made for the automatic recording of data to facilitate analysis by computer because, as one eminent scientist remarked, "true scientific discoveries are made by the trained human eye scanning columns of figures, and once these figures are put into a computer this scanning will cease."

Nevertheless, during the 1950s Ferranti Ltd. produced four models of computer: the Mark I, Pegasus, Mercury and Perseus. In the case of the Mark I, the first machine was installed at the University of Manchester where the design had originated; the second, which was the first to be sold to an independent customer, went to the University of Toronto. Similarly in the case of the Mercury, after the first had gone to the University, which again was responsible for the design, the first sale was abroad, to the Norwegian Defence Research Establishment. Perseus was designed by Ferranti with the help and advice of a British insurance company for data processing work; only two were sold, both to insurance firms, but both abroad: in Sweden and in South Africa respectively. It was only in the case of the Pegasus, the smallest of the four, that the first sale was achieved at home.

In securing and meeting these overseas orders, Ferranti Ltd. demonstrated remarkable technical and commercial ability. To sell the first machine of its type, in a radically new and intricate technology, and to install and commission it, in a foreign country hundreds or thousands of miles from home, is not the easiest way of building up an industry. Ferranti did not choose to do it this way. They did so only because domestic orders were not forthcoming.

Perhaps if the manufacturers had been willing to invest more heavily the domestic customers would have been more ready to buy; no doubt also if the customers had come forward more quickly the manufacturers would have made a bigger investment. As it was, Ferranti Ltd. nevertheless took the biggest single financial gamble in the company's history in launching the Atlas project, to produce one of the world's finest scientific computers, which was only belatedly vindicated by an order from the UK Atomic Energy Authority. The facts suggest strongly that it was the customers who showed the greater lack of initiative, and among the customers it was the large scientific and technical users, predominantly in the public sector, who were the natural leaders in computing and whose slowness to act did most to hold back the manufacturers.

Whatever the cause, it was clear by 1958 that hopes of the UK recovering its leading position were fading fast. Up to that time, Americans had been fulsome in their praise of the pioneering work done in the UK; from 1958 onwards the praise became less warm and less frequent, and by the early sixties the majority of American computer scientists were unaware that the UK had ever made any contribution to the subject at all.

It was in 1958 that the author of this chapter expressed his concern to an official of H.M. Treasury, who was responsible for Government policy in the computer field. "Yes," said the official, "we are concerned about the computer industry, but what can we do? None of the companies is very strong, and we can't put Government money into an ailing firm."

During the 1960s the British Government began, little by little, to do just that — though never enough to cure the ailment. The only decisive Government act during this period was to change the nature of the problem, by forcing a merger of the two largest British computer manufacturers, International Computers and Tabulators Ltd. and English Electric Computers Ltd., to form International Computers Ltd. (ICL).

By this time America's International Business Machines Corporation (IBM) was well on the way to becoming the most powerful industrial and economic force that the world has ever seen, and the entire UK computer activity was by comparison pitiful.

Meanwhile, France had lost her largest domestic computer firm, Compagnie des Machines Bull, in 1964 and found herself virtually without a computer industry of her own. Immediately a Government development programme, Le Plan Calcul, was instituted to recreate the industry. The trials and tribulations of this programme are an awful lesson for any country that should find itself in a similar position.

Germany has recently launched a programme of public support for computer manufacture and use on an even bigger scale. France, Germany and Holland have public procurement policies favouring locally manufactured computers (though the effect is often to favour computers built locally by IBM in preference to those made by other European firms).

Only Japan, after a late start, has succeeded by a skilful combination of good Government direction and industrial collaboration, aided by tough import restrictions, in bringing about the kind of expansion of her domestic computer industry that could pose a real threat to the present American domination of world markets.

In the United Kingdom by contrast, at the beginning of 1971, the wave of concern for computers that had begun in 1964 seemed to have completely lost its momentum, with very little accomplished. It had been finally exhausted by the damping effect of numerous civil service committees, by the growing impatience of businessmen with the imperfections of the struggling computer industry, and by a public contempt bred from familiarity with the established image of computers. It seemed that the diehards were recovering their poise, and that the stage was set for the British computer industry finally to sink slowly beneath the waves of foreign competition, leaving it a backward country, run by American computers and ruled by American finance. The decision by default, a collective one made over the years by British industrialists, scientists and government officials, had been made.

However, at the eleventh hour, a new and stronger wave of public concern began, bringing a new ray of hope for those who wanted to avoid total dependence on American computers. In the summer of 1971 an investigation into the UK computer industry, which the Select Committee on Science and Technology had been conducting since January 1970, moved towards its climax. At the same time in the Cabinet Office, the Central Policy Review Staff turned its attention to the problem. The Report of the Select Committee finally appeared in November 1971 and was in marked contrast to all previous parliamentary comments on this issue; it made no attempt to hide the seriousness of the problem and called for Government action on a scale enormously greater than before. Whether the lesson has at last been learned by the decisionmakers, and whether the default decision can now be reversed, are matters for conjecture.

We shall be looking again in Chapter 13 at the problems which will be facing the world's computer manufacturers, and in Part Five at the decisions which politicians, not only of the UK but of all countries, will have to take. But this case study, in the important area of who should control the manufacture and design of the equipment on which all else is based, shows in dreadful clarity what can happen through failure to look ahead, failure to perceive potential, failure to recognise problems, and failure to act in time.

It is these kinds of failure that, above all, we wish to see avoided in other fields of computer development, in particular those of computer use. This may be a good time to take stock, because there has recently been a lull in the torrential advance of computer technology. The industry has suffered its first worldwide recession, during which few new projects have been launched. But the technology still has a long way to go. It is surely going to resume its advance before long, and perhaps it is worth while at this stage to take a general look ahead, so that we can see the scope of the problems we shall be discussing later in the book. We can do so, without anticipating unduly the arguments to follow, simply by taking the pessimistic view that attitudes will not change, and then extrapolating from the situation we are in today.

Firstly, let us consider the technical advances in the computer industry. There will be renewed initiatives in the USA and, not long after, in Japan. They will bring further advances in the technology for which no European company will have anything to offer in exchange; the Western world will advance, technologically, as fast as the USA or Japan wants it to, and no faster. The best computer technologists elsewhere will be driven by frustration to work for American firms, either at home or in the USA, as many do already.

In the UK, continuation of recent attitudes will mean that the lessons of France will be ignored and the country will wake up too late to the need for effective action to maintain a strong UK computer manufacturing industry. When it does wake up, it will then be so busy putting into action an ineffective remedy for the ills of the computer hardware industry that it will fail to see that the UK software industry, which might perhaps have been retained as a separate industry in its own right, is also being suffocated. Later it will spend a large but by then insufficient amount of money attempting to prop up the software industry, or those parts of it that are still British-owned.

Britain's European partners, though acting more swiftly, started from weaker positions and will not become much stronger in computing than the UK. No country is likely to emerge as a clear leader within Europe, able to set a pattern that the others will follow. Nor, judging by the fate of some recent attempts, is it likely that a stable organisation could be quickly set up that could successfully co-ordinate computer developments in all the major European countries. Therefore Western Europe will be increasingly dominated by the USA. Parallel developments will take place in other parts of the world; the later years of this century may then see a race to achieve artificial intelligence, between the USA, USSR, Japan, and possibly China. The world's computer scientists will join one of these teams; most from Britain and Western Europe will presumably join the USA.

Let us now repeat this exercise in prediction on the applications side.

Computers can be used by almost any organisation, large or small. But they offer more advantages, and overcome more disadvantages, for the large organisation than the small. With the widening use of computers, therefore, governments and large firms will become increasingly powerful.

Properly used, computers will enable large organisations to behave more considerately towards individuals than ever before. It does not follow, however, that they will be properly used. There will almost certainly be strong, and probably also indiscriminate, opposition to computers from the civil rights movements. The ordinary citizen will, however, probably be mollified by the blandishments of the politicians, and for those who are not, the increasing efficiency of the police will constitute a resourceful deterrent.

Civil servants will change from being memo writers to being machine minders, though whereas many of them understood what they used to write, few of them will understand the machines that they will mind. Mostly they will accept what is handed out by the computer technicians and salesmen, most of whom will (if the international scene goes this way) be American, or at least American trained. Bit by bit the administrative procedures of government will be replaced by canned American practice operating through American designed computers, buried under layers of coding sheets, program specifications, flowcharts and all the other jargon of the computer profession, impenetrable and incomprehensible to all but the most brilliant and tenacious Deputy or Member of Parliament. The gulf between legislatures and executives everywhere will become not only wider but less relevant, for they will no longer speak the same language. Parliamentary democracy could become a charade. A new class distinction will arise in society, between those who (to some extent) understand computer systems and those who do not. The latter will become cynical, frustrated, embittered and often unemployed. There will be more riots, and tougher police.

Perhaps here we have overdone the pessimism, even granted our premise; let us hope so. But so far there is little sign that the interests of the ordinary citizen are getting adequate representation, as against the interests of bureaucratic efficiency, in the planning of new computer applications. Bank statements, instead of being more helpful, are more cryptic than ever before. Bills, invoices and statements of all kinds, instead of being more accurate, contain even more errors and, worst of all, the unlucky victim of an error often finds it nearly impossible to have it put right. The only bright sign is the fact that deliberate frauds and blackmails by computer have so far been extremely rare, but with the rapid spread of computers this danger too must increase.

One power group, still embryonic, that could have a strong and pervasive influence in this situation, for good or ill, consists of the computer experts,

especially those concerned with software. Their influence will be for ill if
they interpret their briefs narrow-mindedly or selfishly; for good if they
develop humane professional standards and enforce them. Their predecessors, the atomic scientists, made a determined attempt to do this a
quarter of a century ago, but found themselves in the grip of powerful
forces which they had little hope of deflecting. The computer experts have
a better chance of influencing the course of events, if they choose to do so.
Much depends on whether they take this opportunity, and use it well.
There are signs that they might. Though most of them are still inclined
to look upon their work from a selfish point of view, for the income and
satisfaction that it gives them personally, many of the older ones are now
trying hard to develop an ethic and a social conscience for the profession.
They will succeed only if they can persuade virtually the whole profession
to adopt it, for their standards will be worthless if there are several groups
still willing to compromise. It is to be hoped that they will succeed, and
that the ethic that they will establish will be one that remains responsive to
the needs of society as a whole and does not become simply a self-protective
device for the computer people themselves.

In the development of a computer ethic, the United Kingdom is at
present farthest ahead, but progress could be jeopardised were most of the
UK hardware and software industry to come under outside control. Of
course it is to be hoped that this kind of ethical computer professionalism
will become universal; the point is simply that unless this happens it will
be useless if one country's computer scientists adopt a code which those
controlling the industry from elsewhere regard as unnecessary or even a
positive nuisance.

Thus we have, right at the start, two fundamental problems, one
political and one professional. The political problem is, how can we bring
forward politicians with the ability to deal with technological matters, and
give them all the help they need in their investigations, without merely
creating yet more bureaucratic institutions, and making it harder than
ever for independent viewpoints to be expressed?

And the professional problem is, how can we create a computing
fraternity, with high ethical standards, dedicated to the exploitation of
computer techniques for the enrichment and liberation of human life,
rather than for its enslavement?

Unless these fundamental problems can be solved, all hopes of solving
the problems to be discussed in the following pages can be forgotten.

2   The technical background

The problems which our hoped-for new generations of politicians and computer professionals will have to face will depend greatly on what becomes technically feasible in the years to come. Thus it is to the technical background that we now turn our attention — first to the potentialities of conventional computing, and then, in Chapter 3, to those of the rather more speculative field of artificial intelligence.

A computer is a device which can input, store, manipulate, and output information — not just numerical information, which is a popular misconception, but information of all kinds, though admittedly information which can be expressed in terms of printed symbols is easier to cope with than visual information, let alone tactile or olfactory information. Still, a device which can cope with any kind of written information is powerful enough, for it is in this form that the bulk of the world's knowledge is stored.

Among the information which a computer can input, store and manipulate is its own set of instructions — its own program, to use the technical word. This is the essential difference between the computer and other machines — it can store and modify its own instructions, and take decisions between different courses of action depending on the external data it is receiving. It is this which gives the computer its power — or, rather, its potential, for its power also depends on the number of decisions that the ingenuity of the planners leaves open to it, and the speed with which it can take them.

In the design of computers there are two main areas which can be distinguished, even though they tend to overlap. One is that of the hardware, the physical equipment to input, store, manipulate and output information; the other is that of the software, the instructions given to the computer to enable it to input, store, manipulate and output information in the way required.

The hardware side need not detain us too long, at least as far as the storage and manipulation of information is concerned. This is not to say that hardware developments are not and will not be important; far from it. The point is that the technology has already advanced so far that, even supposing that no further progress were to be made, the arguments in this book would not be substantially affected. There is nothing new or surprising about this — the world before the first world war had all the essential techniques to produce the Motor Age, despite the improvements which have subsequently been made.

So it is with the Computer Age today. The techniques which we have already can produce computers which are fast enough and large enough and reliable enough to make feasible the kind of applications discussed in this book. The advances in technology made to date are, by any reasonable criterion, staggering. In the 1950s calculation speeds were measured in milliseconds (thousandths of a second), in the 1960s in microseconds (millionths of a second); now, to avoid talking about fractions of micro-seconds, engineers have to describe speeds in nanoseconds (billionths of a second — throughout "billion" will mean one thousand million). Times between errors, originally expressed in minutes or hours, are now ex-pressed in days or weeks. Information storage capacity used to be measured in thousands or tens of thousands of items; now it is hundreds of millions. The giants of yesterday are giants by today's standards only in terms of physical size and power requirements; machines of similar capacity (though of much higher speeds) to those of 15 years ago which then needed elaborate power units and occupied cabinets the size of wardrobes or lorries now stand on shelves or are fitted into small desk-like units and can be run from ordinary domestic power points. Computers are also cheaper than their predecessors — even in cash terms, without making allowance for inflation reducing the real value of money. This drop would have been even more spectacular had the drop in the cost of the storage and manipulation functions been matched by similar reduction in the costs of input and output. The cost of "pure computation", the manipula-tion once the information is in the machine, has come down so much that £1,000 worth in 1959 could be done for £6 in 1970, and the cost is still falling.

Thus, given no more advances in technology, but allowing for some further cost reductions arising from full exploitation of the latest techniques and from obtaining the full economic benefits of mass production, computers are already fast enough and powerful enough to make feasible the potential changes which are the subject of this book. In fact, further advances can be expected — there is a clear need for cheaper and more reliable means of input and output, and for a really cheap, large-scale, fast access storage system, for example; and in any case, computer designers are unlikely to become complacent when they have before them as a challenge the information processing capacity of the human brain, with its massive resources of input, storage, retrieval, computation, sorting and collating housed in a unit a few inches across. But such advances need do no more than affect the timescale of the changes which computer techniques have now made possible, principally by making them cheaper and simpler to bring about. The one hardware area in which technical difficulties or delays could substantially distort the picture we shall be presenting in this book is that of data transmission, essential to the growth of large-scale computer networks and general-purpose computing and communications utilities which will figure prominently in future chapters. But with the exception of artificial intelligence, already mentioned in the last chapter as a special case and the subject of Chapter 3, technical advances on the hardware side are likely to bring about changes of degree or of timing rather than of essence.

The technical problems which have to be solved lie rather on the software side. The commercial world, including the computer manufacturers themselves, massively underestimated the problem of programming, and this underestimation still continues; as we shall see in a moment, although the cost of pure computation has dropped dramatically, the cost of solving a given commercial problem has not dropped to anything like the same extent, as gradually people came to realise that far more computing power than had been expected was needed for any given application. The point is that for a long time no-one grasped just how complex and sophisticated our existing human systems are, and the extent to which human common-sense is a built-in factor in almost every process and operation, whether controlling an industrial process, keeping accounts, or running a library. Some of the most successful computer systems which have been designed are those for controlling artificial earth satellites, precisely because the entire operation is new and does not depend on procedures developed organically over many years and designed for humans to operate — both exploiting their abilities, and compensating for their weaknesses. Our human procedures often have the outward appearance of facile simplicity, but are in fact sophisticated control systems incorporating quite complex feedback stabilisation techniques. This is a grandiose phrase which, in the commercial world at least, is usually replaced by that carpet-bag, all-purpose word "experience". The problem is, how does one build this into a program without suffering again all the mistakes which built up that experience?

One main trouble, and a main reason for the problems being under-estimated, is that the majority of routine operations undertaken by computers are generally straightforward for most of the time — for the obvious part of the work, in fact. The confusions arise over allowing for all the possible variations, peculiarities and mistakes that will occur, often to a small proportion by volume of the whole. This is not confined to computing, of course; it is true of a much wider spectrum of design that a structure or system is apparently complex in its final form simply to accommodate all of the minority cases with their special problems. To give two examples: British banknotes are of different sizes so that blind people can distinguish them by feel, whereas the "obvious" solution is to make them all the same; and, although the number of disabled persons passing through an airport is a minute fraction of the total, airports have to be designed to enable them to pass through as easily as the completely fit.

However, these allowances for special cases are conscious ones, which designers of physical systems are used to making, probably because the end product is a visible construction. In the kind of organisational systems where computers are now being used the allowance for special cases has until now been very largely implicit, because human beings have been the means of operating the systems and human beings are flexible enough to recognise the special cases, cope with the variations, and correct the obvious errors; and very often these human operators of the system simply deal with each variation on an ad hoc basis, without consciously formulating how they do it. A whole new branch of the computing profession, systems analysis, has grown up in response to the growing realisation of the underlying complexity of human-based systems; a prime function of the systems analyst is to recognise the existence of such ad hoc procedures and to give them conscious formulation. But the problem of designing a computer system is compounded by the fact that a computer program is not a visible construction at all, in any meaningful sense. It may have a physical representation in the form of punched cards, but it is in essence an intellectual construction, only really existing when it is in operation; and when it is in operation only the inputs and outputs are visible.

Most of the famous jokes about computers stem from such under-estimation of complexity — the gas bill for £999999·99 obviously really denoted a 1p credit: "obviously", that is, as far as human beings are concerned, in this case including the programmer. Only a bad program would have let such a bill be produced; a good program would check that a domestic bill bears a resemblance to previous bills, and so on, and will contain a myriad of other safeguards not only against human or mechanical errors in operating the program and supplying it with data, but fail-safe devices, double-checks of many kinds, so that unforeseen results of *the programmer himself* failing to allow for some combination of circumstances have a greater chance of being detected before harm is done. Academic computer scientists are now becoming interested in the possibility of logically proving that a given program will actually in all circumstances achieve what was intended, though this work is in an embryonic state. Nevertheless, continuing instances of computer jokes — often far from funny for those on the receiving end — are still occurring, showing that this problem has even now not been universally recognised. Computer programmers are still not wholly immune from the "it will be all right this time, it can't happen to me" syndrome.

But all the extra checks and safeguards take up computing power. A substantial part of the dramatic reduction in the cost of pure computation mentioned above has been used up in accommodating the steadily mounting degree of sophistication that experience shows must be built into even the most straightforward systems, if they are really to achieve the major improvements over human-based systems that computers can potentially provide. A great deal of programming is required to replace the common-sense of the individual in a given operation. And no amount of programming, yet understood, can provide a decision in a situation that is new to the computer. However, it is not necessarily the case that problems of this kind severely limit the spread of computer-based systems. It could be argued that the greatest single advance in thinking that has occurred since computer development began has been the realisation that, instead of trying to ape human sophistication, using more and more complex programming techniques, one can instead incorporate human beings into the overall system, using them to provide the kinds of skills which at present we find difficult or at least expensive to build into computer systems, but using computers to handle the bulk of the straight-forward, routine work.

Much of the recent and continuing technical progress is related to this, producing "conversational" systems which enable human beings and computers to interact. Typically, the human operates a terminal of some kind, such as a teleprinter or a keyboard with a television screen. Such terminals need not be placed next to the computer; they can be wherever convenient for the human being, provided there is some source of power and an ordinary telephone line along which information can be transmitted to and from the computer. The speed of operation of computers is such that one computer can deal simultaneously with a number of humans, giving each an adequate share of its attention without anyone having to waste time waiting for a response.

Hence extremely flexible systems have become possible wherein information can be fed in where and when it is created by people on the spot, checked and validated at once; and where information and results from the system can be asked for and supplied where and when needed. The humans can ask the computer part of the system to perform routine work or to retrieve relevant facts faster and more accurately than they could; the computer can ask the human part of the system to verify information and to check or approve decisions in situations where human judgment might be called for. Thus can be combined the perfect memory and sheer calculating and processing power of the computer with the common-sense of people to produce operational procedures that are effective, efficient and economic.

The major current developments all relate to these conversational, interactive, real time, terminal-oriented structures and their interaction with data banks and the need mentioned earlier for better input, output and mass memory devices (to which we can add data transmission equipment) arises particularly from this area. A clear trend is developing towards public and general-purpose, rather than private and special-purpose, transmission networks; towards people linking less to a specific computer than to an interconnected complex of computers. The move towards linking into big computers began for economic reasons, to enable people to share massive resources and so obtain cheaper processing, but already this, though still important, is becoming relatively less important than the possibilities which networks, as opposed to single computers, can offer. Also, there are many advantages in having as terminals not just simple keyboard/display devices, but small satellite computers giving local assistance to the human user. The mass production of minicomputers which this implies could drive prices down below the present luxury car level to the TV receiver level. There is, again, a clear trend for special types of input/output device to proliferate in response to demand, and here at least it is safe to predict that all manner of reading, printing, displaying, talking, listening, measuring and recording terminals will continue to be developed. As for transmission, the huge national investments in cable links to each phone for the national telephone services, which provides the largest cost component for a telephone call, can be utilised far more effectively in this way — though developments are now visualised, and technically feasible, for wide-band "information grids" with outlets (as for the electricity and water mains now) in all but the most remote locations, which could carry not only computer to computer, computer to human and human to human traffic as the telephone system does now, but large numbers of television and sound broadcasting channels also. The most critical decisions of the near future in the UK relate to how far the monopoly Post Office Corporation encourages or frustrates the growth of computing through its transmission charging structure. The national interest would indicate a free network plus an annual licence like the roads. A self-interested POC is unlikely to take this route.

The implications of providing information processing as a public utility are discussed in Chapter 9. On the technical side the limitations are again not hardware ones but software ones, for although the interactive, conversational approach does, as we have seen, solve some of the problems of applying computer techniques to human systems, the sheer scale of the network concept creates new problems of its own. Not least among these is that of reliability, and here a good analogy is that of electrical power. When electricity was generated by the generator in the stable block a few breakdowns were tiresome but insignificant and local — and the solution was simple: back to candles! Central generating systems provided cheaper and more dependable power, but being more dependable meant that electricity was used more and more. Now, not just the lights depend on the grid, but many forms of heating (including even non-electric central heating systems which incorporate electrical controls and pumps), cooking, refrigeration, cleansing, waste disposal, transport (including lifts for those who live in tower blocks), communications, ever larger numbers of gadgets operate automatically from time clocks, and even in some cases life-supporting apparatus like kidney machines.

Modern industrial communities have become so dependent on the continued smooth functioning of electricity supplies that one suspects that in a further generation or two people will have forgotten how to live without it; as evidence here can be cited the chaos which ensues whenever the supply fails or is substantially reduced for any extended period. The same could become true of an information/communications/computation grid, and indeed of computerised systems generally, only on a yet more complex level; however, with computing power becoming cheaper and cheaper the correct analogy is not between computing power and electrical power, but between information availability and power generation — the equivalent of the power station is likely to be the mass databank rather than simply the number-crunching processor.

If such a situation were to come about a few breakdowns would at first not be too significant — possibly they would seem humorous, at worst tiresome. But the more a society comes to depend on computing power, the less funny and less trivial the consequences will be. Already, many rely for their pay on a computerised payroll system; suppose one's ability to buy goods, including food, depended on a computerised banking system, or one's life depended on a computerised medical information system? Suppose a system malfunction, or incorrect input, registered one as dead, and so froze any subsequent transactions? Suppose that the inadvertent erasure of a file meant that any reference to oneself was greeted by the message: "No such person exists"? It might indeed be extremely difficult to prove one's existence in such circumstances, and the very least that would happen, even if such errors could be rapidly corrected, would be considerable hardship and distress. It is a social decision how much to rely on such systems, but how reliable they can in fact be made is a technical problem. At least, it *should* be a social decision; one major danger is that it will be taken by default, or taken on narrow grounds of efficiency or cost-effectiveness without due regard to the technical problems involved. This, of course, will be a major strand in the discussion of such applications later in this book.

By providing standby emergency facilities (such as are used in the case of electricity by essential services like hospitals), redundancies and alternatives (so that the correct working of the system is not critically dependent on a few of its elements), and means of avoiding "domino" situations which might provide cascade effects like the famous power failure on the Northeast American seaboard, the dangers of total breakdown of a network can be minimised. However, in some ways total breakdown is not a major problem, for at least in that case there is no doubt that something has gone wrong. Much more difficult is the problem of sporadic incorrect operation, whether due to a hardware or a software fault. By the use of double-check, fail-safe methods as mentioned earlier the chances of this can be reduced — but only reduced, never wholly eliminated. Let us suppose that significant inaccuracies might occur with a given computer once in billions of times; once a year, say. Put a thousand such computers in a network and there are three a day — and the point about networks is that any information within them, including erroneous information, can be propagated throughout the entire system. How many rotten apples would be enough to ruin the barrel? Every extra cross-check will reduce the chance of error, but will also increase the cost and reduce the efficiency. Where does one stop the cross-checking, when the error which slips through the net, however fine it is made, could ruin or even end a person's life? It is here that the technical problem becomes one for society, and for the decisionmakers who act on society's behalf, and it should be borne in mind throughout all that follows that in every case of potential computer application discussed, the need to balance the three factors of reliability, cost and efficiency has also to be considered. At the end, in Part Five, we shall return to this point, pointing out the special responsibility in this area of computer professionals.

There remains one technical area to discuss, which stands to one side of the preceding discussion. We have indicated our primary concern with the role of decisionmakers; however, decisionmaking itself is an information processing activity — which decision is made depends on the information taken in by and stored by the decisionmaker, as well as the way it is manipulated. One of the most important roles of computers is to improve greatly the quality and quantity of relevant information available to the decisionmaker, in any field. Thus there is a very special relationship, in this field, between the subject matter of the decisions and the decision-making process itself.

This has two main implications. One is that computers themselves may help the decisionmakers to solve the problems which computers themselves create. There already are well-established techniques to enable computers to help design other computers. Techniques exist to simulate complex systems and enable the consequences of different decisions to be worked out, without the sometimes painful or disastrous consequences of actually carrying it out in practice — well-known examples are war games and business games. It is certainly conceivable that such simulations could be developed to cover potential types of computer application in a given area; the main problem here being the difficulty of defining the situation and the potential changes with sufficient accuracy.

The other main implication is that advances in information processing techniques may help decisionmakers indirectly, by increasing human understanding of how human decisionmaking processes work — human brains, human organisations, human societies. It is commonplace that many everyday troubles, and many incorrect decisions, arise through faulty communication. Human to computer communication still has to be very precise and explicit, and tends to be rather condensed, whereas human to human communication tends to be rather imprecise, full of allusions and implications, and highly redundant. An example of this is to compare a message expressed concisely in the fewest possible words for a telegram to the same message given in a telephone conversation. Without a great deal of thought our ordinary language throws up at least a dozen ways to ask for two seats in a cinema without even mentioning which cinema, which film, which day, time, price or seats. Human beings are more used to communication of this kind, and so much work has been and is being done to make programming languages more sophisticated and natural; but equally, such work could shed light on human language communication — the pioneering work of Chomsky can be cited here. However, here we are beginning to encroach on the subject of the next chapter.

Computer technology makes it possible to gather and collate information in far greater quantities than ever before. Prompted by computer technology, greater insight is being developed into the way human beings organise, act, and communicate. By such advances, the computer will make it possible for human beings to tame that vast socio-economic juggernaut which men call civilisation, which we may have invented but have so far failed to control.

In fact the time is not far distant when every tiny financial action of the whole population will be processed automatically within the computer network so that the authorities will actually know exactly what *is* happening to the economy, where now economists have to guess or perhaps do not discover until years later.

Given accurate information about the state of the economy gives a vastly increased chance that correct decisions can be taken, but the computer can make an even bigger contribution because its processing power is so colossal that we will be able to create ever more sophisticated models of what could happen given various possible policies. Both capabilities will bid each other up to give us a real chance to make really good plans and adjust them quickly and effectively. However, before considering such topics in detail, we must take our promised look at artificial intelligence.

3   Artificial intelligence

As we have already said, this chapter necessarily stands partially to one side of our main argument. However, as references in the last two chapters should have made clear, the implications of a breakthrough in this field are so immense that everything that follows must be read with this possibility borne in mind.

We can think of Artificial Intelligence (AI) as being broadly defined by Turing's Interrogation Game. The idea behind this definition is that of the party game in which the player, by having a conversation with a person, has to decide whether that person is a man or a woman. Obviously the player is not allowed to see the person he is interrogating, or even see his or her handwriting, but can get all the information that is required by asking any questions he likes or indeed by holding a full scale conversation. Turing suggested that if a similar game was played with a machine, and it was impossible for the player to tell whether the "opponent" was a human being or a machine, then it could be asserted that the machine had achieved the level of intelligence of the human being.

We are not going to assert that this is a definitive rendering of the notion of AI, because one can see difficulties with it. However, there is a sense in which one tends to accept intelligence by its outward manifestations, and if people sound intelligent and seem to behave intelligently, one has to assume that they are intelligent.

The above argument draws attention to the so-called problem of "other minds". Human beings have no way of being certain that other human beings have the same private experiences as they do; they cannot

47

be directly aware of any consciousness in other human beings, nor can they be sure that other people have any thinking and imagining processes; each one is only *certain,* in any absolute sense, of himself.

One has, therefore, to assume, in terms of similarity of appearance and overt behaviour, that other people are in fact much the same as oneself. It is exactly this sort of argument that Turing used in his Interrogation Game.

Turing also emphasised that what is important in intelligent behaviour is the ability to process data as human beings do, and not, for example, the presence of movement, even when that movement is of a purposive kind. It is of interest here to recall that in the early days of cybernetics, to which artificial intelligence is basic, the emphasis was very much on goal-seeking machines such as Grey Walter's "tortoise". These were clever and useful devices which had much of the outward look of organism-like activity, but there the matter of the resemblance stopped. Later came the development of game-playing and heuristic methods on computers, and it is of equal interest that to most people this seemed far less impressive, even though the degree of "intelligence" involved was far higher, given the choice of the Turing Interrogation Game as defining an artificially intelligent system.

The basic problem implied by the problem of artificial intelligence is whether or not machines can be made to "think". The problem is partly a semantic one, since the word "machine" and the word "think" both present major definitional problems. Both terms can be defined in such a way that machines could (obviously) think or could (obviously) not think, and it is certainly true that quite often we use the word "machine" in such a way that we explicitly mean something which is unthinking, i.e. is automatic in its behaviour. Somehow or other it is necessary to get behind these semantic considerations in order to see what the problem actually is. We would argue that AI is concerned with the construction, both in theory and practice, of systems that think as well as, and ultimately may think better than, human beings. The question is really a matter of whether it is possible in principle to simulate either the seeds of, or the actuality of, human intellectual ability.

The most important single question which arises is whether or not there are certain aspects of human thinking which are in principle incapable of simulation or being built into a program for a computer, say. Most cyberneticians will argue that there is no reason, at least as yet, to suppose this is so. The conclusion one obviously draws is that AI systems are possible; that if they are possible they should be able to achieve human levels; and that if they can achieve human levels, by virtue of their possibility of exceeding the human being in size they should be capable of doing a great deal better than the human being.

At this point some of the possible objections that either can or have been made against the possibility of "machines being made to think" should be noted. However, we should first notice again how easily the semantic problem can intrude. By "machine" we must mean "an artificially constructed system", quite unlike a machine in the ordinary sense of a motor car or aeroplane (for whom the thinking is done by the driver or pilot), a system that is capable of interacting with its environment and thus adapting to changing circumstances in the light of its goals and subgoals. At the moment only the appropriately programmed computer is capable of showing this sort of behaviour to any interesting extent. This is not because the computer is essential to the theory. It is simply that the modern digital computer is the only large scale *universal* machine that exists in practice for carrying out the necessary simulation; this is a purely practical (as opposed to theoretical) consideration. The need is to demonstrate that *the machine* can think because by actually doing so we can make the necessary test of our theory.

The first objections that are often made to this central thesis are: (1) Thinking is by definition something done by man only (this is the semantic problem). (2) It would be most unfortunate if the thesis were true (this is clearly irrelevant) and more importantly (3) A computer program can do no more than its programmer makes it do. This is the argument which is sometimes attributed to Lady Lovelace. Let us look at it briefly.

The Lady Lovelace argument as it stands is ambiguous, since there is a sense in which it is true, although the sense in which it is true also apparently applies to all systems including human beings. Human beings are "programmed" from various sources: genetics, parents, teachers, etc., and indeed possibly from all aspects of the environment. But their behaviour is nevertheless causally determined. This is exactly the same for the digital computer, which is also causally determined — by the programmer alone in the simplest case. But in the cases of interest to artificial intelligence it is programmed from various sources — this is precisely why there is the need for it to be able to interact with its environment, including perhaps other people and other computers. This, therefore, cannot be a supportable objection to the thesis.

It should be noted in passing that the Lady Lovelace objection raises the question of actions being causally determined and that this can lead into arguments about the fundamental laws of nature and "free will". We shall not go into this here, but merely say that whatever the interpretation of the phrase "causally determined" there is no reason to suppose that the same interpretation does not apply to both human beings and machines.

The last objection, a rather technical one from the field of formal logic, is that any machine like an appropriately programmed computer is logically equivalent to a precise axiomatic system, such as Euclidean geometry, where theorems are proved by inference from the axioms. Gödel has shown that any such axiomatic system must contain statements (theorems) which cannot be proved in the system — i.e. statements can be made which are meaningful in the axiomatic system and are indeed true in the system but which cannot be proved from its axioms. The essence of the objection now is that human beings can "see" that such statements can be proved while the machine cannot — or, more formally, that the statements can be proved from the axioms of the human being, though not from the axioms of the other axiomatic system, so the two cannot be the same. However, this argument fails because exactly the same kind of reasoning can be applied in turn to the human as to our first axiomatic system, or indeed to any other such logistic system; Gödel's result, therefore, cannot be used to distinguish on logistic grounds between a human being and a machine. All we have shown is that our first axiomatic system was "less rich" than the axiomatic system needed to describe the human being.

Let us now turn away from the more philosophical aspects of the subject of artificial intelligence and consider the more practical aspects, which are the ones which have a direct bearing on our main theme. We begin by looking for properties which an AI system must necessarily have, without implying that these properties are sufficient in themselves to ensure "intelligence". Firstly, an AI system must be able to *perceive* its environment. This is the method by which information about the environment is selected and interpreted by the human brain and which thus allows the human being to learn from experience. This further requirement that an AI system should learn from experience implies that it must have the ability to adapt to changing circumstances and must, as mentioned earlier, be independent of its original program and programmer, in the following sense: that the programmer who starts the program on the computer will not be able to predict its subsequent behaviour. This comes about because that behaviour depends upon what aspects of its environment are presented to the system (or selected by it) for interactive purposes, and this information is not available to the programmer.

Such a selective and adaptive processor must also be capable of making generalisations and therefore has the need to perform inductive inferences. Strictly speaking it may be possible for all such systems to deal always with the particular, but this is wholly impractical in terms of space and time. The ability to generalise is what makes human data processing possible in practice. Furthermore, the detail of the generalisations made must depend upon the nature of the interaction that takes place.

AI systems must, as is obvious from the above, be able to draw logical inferences (both inductive and deductive); they must also be able to use language and to symbolize situations and, as a result, to think and solve problems. Much of thinking is the ability to process symbolic versions of the environment, and the ability to use language has been absolutely crucial in enabling humans to pass on information from generation to generation and thus accumulate and store information in libraries etc. It is through language and the ability to accumulate information that man is mainly distinguished from other animals.

In fact, the ability to think logically, to perform logical inferences, to be able to simulate and symbolise situations and to solve problems in terms of these simulations and symbolisations, have all been shown to be within the capabilities of existing computers, given suitable programming. This, of course, demands ingenuity on the part of the programmer, and it is not always easy, if only because of lack of sufficient storage space, to reproduce simultaneously anything like the same range of abilities as is shown by a human being. Nevertheless, it is of importance that the principles involved in each of these various particular and necessary steps are all capable of being demonstrated, even at this moment in time.

Work has been done on automatic hypothesis formation (e.g. Amarel, Kochen), and on logic theorem proving on a computer by heuristic methods (e.g. Newell, Shaw and Simon), and by pattern recognition methods (e.g. Hao Wang). Programs have also been written for inductive logic, a whole series for natural language programming, and so on. These make up many of the necessary facets of artificially intelligent systems.

What still do not exist are *integrated* AI systems that can do all the above things in an integrated and complete manner, as most human beings can. This demands a sufficiently large computer store and a good deal of ingenuity in fitting the programs together, and above all having a suitable pattern recognition system.

The notion of pattern recognition is extremely important to AI. While the ability to perceive and interpret the environment is a problem of perceptual pattern recognition, the ability to process information logically, to see relationships between similarities and differences etc., is part of the process of conceptual pattern recognition, which is central to all cognitive processes. Both types of pattern recognition are essential to effective human thinking and problem solving.

AI systems are currently studied as automata, in mathematical logical and statistical and probabilistic terms as well as actually simulated on digital computers. The best known such automata are called neural nets and they have been particularly used to study the principles of human intelligence. They have been used partly because of the fact that the neural type of automaton bears a certain resemblance to the human nervous system. The idea is that if an AI system can be built up which bears some definite relationship to the human system, then it should ultimately make it easier to move over and supply a complete blueprint of human intelligence in neurophysiological terms.

The problem of neural net automata, as indeed with all automata and all computer programs connected with AI, is the difficulty of constructing a sufficiently large system to provide the integrated picture of AI, in the same way as intelligence is manifested in human beings. One way of handling this in the case of automata is again to use the computer and write programs to represent automata. Even these programs, to be interesting, need to be extremely large and it is not always easy to see what the behaviour of the system is in a set of well defined circumstances. We have yet to achieve the necessary flexibility to allow such an automaton to interact over a long period of time with its environment.

One source of difficulty must be made very clear at this point: that human beings are essentially *social*. They interact with one another and converse with one another; they do not only commune with their non-human environment. They are educated and they are processed in a variety of different, highly flexible, ways. Thus to try to simulate a society of automata or a society of computer programs is a very daunting exercise indeed. The fact that this cannot easily be done in the short term is both a reminder of the extreme complexity of the problem of simulating intelligence and a reminder of the fact that, if we introduce a single automaton and try to show its capacity for AI, then we have to simulate other automata as part of that automaton's environment.

Within the compass of this general approach, there are still standard decision processing methods, such as Baye's rule, theory of games, linear programming, heuristic methods, etc. Heuristic methods play an extremely important part in the total ability to simulate intelligent systems. These, of course, are all methods that can be independently used on a pencil and paper basis, but the problem of AI is essentially to show how they can be built up into a fully integrated system of a kind that is similar to the human being.

It is appropriate at this point to say something about the central importance of heuristic methods to the whole undertaking, since the majority of situations in "real life" call for quick plans and decisions. These situations are often ill-defined and call for "insight" and ability, often based on experience on the part of the person making the decision. For this, heuristic methods are required. Heuristic methods are also used to solve problems, make plans, take decisions and perform other such tasks wherever conventional algorithmic methods are not applicable.

Algorithmic methods are, of course, traditional in the computer world and are typified by exhaustive searches, deterministic models and the carrying out of precise computations which have a definite answer. A payroll program on a computer, for example, must be algorithmic. But there are three types of circumstances where algorithms are not applicable: where an algorithm is uneconomic to use, where no algorithm is known, and where no algorithm is possible. An uneconomic algorithm may cost £1,000,000 to apply when the value of the result it delivers is only £500,000 (this, for example, might apply to any job for which it is more economic to use manual methods than a computer). It may also deliver a correct answer in an hour when it is needed in five minutes, and this is manifestly useless. An example of this in human terms is the setting up of a precise schedule for a production line. It can be done with an optimum solution, but if the schedule is sufficiently complicated it cannot be done in time, or is far too expensive. Both such situations make algorithms useless and demand heuristic methods.

Chess provides one of many hundreds of examples of unknown algorithms. As a finite game, we know from various theorems in meta-mathematics, it must have an algorithm, but nobody knows what it is. We are thus forced to use heuristic methods in playing chess, whereas when playing a game such as noughts and crosses we can apply a known algorithm to avoid losing. As for situations where no algorithm exists, the best known example of this is the whole of classical mathematics, for which Church and Turing have shown there is no algorithm, i.e. no algorithm is even possible in principle. This does not mean that some parts of mathematics (e.g. propositional calculus) do not have algorithms, but the whole has not. Heuristic programming is, of course, algorithmic at the machine code level, but this level subserves heuristic models at a higher level.

The difference between deductive arguments and inductive arguments is similar to the difference between algorithms and heuristics. Deduction, if correct, is wholly precise and something either logically follows from something else or it does not. Induction, on the other hand, can be imprecise, since a simple statement such as "almost all women are honest" may or may not be true, and even if we knew how to make it more precise and how to verify it, we still could not be certain of its accuracy. Like all empirical statements it is *uncertain,* and the best we may hope to do is to ascribe a probability to it. The collection of the evidence is, or can be, an algorithmic process, but the model itself is necessarily heuristic.

In practice, heuristics and algorithms often occur together and most rational human behaviour is a mixture of the two. Without the heuristic aspect, however, any hope of simulating human intelligence would have completely vanished. In short, heuristic methods are essential to formulating and testing generalisations in a "real world environment"; they are essential to develop inductive and deductive arguments, to deal with uncertainty and vagueness inherent in all humanlike data processing.

It is also necessary to emphasize the importance of natural language programming, which is often close to heuristic programming in its methods. As mentioned earlier, this is now fairly well developed on the computer, and plays a vital part in what is required by an integrated AI system. The ability to symbolise situations to represent events or things by words and to put the words together into a syntactically acceptable form such as a sentence of a subject-predicate kind can already be carried through on the computer. What is difficult, as yet, is to associate the facility to *converse* in natural language terms with the ability to solve "real" problems. Some steps have been taken in this direction so that some natural language programs also have built into them the ability to make deductive and inductive inferences. However, the full range of human intelligence and human problem solving capacity has yet to be put together with a system capable of performing natural language programming.

All the topics which the brief survey in this chapter has referred to are currently being actively researched. Because of the special place which artificial intelligence has in the scheme of this book, in this case some prediction is certainly justified, and the present state of knowledge and rate of progress suggests that almost certainly a number of completely integrated AI systems, in the sense described, will have been developed by the end of the century. They will probably be special-purpose rather than general-purpose, for example in a military environment — we have already noted in Chapter 1 the possibility of an arms race in this area, with the consequent injection of massive funds by the major powers to speed the research. Other obvious fields of application, likely to develop in academic rather than government research establishments, are those such as education; some reference to the implications of AI in education will be made in Chapter 7. Out of the practical applications of such relatively autonomous and flexible AI control systems we will learn a great deal more about the nature of human intelligence and the nature of human decisionmaking, as already mentioned briefly in the last chapter.

It is important here to appreciate the difference between simulation and synthesis. Simulation in this context means the reproduction of the standards of human intelligence by methods which are similar to those used by the human; synthesis, on the other hand, means the achievement of human standards of intelligence by any method whatever.

Simulation, therefore, is a matter of great interest to psychologists, physiologists and behavioural scientists generally, whereas synthesis is of great importance to all people who want any sort of automatic control system to be developed. The two subjects are clearly related, and the more we learn about synthesis of AI the more we automatically learn about simulation. It could be, of course, that synthesis is always in some form a type of simulation of human intelligence.

The main development of AI has, in the last twenty years, been in the hands of cyberneticians, and cybernetics is still above all else the science of AI. However, it is not by cybernetics alone that the integration will be achieved. It will depend upon the interrelated development of cybernetics with psychology, physiology, sociology and the behavioural sciences. In this way, in the course of time, full scale models of human intelligence will be developed. This is precisely the goal at which the science of AI aims. Once that goal comes anywhere near being achieved, any book dealing with the matters to which we are now about to turn will have to be rewritten. For, as we hinted in Chapter 1, the world would then be a different place.

2

The world of government

4

The computer as a tool of government

The three central parts of this book, on the worlds of government, of industry and organisation, and of human values, are all interconnected; in particular, the whole function of government involves decisionmaking, and many of its decisions greatly affect organisations or individuals. Hence the division of subject areas between these three parts and the order of their treatment is to some extent arbitrary; other divisions and orders are possible and in many cases also valid.

There are, therefore, some governmental areas which are nevertheless not dealt with in Part Two, but left until later. The maintenance of law and order is a major function of government, but because of the way it closely affects the individual citizen it will be dealt with in Part Four, the world of human values. Matters of environmental planning are also included under the same heading, despite the central role of government as a planning agency. Similarly, matters such as governmental support for the computer industry, and the provision of public computer networks, are considered under the heading of industry and organisation in Part Three, as is banking, certainly a field in which governments are commonly involved. Political parties, elections and so on are also left to Part Three as part of a general chapter on opinion forming.

On the other hand, health and education, which might have been treated in later parts, since either service can be (and in some cases is) organised partly or completely privately, we have regarded as being, because of their social connotations, in the public sector rather than the private sector in a way that public utilities are not. Thus both are included in Part Two, and are so important that each has a separate chapter devoted to it.

The principal governmental functions that remain are the machinery of government; taxation and its converse (i.e. welfare benefits, social security, etc., and their associated activities); and relationships with other nations. The first two of these are the subject of this chapter; relationships with other nations are dealt with in two later chapters, one on international aspects generally, including international corporations as well as inter-governmental relations, and one on that ultimate expression of govern-mental power and decision, the armed forces.

Even having hived off so many major items for separate discussion, the remaining field is immense. The range of activities of bureaucracy in the modern state is overwhelming, and the vast majority of these activities appear relatively rarely in the news media. To give a thorough appraisal of the potential for these of computer equipment, whether for information handling or for computing proper (i.e. mathematical calculation) is of such magnitude that, in 1972, the U.K. government set up a separate department, with a staff of 600 or so, for precisely this purpose. Thus the present discussion must be confined to general principles and general problems, illustrated with specific examples — taken predominantly from the U.K., since Britain is an advanced nation, geographically compact, concerned with computers from the earliest days, and with a highly centralised system of government. However, the implications should not be unduly specific to the British scene, and we shall not, for example, be concerned with the possible purchase of a computer for the Royal house-hold; though possible advantages of a national databank for the Royal College of Arms will be mentioned, this will be merely to show how specific developments can have a significant impact in unexpected ways in particular circumstances.

First, then, the machinery of government. As with most activities, the impact here is likely to occur in two stages: the automation of current practices to start with, followed later by modification of these practices to exploit new possibilities. In this case, the major requirements for the second stage appear to be facilities for the fast transfer of information, and immediate access to and interrogation of files using the conversational techniques described in Chapter 2. However, the technical problems mentioned in that chapter, particularly on the software side, have in-evitably impeded progress to this second stage. If one adds to this the relatively long time span required by the lay mind to grasp the full potential of computers, natural resistance to change (compounded by the ultra-caution endemic to the bureaucrat), and the enormous cost of really thoroughgoing computerisation on a governmental scale, it is hardly surprising that no revolutionary developments of any magnitude have yet taken place.

Thus, although the first government computer was installed in the early 1950s (for the American Bureau of Census), in the UK at least, government computer use has stayed firmly at stage one. Indeed (and this is hardly surprising in view of the history outlined in Chapter 1) there is little evidence that there has been any influence at all on government data processing by commercial experience, applications technique development, or even past experience. As late as 1966 a senior member of the British Ministry of Health could reply when asked (in private) when the Ministry would start using computers: "Ah well, they're new in this country, when we get to know something about them . . ."! And in a British Civil Service document: "Computers in central government ten years ahead" published in 1970, there was still no indication of any dramatic changes either in hardware or in possible use.

The main criterion of this document is cost-effectiveness, and this may well account for some of the caution. This is the approach of most governments, if not all, to the exploitation of computers, for there is not the same prestige in having a computerised administrative machine as there is in having an air force, an aerospace industry, nuclear weaponry, or even (in many countries) a national airline, areas in which the application of cost-effectiveness is markedly less noticeable. However, the considerations discussed in Chapter 2 suggest that perhaps even within the time scale of the U.K. Civil Service report the establishment of a national governmental databank complete with the necessary communications network and terminals will certainly become cost-effective for advanced nations and some governments are now turning their attention towards this. Much of the rest of this chapter, concerned with socio-economic management and planning, is written with this possibility in mind. However, before we move on to this, further remarks on the machinery of government are desirable. The pros and cons of a national databank from the point of view of the individual citizen — around which much of the "databank society" argument takes place — are, of course, the province of Part Four, but, even considered purely from the point of view of the administrative machine, simplicity, standardisation and easy availability of the desired information may be a mixed blessing.

It seems an almost universal trait of bureaucracies that departments are jealous of their prerogatives, secrets, and areas of power and dislike having to share these with other departments. Mutual suspicion and rivalry seem far more common than co-operation and pooling of resources.

Some of the opponents of databanks indeed claim this as a positive advantage to the citizen since it tends to weaken the power of the state over him, though this also is not an unmixed blessing, as can be seen when a human problem fails to fit tidily into one of the official administrative boxes. An illustration of this rivalry at its most extreme is given by the joke current at the beginning of the space programmes in the USA: the first US Air Force manned expedition to the Moon were just landing when (it is said) they were horrified to see another, totally unknown spaceship landing in the next crater. A crew member was despatched on the first ever moonwalk to find out if it was the Russians, or little green men. Eventually the tiny figure appeared on the horizon and as he came into radio range they heard his angry voice yelling through the static: "It's the goddam Navy!"

Thus, quite apart from the question of control, one of the problems which the administrative decisionmakers will have to face is, how much departmental independence will any longer be possible, necessary, or desirable, when all records are centralised. Will it be run on a committee basis with all the departments of state which it serves represented, or by a separate agency, bearing in mind that, where there is information there is the effective power? What will happen if the information network is set up in such a way that a clerk in another department (or even a member of the public) can in effect go straight to the top for a decision (where decisions are pre-programmed) instead of through a hierarchy of officials? One suspects that the administrative decisionmakers will spend much more time worrying about such problems than the far more important ones relating to the individual citizen which we shall come to later.

There are similar problems at a more political level when one considers the division that exists in most countries between national and local government (which itself may have several levels). Local authorities tend to be jealous of the autonomy they possess, even when, as in the UK, this is extremely limited; one can imagine the kind of "states rights" troubles that could ensue in the United States, or the difficulties which could crop up in similar less centralised states such as Switzerland or Australia, if the merging of government records at all levels were to be planned.

Yet another division which exists in many government machines is between the legislature and the executive. Indeed, in America this is explicitly built into the constitution. At present legislatures tend to depend on the executive for information, though in the US a virtual "shadow executive" exists to keep Congress informed. In the UK, members of Parliament tend to be very much at a disadvantage when pursuing subjects in committee or by parliamentary questions (especially if they belong to opposition parties) compared with the Ministers who have armies of officials preparing briefings for them; even in the US, where the imbalance is much less marked, the superior weight of the executive in marshalling facts is often evident at congressional hearings. With national databases, one has only to provide each elected representative with a terminal and the appropriate passwords to access the files he needs, for him to be (potentially at least) as well-informed as the executive. Further, the possibility exists of having relevant information available on-line and interactively during committee sessions, public hearings and even in full debates in the legislature. Such facilities would do far more than reduce in debates the number of arguments about whether such-and-such a politician did or did not make such-and-such a statement in 1970. Possibly, then, a national database might help to produce the race of *informed* politicians the need for which we noted at the outset, though the twin difficulties of ensuring that the database is accurate and complete, and of requiring an *independent* check on the executive, would still exist.

However, let us now turn to the socio-economic aspects. The three major requirements for any computer-based administrative system are reduced costs, better control, and more accurate information and decisionmaking. This is true whether one has a national database or not, and unless one or more of these are present the likelihood of a computer-based system can be discounted. The factor of reduced costs, although until now the major determining one, does not of itself, as we have seen, lead to changes in administrative practice and so for the purpose of this study can be ignored, although it should perhaps be mentioned in passing that a computer system introduced to reduce costs could, if badly planned, lead to worse control and less accurate information. In fact, it is at the point of financial control that computers will probably make their most significant impact on the practice of government over the next thirty years.

If one looks at the various socio-economic functions of government, one finds that virtually all would benefit enormously from a national database, both in the provision of more accurate statistical data and in the improved accessibility of information on which so much of the work depends.

Take, for example, the field of employment. Practices vary from country to country, but most modern states have to go in for some form of manpower planning; in the UK the government not only provides subsistence pay for the unemployed, plus extra benefits for those made unemployed through redundancy, but acts as an employment agency (especially in the manual and semi-skilled sectors) through the same local offices of the government department concerned. Special youth employment and careers advisory services are also provided (optionally by the local authority). In this kind of activity a computer-based system can begin by doing no more than the relatively routine task of matching job seekers to vacancies (as is due to begin on an experimental basis in the London area in 1973). In the short term this could be extended to include much more sophisticated vacancy matching, and to extend the geographical coverage so that, if a job seeker is willing to move homes, he can be provided at once first with a list of areas where suitable jobs are available and then, when he expresses interest in a particular area, details of the specific vacancies there. In the longer term, the system could be used to analyse the available data to show patterns of desired mobility, redeployment, retraining and ultimately of trends in educational requirements for vocational training. The principle by which such a system might operate is of maintaining a database of available jobs and available people over a given area, so that the most suitable job and the most suitable candidate are matched. The definition of "suitability" is one which must by its nature be flexible, particularly bearing in mind that the best-educated, or the youngest, is not necessarily the best qualified. National trends in vocational training requirements can be established by analysis of job content, related to the general capability of the market. To give a current example, it has been suggested that after Britain joins the European Economic Community in 1973 it will become the centre of research and high technology, due to the lack of natural resources and the relatively high cost of importing raw materials and the re-export of finished goods. The validity of the proposition could be tested, given adequate data-collection and analysis facilities, for appropriate action to be taken in good time if the proposal is valid.

It is at this point that interdepartmental demarcation difficulties could arise. In Britain, employment services are separated from general welfare services, yet obviously in many cases an unemployed man will have a number of dependants for whom supplementary welfare benefits will be needed. Wherever the demarcation may lie in a particular state, somewhere along the line there will be an overlap where a nation provides both employment services and social security services of a more general kind, and in a computer-based system some connection between the two is clearly desirable.

In both of these areas, particularly in the event of a cashless society, an immensely beneficial (in the social sense) system could be created on the back of what would be a restricted but highly personal databank, and at the same time provide an input system to the overall financial picture. (This last factor would, of course, form further connections with other departments.)

From a financial control standpoint, a constant feedback of social security payments would provide the basis for accurate extrapolation and projection in detail. The basic information required would not need to be other than totally impersonal in presentation, though an abstract of personal details, even if publicly available, need not lead to an invasion of privacy. In this instance, summary information from the employment file would provide the forecasting basis, using type of unemployed person, mean time unemployed, family size, etc. Certainly, the amount of administrative paperwork could be much reduced, the information would be more accurate — automatically, if only because of a reduction in the number of points of possible introduction of error — and decision-making would be much tighter.

At this sort of level the spin-offs start to occur, perhaps in unexpected directions, as in the UK the possible gradual construction of complete genealogies for the great majority of the population. So to the Royal College of Arms, armorial crests and shields automatically designed and registered, and the beginnings of a large export-cum-tourist trade! A less trivial and more general example is that of updating government records of business firms in a purely capitalist or mixed economy, not least as a cross-check for tax assessment purposes where a corporation or payroll tax may be affected by the number of employees. Certainly in the UK where work has finally started on the data-processing requirements in this area, records are incomplete and often not up-to-date. A further spin-off here could be (since public company records of this kind are, almost by definition, not confidential) a revenue-earning on-line interrogation service run by the government agency concerned for commercial users. This could in turn be linked with stock exchange records.

Returning, however, to the employment/social security system, the amount of traffic between the two parts other than that generated by the unemployed is likely to be low in relative terms, and even that proportion is comparatively small given that the modern, growth-oriented view is that an unemployment rate of 5%, let alone 10%, of the total workforce (which includes the chronically unemployed) is unacceptably high. Nevertheless, in real terms the volume of traffic could be considerable. Given one record transfer per fortnight for each unemployed person, not likely to be a wild overestimate, the January 1972 unemployment figure in the UK would mean 500,000 transfers per week. But unemployment means also a serious social problem, and one which can on occasions be solved by selective action in particular areas: to do this, however, it is important that sufficient, accurate and up-to-date information be available, to determine the action required. It is theoretically possible to provide such information, but the mammoth clerical task of collecting, collating, sifting and analysing the data, by people whose work-load is increased by the existence of the problem itself, within the required timescale, does not make it a practical reality.

Turning now to the area of financial control, a relevant example of the value of a restricted database is in the import/export field — in particular the levying of duty on goods subject to tariff restrictions. (In the UK other activities are combined with this, such as the tax on alcohol and tobacco.) The proceeds of this levy go towards the financing of other government activities, where the amount of expenditure is planned in advance, on the basis of the amount of money calculated to be available from (predominantly) taxation.

However, the accuracy of revenue forecasts, and hence the extent to which planned expenditure is carried out, leaves much to be desired in most countries of the world, including the UK.

Let us not, here, lose sight of the fact that a large unplanned budgetary surplus is as large an error as a large unplanned deficit — the effects may be less serious, but in itself the error is as great. Many of these large deficits and surpluses could be substantially reduced if not totally eliminated if two courses of action were to be adopted:

(i)   The implementation of closer, more detailed, breakdown of revenue centres;

(ii)   The establishment of a finer, more imaginative method of imposing and changing taxation levels.

In other words, the action advocated is the abandonment of the headsman's axe in favour of the scalpel — the scalpel in this case being wielded with the aid of a computer. Applied in the import/export field, this could well mean the storage of quantity and value for not only broad categories of goods but individual items, enabling the effects of changes in duty rates to be calculated in advance, to within fine limits, should it be deemed necessary to make short-term changes to them: additionally, the true effects could be monitored, to correct forecasts for the future, and to curtail special levies as soon as the desired effect had been achieved.

Looking at the larger implications, this could eventually be extended to analyse each segment of taxation legislation, thus enabling the government to isolate and eliminate unproductive taxes, to assess rapidly and accurately the value and effectiveness of taxation in various product-areas, and to rationalise — and possibly simplify — the whole structure. The present situation in the UK, on the other hand, is that parliamentary questions regarding the yield of taxation are sometimes unanswered, frequently only partially answered (that is, in terms of analogy, or larger grouping) and invariably involves the expenditure of research time — usually in inverse ratio to the yield of the tax in question.

All this could be realised, while still making allowance for political whim, within the next thirty years, by the implementation of an effective data-collection system associated with an on-line retrieval system, and it seems probable that considerable headway will be made during the 1980s. In the UK this will probably be based, at least in part, on the experience gained by the relevant agency (Customs and Excise) of the London Airport cargo system (LACES).

In general, by the implementation of across-the-board changes in taxation as a short-term measure, it would be possible to maintain revenue in line with budgeted or extraordinary expenditure, but the problems of external administration — the collection and control of implementation — before 1990 is unlikely to make this possible, so that, allowing for the human factor, it is not more than an outsider for implementation within the next thirty years — assuming that in fact it is ever considered desirable. In addition, the practicability of this proposal depends as much on the ability of the commercial organisations concerned to implement it as it does on governments to develop and monitor it.

In the case of personal taxation, it is probable that, well before our thirty years have elapsed, on-line input of tax returns will have become a reality, either by transcription of forms onto visual display terminals, or alternatively by direct reading of the returns forms themselves. The practicability of such a system under the present circumstances is not in doubt; the question now for the decisionmakers is, rather, when will such a system be implemented, and what strategy will be adopted. The rules for calculating tax exist: past information can be stored for comparison purposes (thus eliminating the need, for example, to input each year the names and ages of children, as is the case at present with UK tax returns), so that the requirement is for the input of exceptional information, to enable the new tax to be calculated. In countries where the citizen simply reports income and claims allowances, the actual tax due could be calculated and reported at once; where he has to do the entire calculation himself, the calculation can be checked. In many countries, of course, changes in tax law would become necessary. In fact, it has already been proposed in the UK that the change should be made to a system where the citizen calculates his own "tax code" (which in turn determines the tax he pays). With the advent of the domestic terminal (to be discussed in more detail later) a conversational package of programs could be provided to enable any form of personal or corporate taxation return or amendment to be input. Any taxation system based on self-assessment (as in the USA) or self-coding (as proposed for the UK) could be adapted fairly straightforwardly to on-line working, and there seems little to stop this becoming a reality within the timescale we are considering.

Here at least the existence of a personal database could be beneficial to the individual, provided it was kept secure from outside access and exploitation: the chances of receiving demands for mammoth arrears of tax would dwindle almost to nothing, the task of digging out past history each year only to repeat what was input the previous year would vanish, error-correction could be carried out more quickly and simply. In exchange, the principal disadvantage would be the reduced chance of "getting away with it" — though even here the dodger would be less likely to make revealingly inconsistent returns from one year to the next!

The principal key, however, to the use of computers in this sector of government, is the ability to experiment with a number of alternative forms of taxation. For example, one of many reasons for the delay in the introduction of value-added tax in the United Kingdom has been the difficulty in assessing the levels of taxation to be imposed at each point of value-addition. It should be possible — and indeed would be indispensable — to carry out a simulation of the effects of alternative rates or patterns of taxation, to obtain the optimum (both in terms of simplicity and in revenue) before changes are introduced.

The practice of simulation should, however, be adopted not only here but as a first principle throughout the whole field of government operations. Certainly in the UK, on the other hand, it appears to be the poor relation, the main area of utilisation being (apart from whatever may be done in defence installations) in the field of weather forecasting, where accuracy depends on the existence of a detailed historical database and on the provision of detailed and accurate climatic reports. To consider the use of simulation for government planning, it is worth while straying briefly into the environmental field which will be covered more comprehensively later on, for it is here that the most striking examples (in any case socio-economic in their impact) can be given.

The use of simulation requires the existence of a database — or indeed of several, in the case of environmental planning and control. Here, the planning of roads, of housing policy, of the provision of public services, all depend on accurate forecasts of the changes in what is, after all, as dynamic a situation as changes in climatic conditions. Better simulation facilities (based on more accurate historical data) would have prevented the expensive error of judgment which caused the first phase of the London-Bristol motorway in England to be two-lane only. Railway communications have been run down in many areas of Britain for economic reasons, but in a way which has not been co-ordinated. Thus, in the West Country, for example, what was once a busy two-track railway is now a little-used single-track line, but the road-communications facilities have not grown in step to compensate for this reduction in capacity. Simulation of the effects of this closure could have provided at least the warning of the congestion which subsequently occurred.

Thus one can foresee the construction in advanced states of national models of population, communications and employment. Local as well as national factors would be included, since (for example) housing policy would be based at the detailed local level not only on individual needs and local politics, but on the availability of resources such as power and transport; simulation techniques can equally analyse the interaction between these and other policies at the local as well as the national level. This leads on naturally to comprehensive planning of land use and (where this is politically and socially permissible) population — including allocation between agriculture, recreation, housing and services of available land and water resources, optimisation of domestic agricultural production, studies of the effects of possible land reclamation projects, and so on. On the population side, the periodic census which occurs in modern states would tend to become a confirmation of knowledge (and a check on the validity of the simulations) rather than a revelation of past events. Finally, one comes to a complete model of the socio-economic state of the nation, which could be used to test planning decisions, budgetary proposals, etc., prior to their adoption.

All of the foregoing is simply said, and therefore may appear simple to implement; the timescale might easily be assumed to be within the next thirty years. There are, however, two problems of such magnitude that in less than twenty years they may well be insuperable. These are, firstly, the need to set up and maintain the databases and secondly, the need to obtain the information on which to build the models — models which must be capable of self-rectification and self-development — and to lay down the parameters for their operation.

Data collection for any type of operation must be the key to the success of the system, and this is especially true of a database operation, where the collection of the initial historical information is a significant hurdle. In this case, of course, the vast bulk of the required information is, at least theoretically, readily available. Surveys and censuses carried out over the past fifty years — and particularly since the Second World War — cover the majority of the information required, although in continental Europe many records were lost during the war. Where the information is not easily available to central government, it may be held at regional or local level, or, in a few cases, by private individuals or firms.

Given, then, that the information exists, and can be obtained, there are two further problems: first, its conversion to machine-readable medium; second, its verification. In the first case, this could well mean a hard clerical grind — keyboard-bashing on either card-punches or key-tape devices. A more acceptable solution in effort, accuracy and ultimately in economic terms, is the use of intelligent VDUs — programable visual display terminals, which have substantial editing capability and possibly also displaying the forms — or at the very least the column headings — for the operator to fill in. The effort to carry out the work would come in the second year from those released by the use of a partial system in the first: thus, for example, automatic tax-return procedures would release staff who could then concentrate on historical data input.

It is too easy to underestimate the problems involved in collecting and entering the basic and historical information; it is a truly enormous task, and an even larger task to verify. On the personal record file alone it would extend ultimately to the entire population of the state — hundreds of millions of people in the case of the USA or the European Community (where, in time, it might be considered desirable to have such records at community rather than national level).

Some of the information required exists now in machine-readable form: the last UK census, for example, was entered onto magnetic tape for analysis purposes, other information is held on punched cards or paper tape, though some of this is suspect. It is safe to say that even with data already in machine-readable form, it will be necessary to set up comprehensive data-checking procedures on a random basis. For data being input for the first time, self-checking entry-routines will be required, in addition to the higher degree of accuracy associated with direct-entry systems, if only because of the wide variations in basic information origin. We shall return to the maintenance of these databases after their initial establishment, in a moment, since this is a suitable point to examine the collection of basic information for model-building. The specific topic of model-building and simulation in government is, once again, the domain of specialised departments, and is one which cannot be treated exhaustively here: pointers, however, are appropriate.

To attempt to establish at the outset parameters for a complete and comprehensive simulation of a national economy would be foolhardy.

The most fruitful area for this work, and one which is most amenable to simulation, is that of population and transport; alternatively, and possibly even better researched, but more diffuse, is finance. Data would, of course, be collected by random sampling of the available information, which would be analysed as it is input in an initial trial to establish causal relationships. Further specific data could then be gathered to test the validity of relationships calculated from past data, using classical research techniques.

For the maintenance of an established database, or for gathering information to test a model of the nation's transportation system, one reverts to the same problem: data collection and input on a continuing and stable basis, with the facility of being selective or random, localised or nationwide. There is one logical method of organising it — by a national data-collection network at regional and district levels. Such a concept would also fit into the notion of data concentrations located at regional administrative centres in e.g. state capitals or county towns, as the focal point and editing centre for data input by all the district authorities in the area. An even lower level of hierarchy for data input would, logically, exist in states with sub-authorities below the district authorities, such as parish councils in rural areas of the UK or neighbourhood councils in some urban areas. Alternatively there may be autonomous public bodies in a given area (such as those running water undertakings, port and harbour boards and the like) who should also be linked into the system.

Such a network would have considerable side-benefits, serving, as it inevitably would, as the basis of a local authority administration system. Here, local authorities would be able to carry out their own processing, using a central system based on the region — a local authority utility, if you wish — using, quite possibly, the same terminal, and certainly the same data-link, as for the national data collection system.

By maintaining regional archives of local personal and impersonal information, it would be possible to cater for the administration of local authorities, in a dynamic situation, where boundaries are changed, volumes of information fluctuate and people move about within the area, while maintaining optimum use of the data processing facility, and minimising the need for specialised programming (for so long as this over-laborious concept persists) by segmenting at regional level, while catering for the need of the local administration.

How, then, can we summarise the main features of government computing by the year 2000? In order to be specific we shall try to make a forward projection for the UK, as being a highly developed country with a great deal of computer expertise, but one in which, as we have seen, the government attitude to computers has been, to say the least, cautious. Developments in other countries will take place at different rates, and there will be variations of detail because of differing conditions, but the general pattern can be expected to be on the same lines.

First, the practical availability of on-line or demand processing is now established — even in the minds of the decisionmakers. The main early takers will be the departments of Social Security and Employment, where the value of on-line working will be proved.

Second, a number of small jobs will go on-line, including Companies House, for example, where the central register of commercial organisations is kept and where a preliminary study of data processing needs is already under way. At this point, there is a possibility of the facilities being offered as a commercial system.

Third, large-scale simulation and model building will commence, on the basis of information made available by (by then) existing on-line systems, and this in turn will lead to the establishment of restricted database systems for experimental purposes.

Fourth, database systems will be expanded, to meet the requirements of more sophisticated simulation work and to cope with the problems of overpopulation.

Fifth, at the same time (or earlier if the local government bodies proceed independently), a network of terminals will be established throughout the country. It is difficult to see whether this will become a major user of the Post Office network (the Post Office Corporation is the UK telecommunications agency and is already developing a national data processing network, which by this time should be well established) or whether, on the grounds of "national security" or to satisfy public opinion, the two systems will be separate. In any case, this phase will take many years to complete, and outstanding computerisation within the government will be completed before the end of this phase.

The timing of these phases will be approximately:

Phase I	complete by 1980, in major population centres.
Phase II	started by 1978, complete possibly by 1985.
Phase III	unlikely to start in earnest before 1980.
Phase IV	expansion from 1990 onwards.
Phase V	starting between 1985 and 1990, to last 25 years.

Expressed differently:

1975   on-line implementation under way for Social Security and job-matching.

1978   commencement of service for on-line taxation calculation (in-house only, for income tax purposes).

1978   system for Companies House operational (?).

1980   large scale simulation work commences, using easily assembled data (i.e. from existing on-line systems or already in machine-readable form).

1981   census analysis on-line: will provide much incentive to increased modelling work.

1985   in-house experimental database system operational — possibly in the Home Office — to finalise the form of the eventual national database.

1990   first phase of national database available, possibly using census data.

1991   publication of proposed national (government) data network.

2000   census data input locally from local government terminals.

The increased need for social control may tend to make events take place faster than has been indicated here: an almost equal and opposite force acting against their ever taking place at all will militate in favour of the time-scale proposed. On the basis of present-day technology, however, it is unlikely that the deadlines predicted could actually be met in practice, and some technological developments are predicated — including, above all, improved input techniques and faster, bigger, cheaper file storage.

The problems facing the government decisionmakers should, for the most part, be clear from this survey. Paramount among them will be at what point one can rely wholly on computer-based information systems and can discard back-up manual systems (here the decision is likely to be dictated by economics at whatever level of reliability or public confidence the computer system is running), where and to what extent one can decide policy from simulations and models rather than by "feel", and how far and fast one can press ahead in practice when one takes into account how much the public can be persuaded to accept. In this last case at least, governments with any real measure of public accountability will be, though powerful, not all-powerful; the public acceptability of computer techniques in determining (say) who should be taxed, by how much and by what means will depend not just on the way governments use computers, but the way everyone uses computers.

5　The military use of computers

The difficulty in discussing future developments in the military sphere, in particular those in the fairly near future, is of course that the most up-to-date and comprehensive information is not readily available. Those in the know are either subject to security constraints, or are illicitly in possession of the information and do not wish to publicise the fact. This is particularly true of weapons systems. However, a computer scientist can, without being a military technologist, extrapolate from readily available information into this area to a certain extent, while many of the principles involved in the military use of computers for command and control, rather than for weaponry, are similar to those which apply to management in a wide sense. In fact, it is principally from the point of view of command and control — for this is where the military decisionmakers are — that we shall discuss this area.

When computers are introduced into any management area, changes become certainly possible, probably desirable, and often necessary in the organisation of command. The computer modifies the flow of information within an organisation, and leads to new divisions between man and machine. Certain tasks are allocated to the machine; fresh tasks are given to man.

If we look first at the prevalent command structure in any organisation, we find that it has not changed very much from the time of the Romans. The pyramid form of command grew up because one person could not look after more than a certain number of functions. Within the major pyramid there were, of course, minor pyramids representing smaller units, and often they would overlap and conflict. There was a forlorn government

75

notice in the last war which said: "Remember the man in the next department is not necessarily an enemy." Certainly one has this pyramid
structure today which is a legacy from the very early times.

Computers make it possible to fuse and amalgamate departments
within an organisation, and so simplify this pyramid structure, simply
because they provide the means to centralise and co-ordinate control over
more functions than an unaided human being can cope with. The effects
of actions in one area on another area can be seen more readily, and so
planning becomes more comprehensive. This process of amalgamation
can lead to a temptation to centralise control completely.

However, there is equally a case to be made on the other side, for
upgrading the level of decision made at subordinate levels of command.
This is partly for psychological reasons, but partly also because the same
technical means for making full information available at headquarters can
be used to make it available at subordinate control points. With more
information, a subordinate is likely to make a better decision, just as, with
better tools, any workman is likely to improve the quality of his product.
Further, the simultaneous availability of the information at subordinate
and superior levels makes it possible to carry out a subsequent check on the
subordinate's decisions, with a reduced chance of someone who has made
an error of judgment being able to talk his way out of the situation.

This, then, could become one problem area generated by computers in
defence. Soldiering is an old profession, if not the oldest, and its explicit
ordering of ranks and tradition of command is of long standing and is
regarded as being of great importance. It is inevitable that discipline, and
rules about instantly and unquestioningly obeying the order of a superior
officer, should be much stricter in an environment where human lives are
at stake than in civilian environments where the management structure
may be very similar. Anything that might tend to modify this structure
could have much wider implications than its immediate area of application
might at first sight suggest, and while military traditionalists have a
deserved reputation for being suspicious of anything new, in this case one
can see a basis for such suspicion. What might happen, for example, when
a tactical computer at a battle front indicates one course of action, while
the commanding officer orders a diametrically opposed course which the
computer predicts would result in disaster? There is a difference of kind
here rather than degree from the situation when a human subordinate
disagrees with his superior's assessment; it is not one which could be
solved by according all computers the rank of private.

Computers are not yet so prevalent that this has yet appeared as a
problem, though in the wider, structural context what evidence there is

certainly seems to point to some reduction in the number of levels of command. In the North American Defence Command, for example, the introduction of the SAGE (Semi-Automatic Ground Environment) computer system led to a reduction in the number of command stages from five to four; at the same time, the direct command structure for the Air Force was moved up two stages. In more detail, again in the American Air Force, a horizontal shift of responsibility can be detected. In the early 1960s, two flying units with ground services were brought into operation for locating unidentified aircraft approaching the United States. The introduction of a computer system into one unit meant that all radar paths of aircraft were automatically notified and relayed to the SAGE computer headquarters. An air battle would, therefore, no longer be directed by flight crews, but from the SAGE installation; and the responsibility would thus be shifted from the operational personnel towards the ground maintenance crews.

A consequence of this change was that operations plans were now based on what maintenance was feasible, rather than, as before, being determined first with the maintenance plans fitting round them. The relative importance of the maintenance and operational personnel had shifted, in particular the role of the operational personnel had become more passive; it appears that the morale of flight crews may have decreased as a result.

Hence three tendencies can be observed in the organisational structure of armed services as a result of computerisation, though it is difficult to assess their relative importance: the decision-taking level in the command structure may move upwards, the number of command levels may be reduced, and there may be horizontal as well as vertical shifts of authority. In addition, the whole structure tends to become more dependent on the quantification of information and the rational backing of decisions by facts, just as in civilian organisations.

Having made this preliminary survey of organisational structure, let us now consider in turn the five main specific ways in which computers can be used in a military context: weapons, intelligence, logistics, planning, and finally the command and control area which we have already been discussing. Before returning to that theme we shall now look briefly at each of the others.

As far as weapons are concerned, the major area is that of weapons control systems; the military connotations of the various space programmes are hardly obscure, and a computer system which can guide a rocket to the moon can guide one to a hostile target, a computer system which can cause an earth satellite to photograph a star field can cause it to launch an attack on an enemy country. In fact there are already many hundreds of devices which are used in a variety of monitoring and control roles for weapons, ships, aircraft and the like. The reason there are so many is that the effort of technology, so far, has gone into building equipment that is miniature (for instance, an airborne computer weighs a few pounds and has several thousand words of memory) and also which is robust because of the conditions under which it has to operate.

Now many of those problems have been solved, and one can begin to see a greater compatibility between the different devices themselves, and also between them and their civilian counterparts. They can also be expected to become less complex. A simple example of a tactical weapons control system is that known as Tac Fire, where information from the front, e.g. provided by observers in radio contact, can be fed into a computer at battery headquarters which can direct the guns onto the targets. Other possibilities in weapons guidance systems are obviously vehicle-borne computers (in aeroplane, ship or tank, for example) to guide rockets or torpedoes after firing. Such systems could also be linked into a central system so that attacks can be co-ordinated. The American army are known to be working on a number of systems where something like 100 computers are provided for a field army, starting with computers at battalion level installed on trucks.

At the other end of the scale one has the kind of system proposed for the American ABM (anti-ballistic missile) defence network, described thus in the book "ABM: an evaluation of the decision to deploy an anti-ballistic missile system":

"The proposed system would include up to twenty data-processing units and have a capacity equivalent to one hundred large commercial computers. The instructions for the computer — the program — would also have to be more sophisticated and complex than anything accomplished so far. The computer has to perform many tasks at the same time — interpreting the radar signals, identifying potential targets, tracking incoming objects, predicting trajectories, distinguishing between warheads and decoys, eliminating false targets, rejecting signals from earlier nuclear explosions, correcting for blackout effects, allocating and guiding interceptor missiles, and arming and firing them if they get within range of a target. All this must be done continuously and with split-second precision during the short period — ten minutes at most — between the time the attacking missiles first appear to the radar and the moment of impact. In addition the computer must check its own performance for errors and defects . . . A central, governing unit will be used to oversee a group of subordinate computers. It will broadly outline the solution of individual problems, determine the amount of computer time and storage space to be devoted to each problem in light of its importance, and assign the problems among the subordinate computers for detailed analysis."

The possibility of artificially intelligent weapons systems we shall defer until the last part of this chapter; meanwhile there are two further points systems or particular elements of them, the other is the possibility of using computers themselves as weapons in a certain sense. Clearly computers themselves, without some destructive agent, are not weapons which can attack and damage human beings or physical objects directly, but since they are able to manipulate information they do have some potential for attacking and damaging or destroying enemy information which is held in a form amenable to computer manipulation. The problem here, as with any weapon, is deploying it so that it can be applied at the right point — the spear at the throat, the bullet in the thorax, the grenade on the outpost, the bomb on the city. However, if computers could be deployed in this way they could destroy (or, perhaps more effective, corrupt and distort) enemy information — or even turn a weapons system against its owners. This may seem fanciful, but certainly the sabotage possibilities cannot be altogether disregarded.

This brings us to the question of intelligence, our second main area. Computers clearly have a role to play in automatic coding and decoding, in codebreaking, and in the collation of information, testing of intelligence reports for accuracy and significance, monitoring the performance of agents, and so on. In many applications in this area the speed and capacity of computers will be of the greatest importance in a war situation. As implied above, however, computers, as well as being an aid to intelligence services, provide them with a new problem, because of the extensive espionage possibilities with computer-based systems, especially if networked. There is not merely the possibility of destruction of information, but its abstraction and transmission to the enemy. The security of the system must obviously be one of the major design problems for any military use of computer techniques.

Let us turn now to logistics. This is defined in dictionaries as the "art" of movement and supply of troops, etc. However, in the Computer Age it is (or should be) a science rather than an art. Since a logistics problem is an optimisation problem similar to that of a firm deciding where and in what amounts to keep stocks of components and other supplies, or how to decide the areas and itineraries of its representatives, it is not surprising that this appears to be an area in which computers are being most fully exploited, particularly by the US services. A fully integrated logistics system should, given requirements in general terms, be able not only to produce an optimum plan but generate the orders necessary for its execution. One side-effect could occur in multi-national forces which exist today, such as NATO forces: if the algorithms on which the computer operates are known and generally agreed by all participating states, it could reduce the political element in logistic decisions by removing the suspicion that a decision has been made in part or whole for national rather than multinational reasons. This, of course, holds more generally than in the logistics field alone.

The next area is that of planning, already touched on in a more general context in the last chapter. Essentially, there are two kinds of planning — taking a situation as it exists, postulating certain courses of action, extrapolating, seeing what happens, and then deciding what to do; or taking an ideal situation, extrapolating backwards, and trying to see what steps one has to take to reach it. The second is in the military context called the "McNamara approach" (after the former US Secretary for Defense). Both can be aided by computer techniques, for example by the simulation methods described in the last chapter. A "war game" is a special example of this; here the computer is neutral, calculating and reporting the effect of decisions made by protagonists in a simulated conflict. This is a valuable training technique for would-be commanders at any level; more sophisticated is the simulation in which a human makes decisions, and the computer not only calculates the consequences of these but determines the optimum counter-measures by a supposed enemy and generates these. Most sophisticated of all is the equivalent of the logistic program which, given objectives in general terms, reports the optimum plan which will achieve them — supposing that a plan exists at all.

This brings us back to the question of command and control, the last of our five categories and the topic with which we began. The term "command" here means the effective management of resources, and "control" the effective utilisation of resources, and the function of a commander is to make decisions in both areas. As far as a computer system is concerned, there are two possibilities: that the decision is made and taken by a human commander, or taken by the computer system. Taken, but not made, because the decision would have been built into the system by its designer and so made by him — though possibly not consciously as it may be the result of an error in design. However, in any situation preparatory staff work is done for the commander before the decision is made, and administrative work follows once the decision is taken and has to be implemented. Thus, even when the decision is actually taken by the human commander, computers can assist in all the steps leading up to and arising from that decision.

A number of points arise here. Firstly, it is particularly important in the military context that the commander and his staff are closely involved in the design of the computer system at all stages. If built-in decisions are to be included, his must be the final responsibility for their correctness, and he must see that the system is as error-free and fail-safe as possible, so that no decisions not consciously built in can be taken by the system. In most civilian contexts (though of course not all) the consequences of a system error can be put right afterwards; in most military contexts (though not all) the risk cannot be afforded, as there may not be a second chance.

A second and related point is that it must be possible at any time for a human being to override the system, if the situation has got out of hand or it becomes apparent that the system is functioning incorrectly or the plans it embodies are incorrect or inadequate. This is in addition to any facility which may otherwise be included for the system to refer to a human for a decision, or confirmation of a decision. Designing a system with this capacity of handing over to a human at any time is far from trivial; further, the hypothetical case described earlier of a conflict between human orders and computer predictions show how difficult it could be to know when and how the human should take over.

The third point is that any such system must be flexible and evolutionary in design philosophy, so that as situations and requirements change and resources and techniques improve, the system can cope with them without the need for complete redesign; in warfare the time for redesign may not be available. Finally, and rather obviously, the system should be made as invulnerable from attack as possible, and so designed that it can continue to function even if damaged. This might even involve complete duplication of systems.

At this stage it is possible to look at the way in which a command and control system can be built up. Simply for reasons of time and cost, what tends to happen in any complex operation is that one starts with simple, basic components, and then merges and expands them. In the military field, as in many commercial fields, one might start with payroll operations, holding on file information such as rank, name and number, with unit and location. Then one can add further items of information about the personnel. In fact, most military forces in advanced countries now have computerised payroll systems — for example, the Italian Navy has some 550 items of information for every officer, warrant officer and seaman on file in what is in fact one of their smallest computer systems. When one has a system like this, even if solely about personnel, one can, for example, produce lists of those who are under a certain age, have a minimum standard of fitness, are experienced in certain forms of combat, and who are unmarried — if one is seeking volunteers for a specially hazardous and specialised mission. All this is to a large extent a fallout from an operation justifiable on payroll grounds alone in the first instance.

This is the beginning of what in the civilian world would be called a management information system — a system in which the managers (in the military case, the high command) can retrieve at will any data relating to the forces available to them; this is the "database" situation introduced in the last chapter, and leads naturally on to the use of the simulation techniques which were discussed there. As an example we may quote the situation in one country's early warning system, where there is a £2,000 million inventory, 400,000 items supporting 150 systems, and a spending rate of £150 million per year with an additional £15 million for maintenance. All of the relevant files are held in a computer system, including both base and regional depot information. Simulation and modelling techniques can be used to determine the optimum distribution of equipment and spares between depots, when and in what quantity to order new supplies, how to schedule maintenance, and so on.

A rather more complex example is provided by the preparation by the Israeli Army for the June six-day war in 1967. The whole war was fought and refought several times by computer simulation before the actual war took place, in relation to stores control. Access to some quarter of a million items was subject to computer control, right down to a request for a nut or a bolt. All the issue of parts, re-ordering of parts, cannibalisation of captured equipment, etc., was simulated. The only question was, whether the system would stand up to actual war conditions, which in fact it did, completely adequately.

However, such modelling and simulation techniques are not necessarily as successful as that. For example, a war game in which the course of a battle, based on the Battle of the Bulge, was simulated ended in a decisive victory for the side corresponding to the German army, which in fact lost the actual battle. Hence such models, at the present stage of development, may be no more than an indication of a possibility, rather than a prediction of a probability. One of the most difficult problems in the military sphere is the twin one of deciding (at a practical level) when to trust the model and (at the theoretical level) how to calculate a reliable probability estimate of a given prediction.

Nevertheless, models are still valuable in a training context. For example, a war game can be set up in which all units above battalion level are represented on the computer, and commanders given exercises to deploy the forces. There are obvious savings here compared with holding field exercises, though these are clearly still needed for other purposes.

So far we have discussed the use of computers in command and control in limited ways, based on information available from routine computer applications like personnel records, stock control systems and so on. Let us now consider a more complete operational system. The process of command and control takes place in three stages: the perception of what is happening, the decision about what action to take, and then the control of resources to implement the decision. However, it is not in practice as tidy as that; the implementation of decisions changes the situation, new decisions are continually required. In both the perception and the control of resources stages, monitoring of the actual situation is required, though the motivation is different; in the first stage one is simply gathering information so that plans can be formulated on the basis of adequate knowledge, in the second one is concerned to see that the plan is being carried forward successfully, and that predicted developments in the situation on which the plan depends are in fact taking place.

Thus the system designer, in dealing with situation monitoring, has to allow for a continual inflow of information of many kinds — weather information, intelligence reports, enemy movements and strengths, the location and present activity of one's own resources, etc. — of which some, as well as forming part of the picture on the basis of which the next decisions will be made, will be required as part of the control process for a plan already in operation as a result of past decisions. At one time a given item of information, such as the movements along a supply route, may simply be needed for routine situation updating, at another it may be a crucial factor in the success of a plan. Such considerations may affect the priority with which incoming information is processed, or the frequency with which it is collected. In the latter case, if something has not gone according to schedule further action may be needed to correct for this, or other aspects of the plan changed in timing or form in order to make the best of the new situation.

Typically, then, a commander can use such a system to produce summary situation reports, or reports on the progress of a particular operation, or details of a particular kind, such as the number of men available in a given area. The other prime requirement of the system will be to assist in the decisionmaking process by evaluating particular plans or choosing optimum methods. He will require the system to provide such information as the number of men required to mount an attack to achieve a given objective, how long it will take to assemble them and their equipment, how this may affect other operations, and so on. He will require it to be able to select the most effective targets for attack in given circumstances, and to give forward projections of the effects of, for example, a withdrawal or a counterattack. He will require it, once the decision is taken, to take the necessary subsidiary decisions such as which resources to allocate, when to start the operation, and so on. The more sophisticated the system, the more sophisticated the decisions it might take — for example, a decision to launch air attacks on a given area might involve selection of targets in order, decisions on whether to send a second strike in the case of only partial success, etc. One way in which this could be done is to make the system carry out forward projections, varying parameters such as weather conditions or mode of enemy response, and make contingency plans for each one. Just as when this kind of planning is done by humans, the purpose is to be ready to react promptly to a changed situation without having to do too much re-evaluation; though the computer system might be capable of carrying out all the necessary re-analysis faster than humans, this may still not be fast enough, even if fast enough the time saved might be valuable, and in any case if the other side has a computer-based system it will also have the advantage of fast response speeds. It will be apparent from all this that ideally the system should contain within it certainly the logistic and planning functions discussed earlier, and preferably the weapons control and intelligence functions also.

One point about such a system which should not be overlooked is that, while a human command chain reporting up to the field commander means that he and he alone can see the whole picture, an electronic command system can, with very little extra overhead, make the same picture available at numerous points, even if there is only one from which decisions are input. This has a number of consequences, particularly of a political kind. One is that political leaders could equally well be apprised of the situation just as their army commanders are, instead of having to rely on them to inform them of the situation. That this is by no means an empty point is shown by the Vietnam war, in which information reports have been sent back direct from the field to the White House, bypassing the field commander and the Pentagon — the reason being the political impact of American involvement there, and the fact that the field commander is too close to the actual fighting for his decision to be a final one.

Another consequence is that, again perhaps for political reasons, decisions could be split between different command points, or have to be taken jointly. Splitting could be for the simple reason that commanders in different areas may make better decisions if they can see how the entire war is going, just as their subordinates, as mentioned earlier, may make better decisions if they know more of what is happening. Joint decisions, on the other hand, might be built in for much more important reasons; for example, it might be that any decision to use nuclear weapons would have to be input simultaneously and independently at all command points, including the political ones, while any attempt to bypass the procedure would be recorded and action taken.

These, then, are the kinds of possibilities that exist. In the defence systems throughout the world most of what has so far been achieved has been in the logistics field, although the USA and no doubt the USSR also have gone well beyond this. However, it is certain that the military decisionmakers will be pressing on in the general directions indicated as fast as techniques and their budgets allow; the question is not whether such systems will develop, but when. Political questions, both of financial support and of control, are more open.

Everything discussed so far is based on conventional computer techniques. Let us now turn to the more speculative area which we said we would leave until later, i.e. weapons systems based on artificial intelligence. The ultimate development of the kind of systems we have discussed up to now is presumably something like a totally automated version of the ABM system described above which would, once activated, be capable of continuing the defence of a country, and launching further attacks on an enemy country, long after its human operators were dead. Yet it is possible to envisage such a system which would be in no real sense of the term "intelligent". On the other hand, although it might be such a system that would come to mind when the military use of artificial intelligence is discussed, its use if and when developed would initially, at least, be limited to much smaller systems — intelligent aerial or sea mines which could seek out and recognise enemies, self-guiding rockets or torpedoes, aeroplanes, tanks or submarines capable of finding their own way to and from a target, weapons or weapon carriers or personnel carriers of all kinds capable of recognising and avoiding danger and devising ways of concealment, disguise or escape, booby traps able to distinguish friend from foe or to carry out an ambush.

In many such systems the level of intelligence required would not be very high. This does not necessarily go against our ad hoc definition of artificial intelligence in Chapter 3 (that it would be impossible to decide by questioning alone that the device was a machine rather than human) since by questioning one can certainly distinguish between a stupid human and a clever human. A quite possible development at this level would be symbiotic relationships between men and intelligent machines.

At a higher level one can postulate intelligent artificial earth satellites, capable of self-defence, watching for hostile developments without the need for continual human monitoring, and able to take offensive action, when required, having been given orders in a quite general form. Another intelligent system at this level of complexity would be an integrated strike force of (on land) tanks and other armoured vehicles, missiles, and air cover, forming a kind of group intelligence. The ultimate development would indeed be the complete national defence system composed of an integrated network of units with shared intelligence — a hardware embodiment of "national will and consciousness", if this does not beg the philosophical question of whether an artificial intelligence can be said to have consciousness.

All this is necessarily speculative; yet in fact it is in the philosophical problems of artificial intelligence that the greatest difficulties of the military decisionmakers may well arise. What is more, it may well be in the military sphere that the philosophical problems of artificial intelligence will assume greatest importance — partly because in a world of nuclear deterrence anything with potential major impact on warfare is also potentially a major danger, and partly because, as we pointed out in Chapter 1, it may well be as the result of an arms race in artificially intelligent systems that the necessary technical breakthroughs will be made.

These problems are obvious enough. First one has the prospect of an intelligence which would be totally, or almost totally, rational, logical, and unemotional. (We say "or almost" because conceivably artificial intelligence may prove not to be achievable without some inbuilt irrationality; but the existence of extremely rational human beings suggests that only a trace would be needed were this so.) An intelligent fighting machine would have neither antipathetic qualities of emotion, belligerence or hate, or sympathetic qualities of compassion or conscience. Again, a human being's behaviour in a state of conflict is conditioned by fear of self-destruction or injury; and while an artificial intelligence may seek to preserve itself, the emotional fear of destruction would be absent, and there would be the certainty in case of injury that components could be replaced — rather more easily than human limbs or organs. Finally (something which may exercise the military decisionmakers more than the existence of compassion or conscience or fear) there is the problem of ensuring loyalty — how does one know that one's weapons may not turn on oneself, or if rationality demands it, defect to the other side?

Perhaps the greatest cause for concern here is the fact that in an arms race situation — which is when, as we have said, artificial intelligence is most likely to develop quickly — such questions of philosophy are likely to be forgotten. If this is doubted, there is the example of the atomic bomb, when, in the race to get it developed, the question of the morality of actually using it was forgotten by the military decisionmakers, though not by all the scientists involved. It is clear that, in such a situation, the computer scientists involved would have a very heavy responsibility to bear — and perhaps, with the experience of the nuclear physicists of the 1940s to look back on, they might be able to exert more influence.

This brings us to a final point. Whether or not an artificial intelligence race is to add another gruesome twist to the unending sequence of armaments spirals which disfigure human history, it will still be true that computer manufacturers will be intimately involved in and to a considerable extent dependent on weapons development and supply. Indeed, this is the case already — many of the technical advances in the field have arisen directly from military or paramilitary (e.g. space programme) requirements, and much of the wealth of the computer industry and the electronics industry has derived from government contracts for defence. The moral responsibility of the computer manufacturers is as obvious as the fact that their vested interest in continued high levels of military expenditure makes it tempting to try to avoid it. It may be said that the computer systems only guide the weapons; but then a gun is only lethal when loaded with a bullet, and the bullet is only dangerous if filled with gunpowder — can the gun and bullet manufacturer therefore shrug off all responsibility? The argument "we only make them, it is up to others how they use them" may be more obviously specious in the case of arms manufacturers, but the difference is only one of degree. Clearly the prime moral responsibility lies elsewhere — but a share of the responsibility for the safety of mankind in a nuclear world must rest on those supplying the world's governments with military computer systems.

As military systems become more dependent on computers, that share of responsibility will increase.

6   Computers and medicine

Any discussion of the future has difficulties not only associated with the identification and extrapolation of the present major trends, but in allowing for the emergence of new ways of responding to changing patterns. Nowhere in the present work is this more true than in the case of medical care.

The health care industry has always been labour intensive. It has yet to enter the area where clinical and management information is plentiful and where human resources can be distributed on a basis of a better return for the manpower and effort invested. Yet the objectives for medical care must still remain the same, to give the patient the best care compatible with the state of the art and the resources allocated by society. Such a statement leaves many vague generalities in need of more precise definition, such as the questions of who gives the best care and what in fact comprises this kind of care. A formula to determine the distribution of resources to preventive and curative services in such a system still eludes us. Without a great deal more basic information any extrapolation can only be marginally better than guesswork.

If health services are to manage within a budget of 4–6% of the gross national product, as in the case of the UK, it is difficult to determine what are the best methods of allocating resources in such a system. This system is essentially driven by patients and at a lower level the decisions of those responsible for their care. In strange contrast the resources are often allocated centrally, usually on the basis of what worked well last year, will do for the next. Thus there are a lot of outstanding questions to be solved by research and patient investigation over the next thirty years.

What is most urgently needed is more data about the organisation and distribution of resources, and the decision bases on which resources are given to patients, both those aimed at the prevention of disease and the care of established illness. Computer technology has begun to play a part, and can play a greater part, in this endeavour.

The development in computer techniques and systems in health care services which can be expected to take place in the next thirty years can be considered in three phases, the first of which is in progress now and will run until about the end of the decade.

During this phase experimental projects will gradually explore many areas of medical care, solving some of the problems of medical and administrative records, especially those involving patient care in hospitals and general practice. It should be possible to combine these with the preventive medical records such as those at present held in the UK by local government medical authorities. Already there exist many records, but while these are useful in the immediate clinical care of patients, they are very difficult to manipulate and analyse because of lack of organisation and standardisation. Computer technology will obviously make a big difference here, but there will have to be a great deal of restructuring and reorganisation of information collecting and recording to enable this to take place. Here, then, is one important area for decisionmaking in the medical sphere.

Various areas of health care are now being investigated including the problems of medical records, new ways of gathering data from patients, whether this be by questionnaire, by doctors or other health care personnel. Manipulating this information into medical decisionmaking is being explored. In very limited and strictly circumscribed areas of medicine, the computer has been used to give a decision about diagnosis. However, such diagnostic systems as have been created cannot be generalised to the whole of medicine, and at present interest in these has waned. Our concepts of diagnosis and its purposes are in need of revision. The scheduling of medical and nursing personnel has been investigated and also the problems of using computers in intensive care units and for patient monitoring. Others have used it in the management resources in the hospital such as automated dispensing of drugs, and the recording and monitoring of treatment given to patients. On the physiological side new knowledge of biological control feedback systems is being explored, and such systems modelled by computer techniques. As yet the total medical system has not emerged but its difficulties are now becoming more clearly defined, and the problems recognised.

In these areas the problems facing the decisionmakers should not be particularly sticky. The systems designer for automated drug dispensation will have problems of accuracy and security to contend with, of course, but the administrator need have no doubts about introducing a properly designed system since its advantages in reducing the chance of human error in dispensing the correct dosage or the correct drug are so obvious. Similarly with patient monitoring systems, with their capacity for continuous tireless watching over the patient's condition, where the only problem is where to set the critical levels which will cause the system to alert medical staff.

There is more room for doubt in the cases of computer diagnosis or treatment; however, in the timescale we are considering there seems little prospect that the problem will become acute. For the foreseeable future every computer diagnosis will be monitored by the doctor in charge of the case (the system might in fact amount to little more than a specialised information retrieval system aiding him in making his own diagnosis) and so the decisions will be individual ones in individual cases as to whether the diagnosis can be accepted. In this situation — which could be styled "an automated second opinion" — there are no extra problems added by computers to those which doctors already face every day. As for computerised treatment, it is only when allied to unmonitored computer diagnosis that the really difficult problems of principle may arise; for the foreseeable future one can expect this first to be the administering of treatment decided on by human doctors and, secondly, to be accompanied by intensive patient monitoring.

The second phase will begin when most of the essential research and development of experimental projects has been achieved — perhaps by the end of the decade. Thereafter it can be expected that the application of computer techniques to health care will begin to expand and generally spread throughout the whole of medical care. This will be accompanied by management revolution using computer analysed information to feedback to local health administration areas, so that instead of managing in a vacuum there will be adequate information generated at the appropriate time for decisions to be made.

It will take a decade or longer for medical and other health care personnel to be working in a welter of information, as against the present system of inadequate data. This will make it possible to look much more closely not only at medical decisionmaking about patients, but also decisions on the health care resources allocated by society. The management revolution which should begin in the late 1970s will continue to progress due to further increases in knowledge.

During this phase also the effect should begin to be seen of the introduction of computer techniques into general education at primary
and secondary level, as discussed in the next chapter, since that generation
will be reaching the medical schools and medical services generally. It is
to be expected that all personnel, including those actively working in the
field, will be much more aware of computer systems, and the kinds of
activities in which they can be used. This educational revolution will make
it much easier to implement and develop new techniques, with much less
resistance than at present.

The second phase may again last for about a decade, taking us up to
the last decade of the century and the beginning of the third phase. This
phase will herald further research and development in medical information
systems, and the allocation and management of resources. It is to be
expected that new facts will arise from the research already undertaken,
and will develop medical theory. This should facilitate the reorganisation of
concepts about medicine more on feedback control lines. A peripheral
managerial organisation will have been much more firmly established
which blends local initiative and funding with central allocation of
resources on a broad based total health care system. Because of computer
systems much more use can be made of local initiative especially in relation
to the management of resources. This would allow creative experiments
to exist at a local as well as international level, and no doubt forward
many new and interesting applications of computer systems.

If this is a reasonable assessment of how things are likely to develop, let
us now discuss each phase at somewhat greater length, beginning again
with the first phase, which may take us to about 1980. During this first
period the most difficult steps have to be taken in the field of computer
systems, namely that of research. It is always more difficult to develop
new technology than to apply it. The development of computer technology
in the British health service has been relatively slow. The first reason
has been a lack of knowledge of computer techniques among doctors, in
spite of fifteen years of development. The second has been the state of
development of computers themselves. It has been possible for the past
ten years to develop local information systems, usually card-based
with limited applications. Some experiments have taken place in the
field of medical decisionmaking in relation to diagnosis in small groups
of clinical conditions. In the preventive field, the control of immunisation by computer techniques used by local authorities has been
very successful. In the clinical area a limited experience in applying
computer techniques to medical records has been very productive in
new ideas. It has also alerted doctors to the kind of problems that are

likely to be solved by computer technology fairly easily, and the areas which are difficult.

A further retarding force so far has been the complexity of the health care system and its challenges to the development of computer systems. The expense and difficulties of these developments have required them to be funded in different ways to the usual type of research in the past. Also, the need for confidentiality and security of health records in the health service has meant that they have to solve this problem by buying their own machines rather than using bureau services. Health Service personnel have also had to learn how to deal with new types of machines for recording data, in addition to pen and paper. A further difficulty has been the general over-enthusiasm of amateur prophets, unaware of the difficulties of system analysis and design, and having little experience of available computer systems. They raised many expectations which were unrealisable in the short term, usually taken to be three years, for the standard run-of-the-mill research project.

Early experiments in the United States by the American government and by voluntary agencies, spending several million pounds a year, both in direct and indirect support of computing systems in health care, has taught us useful lessons, but few reliable systems have developed. Many hospitals have had their own individual computer projects, but the only major successful application so far has been that in accounting for services rendered. Here computer systems, such as those used in business, have been translated into the health care field. Elsewhere progress has been much slower, especially in relation to medical records. The use of information generated at the patient's bedside for guiding health care policy in any major way has yet to come.

In the United Kingdom the need for medical computing systems has been recognised. Most computer systems so far have been used for administrative tasks, which again are an extension of those developed in business. Thus, store and suppliers' accounts, cost accounts and payroll have been a major interest of hospital computer installations. On the other hand clinical projects have not been encouraged to develop as rapidly. The applications by local health authorities of computer systems for immunisation purposes to register and maintain records has been successful in ensuring a high rate of vaccination and immunisation. The application of computer systems to establish the usefulness of cervical cytology, child health and school medical records, has been in progress for several years.

In recent years the Department of Health and Social Security in the UK has launched an experimental computer programme with the objective of determining the role computers should play in the service. This programme was intended to discover how and where computers could help to improve clinical care in relation to the distribution of resources and administration of those resources, to provide facilities for management. It was also intended to do research in various clinical areas to determine to what extent the computer can contribute to the clinical side of health care. The first phase of research and development will probably last until 1980 — about the timescale, in fact, suggested for the first phase we are discussing here. By this time it should be possible to decide which experimental projects should develop into operational projects.

In medicine one must emphasise the importance of medical data contained in the medical record. This contains the necessary information which after processing can be the feedback that guides the clinical team. While it has not been very difficult to create different types of medical record in the health service, namely those of general practice, hospitals and administration, it has been difficult to produce a structured type of record suitable for most areas at different times. It is not difficult to keep masses of records on paper or on cards, but analysis due to lack of system is difficult, and expensive in resources and time. Several research projects undertaken to develop computer medical records have failed because of the lack of appreciation of the necessary effort and the reorientation of the doctors' attitude required to drive such a system.

Nevertheless, as medicine expands, and teamwork increases, the common data base, the medical record, will become more and more essential. In general practice and in hospitals, it is necessary that doctors be aware of what has happened to the patient, what drugs and treatment have been given. A reminder of genetic liabilities and difficulties are important in the treatment of disease, not only in the physical area, but also in the emotional and social fields. For instance, blood group information will always be important. It is necessary to know if special individuals have abnormal haemoglobins circulating in the red cells in their blood, which can give rise to different clinical disorders. When a strange doctor first sees the patient, genetic information of this kind can often cut short a great deal of investigative work. In addition to genetic information, known information about an ill patient is very important when beginning treatment. Communications between general practice and hospital care often get delayed and data may not be transferred by the standard written messages or by telephone. It is necessary to enlarge the communication interface, because doctors, in primary care, are using hospital laboratories and investigative resources to a much higher degree than previously. This trend will continue. Indeed, many more facilities are going to be offered to primary care, because it is cheaper to treat the patients in their homes.

Not only is it important to collect both medical and nursing clinical data about patients, but a great deal of effort and resources are spent on obtaining special investigative information to make diagnosis more specific so that the best treatment is given. Thus, computer systems are being tried in investigative laboratories following the wave of automation which generated a new data overload. This automation gave rise to difficulties for the equipment was designed to give a printout of data at laboratory level, and not linked by a communication system to the doctors at a patient's bedside. Ways of working in laboratories have also been designed to suit the existing manual paper system. As such, these systems are not necessarily suitable to information processing and need changing. The communication between doctors in laboratories and those looking after patients is still carried out by pieces of paper delivered by human hand. Facilities are rarely scheduled and everything is geared to meet the random demand rather than spreading the load using fewer resources to meet it. Systems which are hand-driven and labour intensive need changing, and computer systems can help. Thus studies are required to apply standard organisation and research methods, and this will improve the implementation of computer systems.

A change in the medical record and communication system by means of computer technology must inevitably imply a reorganisation of all the services concerned. As well as the organisational decisions which this will involve, inevitably this also means re-education and retraining of personnel to establish the new orientation. The importance of computer technology to general education has still to be recognised, and though this will be dealt with in greater generality in the next chapter it is helpful to mention it here in relation to a particular field.

The point is that the growth of computer techniques has developed new, algorithmic ways of thinking in many fields to which computers have been applied — what is often called the "systems approach". These ways of thinking are not so much new in themselves as new to their areas of application, and, while introduced because of the use of computers, are more general in scope and value. In the medical field people want to know not just the computer techniques themselves but the new ways of thinking behind them. It should be accepted that health service workers can think in an algorithmic way and so be appreciative of and sensitive to the problems which can be solved by the development of computer techniques, in relation to both information processing and communication.

Nevertheless, this important educational aspect has so far attracted little attention and has proved unexpectedly difficult to fund and implement.

In countries such as Britain many university students in all disciplines, including medicine, are now beginning to find computing in their curricula, and medical teachers are finding it necessary to know about computers in order to introduce their students to these techniques. One of the major difficulties now is to find new and easy ways of persuading people to view the solution of problems in an algorithmic way. Then systems design can be approached in a logical and analytical fashion. Indeed, the greatest impact that computers will have is in developing new ways of thinking and doing things, because of the analytical techniques that are possible. They highlight the continuing importance of getting down to fundamental details and taking into consideration as wide a range of factors as possible.

In a human-driven system, generalities tend to hold sway and there is a great tendency to work from the general to the particular. In an algorithmic way of thinking, while the objectives have to be stated, it is important to get down to detail and work out the algorithmic path through a problem. Hence, in many fields such as medicine, the really significant educational aim should not be to get people to write computer programs, but to create new and logical ways of developing systems, using computer technology in their implementation when appropriate.

We shall, of course, look again at this in the next chapter. Meanwhile, let us turn to our projected second phase of development of medical computing, which we have projected as possibly lasting through the 1980s. It seems reasonable to allow a decade or more; it has taken some 200 years to develop the application of Boolean logic to information processing and it is unlikely that generalised applications of computer systems to health care will take place very fast. Resistance to using a new analytical tool will be difficult to overcome, as people find it much easier to criticise a machine than a person. As already discussed in Chapter 2, computer technology is not yet wholly adequate to deal with the enormous demands of information systems large enough to cope with the needs of medical services, but there is reason to expect that at current rates of progress sufficient advance will have been made by around 1980 for this not to delay the start of phase two.

It is not recognised that many of the skills required in medicine have not changed for hundreds of years, and it is difficult to envisage new ways of solving old problems. Personal skills of relating to patients are unlikely to change in so short a period, but investigative and therapeutic tools will continue to develop rapidly. It is here, where machines become obsolete quickly, that innovation and change will continue to take place to improve both the accuracy and effectiveness of investigative and therapeutic procedures. Rapid communication, checking, and analysis of data will contribute greatly to the effectiveness of new machines. Information fed back too early has no effect because it is in the latent time of the system, or if fed back too late causes the system to be inappropriate to the present actions of the system.

The application of control system ideas to management, allocation and uses of resources in the health service has been slow to come. The existing management in health services has largely been an information vacuum driven slowly by individual expertise, based on experience no matter how fallible. In future, information systems based on medical records can generate administrative and cost information that can be compared with and related to the expenditure of resources. Thus, by determining how we utilize resources and patient care and also by having an account of the on-going expenditure of resources in the service, both human, in the way of salaries, and equipment, etc., it will be possible to balance these two budgets against each other, observe trends early and take the necessary appropriate action to make sure that the effective use of resources is taking place.

However, this means a serious revolution in management, which will require a great deal of experiment and education before it becomes established in phase three. These new problems of learning how to handle an avalanche of data, how to run medical and financial information systems, and how to design these to work by the exception rather than the rule, remain. This managerial revolution dealing with complete management systems has yet to take place in the health services and elsewhere. It will be very demanding and need new approaches to the application of computer systems. Nevertheless, in phase two much more research will be undertaken in this area as well as that of patient care, so the two will develop side by side.

Turning now to phase three, taking us up to the year 2000, it can be expected that by that time there will be a complete reorientation of the theory of medicine and of our ways of maintaining and using our medical records. By this time it can be expected that the preventive and curative aspects of medical care will be united and they will be undertaken by all health personnel. The division of labour in the past between the preventive and curative aspects of medicine will be gone forever, because of good information and communication systems.

Medical management will become a much more important subject now that a great deal more information is available about disease, and standard epidemiological techniques will have a much wider application in the control of genetic and familiar disorders.

On our timescale, by the year 2000 a new system of medical records will be active, based on new medical theory and much more oriented to the control of patient care using computer systems for information processing and communication. With this will go a revolution in automation, and many new machines will be used to give a dynamic picture of changing processes in health and disease usually using non-invasive techniques on the patient

There will be a great deal of resurgence of interest in whole patient medicine, not only in the physical aspects, but in the emotional and social sides of life, so that the doctor will have a greater chance of delineating and controlling illness, which arises in other spheres than the physical. For the treatment of such major disorders like cancer, there will be new and powerful drugs, which will be monitored by new equipment. However, work will have to go much further into understanding the individual variations of each patient, so that treatment can be designed that is appropriate to him. Only with computer systems is such information going to become available. There will be an increasing demand for facilities for further investigation and treatment and storing information about patients which is required to monitor their progress. It is likely there will be more harmony in the medical and administrative aspects of management by the use of data processing. Certainly management will become more peripherally rather than centrally oriented, as computer information systems develop.

While planning and control will go on in the central administration based on evidence from large data banks, much more development will occur at a district level, where local initiative and use of resources and central planning meet.

The application of computer techniques to medical care will be the next major revolution by the year 2000. Without computer systems medicine cannot develop. It is already running into large problems due to communication difficulties, data overloads, and inadequate information banks. The need is to develop not only new tools, but new systems and ways of thinking to deal with the problems. If computer systems are adequately developed, health services in the year 2000 will be meeting the need rather better than they do at present.

In medicine at least, then, the decisionmakers, though faced with many problems, can regard the potential of computers during the period under review as almost wholly on the positive side, with possibly the acceptance of the new techniques as the only major headache. To them the question will virtually always be not "is it desirable?" but "is it possible?".

In education, to which we now address ourselves, the situation is rather different.

7   Computers and education

It is not particularly surprising that considerable work has already gone into educational aspects of computers. Virtually every communications advance has been exploited educationally. Films, recording and television have obvious educational application, and even postal services (for correspondence courses) and transport systems (for field trips and educational visits) could be said to have had some impact upon education. Indeed, of the communication technologies only the telephone and telegraph seem to have had no effect. The raw material both for computing and for education is information, so it was only to be expected that computers would be used educationally from quite early on.

Another factor, of equal importance, is that much early work in the development of computer applications took place in universities, by people who were themselves involved in education. Although the machines were initially installed purely as research tools, the computer scientists inevitably found themselves involved in teaching people to use computers, and it was a natural development that some would go on to consider the use of computers as a teaching aid in other educational areas.

We shall, therefore, begin by considering the most obvious impact of computers on education — their contribution to educational technology. It is here that the most dramatic effect could take place, although there are some other important effects which they could have to be discussed later. The first point to consider is whether in practice a dramatic effect is likely to take place. After all, despite the many technological advances in communications which have been made over the years, the changes in the pattern of teaching which these have brought about have been marginal. The basic teaching situation is still that of the teacher surrounded by his pupils, the exposition by the spoken or the written word, the development by discussion and by written or direct practical work performed by the pupils. Of all the technological developments which have taken place, only one could be regarded as being indispensable for everyday use: the oldest one of all, the printed book.

However, the significant factor which sets computing apart from the other techniques mentioned is that the communication can be made to be a two-way process. Even the simplest computer-aided instruction (CAI) system, where the pupil sits at a teletype, receives messages, and types responses, possesses this feature; and despite the obvious drawbacks compared with, say, television, which can present information in the form of static or moving pictures with or without sound, it is nevertheless, through allowing the pupil to respond and not merely be a passive receptor of information, already superior to the other communications methods in that extremely important respect. The computer-based system is the only communications medium which comes remotely near being able to match the interactive situation which obtains in the ordinary classroom. If CAI is to become a generally available, everyday feature of education, like the printed book, rather than an occasional aid like a film show, it will be because of this. There would be some, indeed, who would argue that CAI could go further, to the extent of largely replacing the human teacher. There are a number of grounds for such an argument: that one computer can give what is effectively individual attention to many human beings simultaneously (see Chapter 2), in this case pupils under instruction; that a computer never gets tired, does not possess personal likes and dislikes, never makes a mistake, and need have no effective limitations on its knowledge. Carried to their perfectionist extreme these arguments are, of course, untenable. If too many humans make too many demands on a computer system trying to cope with them simultaneously, some or all may have to wait for an answer; every so often a computer needs a "rest" for maintenance or repairs; someone designing or programming an educational computer system could quite easily (and not necessarily consciously) build in his own predilections and prejudices; the problems of writing software as massive and complex as a CAI system would require are so immense (again see Chapter 2) that it is likely to contain errors; and the system's knowledge will be no more extensive (or, for that matter, more accurate) than the data fed to it, even supposing that there is no cost limitation on size of the information store.

Despite these counter-arguments, the case remains a formidable one. In principle, at least, the computer is reliable and predictable in performance; hardware breakdowns are becoming less frequent; software techniques for interactive systems and for large systems generally are improving; and built-in prejudices or limitations of knowledge are at least more open to scrutiny and correction than in the case of human teachers. Nor need the limitations of the teletype systems — typed messages and keyboard responses — be held against CAI generally. Experimental systems have been based on this for reasons of cost and because the experimenters already had them available, but much more sophisticated and flexible means of communication between pupil and computer are already in existence. The computer can communicate by diagrams and messages on a display screen instead of by typing, and can use simultaneously sound or video recordings. The pupil can respond not only through the keyboard but by using a "light pen", to point to different places on the display screen, draw lines on it, and so on.

Flexible though such facilities are, others could be used and indeed for special purposes would be essential. For example, speech recognition could obviously be used to accept verbal responses, and would be essential for language teaching or for very young or backward pupils in situations where picture-and-pointing would be insufficient. As far as skills which are partly or wholly manual are concerned, the light pen has obvious limitations. Given adequate development of pattern-recognition techniques it could be used to teach writing, technical drawing is clearly feasible (although if computer exploitation had reached this level of sophistication that skill would have anyway been replaced by the use of computer-aided design techniques); even painting would be conceivable with a fusion of light pen and colour television techniques, though the problems of aesthetic analysis and guidance by computer would not be exactly trivial. However, flight and car-driving simulators come immediately to mind as instances of situations where special equipment is needed. Until now we have been talking about equipment which has uses — the main ones, in fact — outside education, so that costs to an education budget would at least not include hardware development, but if CAI were to become at all widespread it would not be surprising if special hardware should follow. It is a leapfrogging process — one does certain things because standard hardware is available, then having obtained the standard hardware one justifies the special hardware to do other things because it enables the system one already has to be used more widely and effectively. (This, of course, is a technique sometimes used consciously in a variety of contexts, by "empire-builders"; on the other hand, it is also a perfectly acceptable form of gradualism. The problem for the decisionmakers, in education as elsewhere, is how far and how fast the leapfrogging can be justified.)

Hence the possibility can be foreseen of a wide variety of measuring, weighing, and sensing devices being used for pupil response; in fact, in many cases these could probably be adapted from similar devices used for process control in industry, and so even here the development costs might be quite modest — on the hardware side. Considering the sophistication of industrial and research techniques it certainly seems feasible that the required measurements could be made and input to enable CAI to be used for the teaching of such skills as cookery and metalwork.

Taking this one stage further, one can foresee the use of devices attached to the pupil — probably, to be sufficiently flexible in use as well as acceptable to the individual, self-contained microtransmitters. These are the kinds of devices which can be used to monitor physical activity or behaviour in a medical context, such as the patient monitoring or intensive care applications mentioned in the last chapter. Among the kinds of educational work these could be used for are physical education and sports, and group activities of other kinds, since they could enable the pupil to be freed from his keyboard and display screen. In professional sports, walkie-talkie techniques are used to enable a coach to give directions from the touchline (this has been discovered — and banned — in actual play but is of course legitimate in training) and this is only a further extension of the technique. They would also improve the CAI techniques even in static situations; for example, a piano could be monitored to detect the striking and loudness of notes played by a music pupil, but this in itself would not yield sufficient information about fingering, which could be obtained by monitoring the pupil.

This brings us to yet another possibility — that of monitoring the pupil's unconscious reactions, as well as his positive responses. This could provide the computer with the equivalent to the teacher's perception that Jones is fidgeting, Smith is actually reading a comic, and the two girls at the back are giggling about something instead of paying attention.

There are obvious advantages in being able to assess a pupil's mood, whether boredom, excitement, anxiety, or whatever. Nevertheless, this does point to an area in which some difficult decisions may have to be taken. It is one thing to know that a human teacher may notice such things; it is another when a CAI system designer makes a positive and conscious decision to monitor for such data and process and perhaps record it, especially when it may well be, however sophisticated a CAI system one has, that human beings will also be around, even if only in a supervisory capacity. It may in fact be, of course, that the monitoring devices for such purposes will initially be human supervisors; the problem will not necessarily depend on the technology.

A related problem arises from the fact that devices such as this might be used for output as well as input, yielding the possibility of administering punishment for bad work or inattention, or reward for good work or diligence. Whatever the philosophy or practice of education into which a CAI system is introduced, it is clearly a decision of some importance whether punishments or rewards should be built into an automated system at all; educational philosophy at a particular place and time might permit punishments or rewards, yet require that these be wholly controlled by human judgment.

Such special input-output equipment apart, the hardware requirements for CAI are straightforward, though substantial. On the software side the difficulties occur that arise with any large system, as mentioned in Chapter 2, whether in education, or defence or medicine discussed earlier, or any other broad field of application. In addition there are the problems of producing the teaching program itself, even if the organisational side is scaled down to one pupil and one large computer. Various attempts have been made to produce special-purpose languages for writing teaching programs, the best-known probably being IBM's Coursewriter series. But although these and other such languages are to a greater or lesser extent "high level" languages in computer terms — i.e. each instruction which the programmer writes is reasonably understandable to humans, yet corresponds to a number of machine operations — they are far from this in educational terms. Each educational step has to be programmed separately: each message, each follow-up, each change in the rate of advance, each treatment of each alternative likely response. For CAI to be thoroughly exploited it will be necessary to go rather beyond simply making such steps easy to specify, to a stage where the course designer can indicate in quite general terms the concept he wants to get across, the educational approach he wants used, the performance required from the pupil before he can proceed to the next concept, and so on. To do this — even if it is possible — would clearly be a formidable task, perhaps requiring fundamental advances in educational theory; and it is anyway likely that the course designer would wish to go over the whole program, modifying steps here, changing examples or varying phrasing or treatment there. One possible approach in developing courses, however, would be to invert the roles of man and machine in the CAI situation, so that the computer as pupil would record the messages sent by the human as teacher, generate responses when required, and record the actions taken by the teacher as a result to a given response pattern; even this, to be successful, would have to be quite sophisticated.

Two further possible technical developments should be mentioned here. One development would be of self-modifying instructional programs, whereby the CAI system would learn to teach better by observing its own performance with its pupils. To a limited extent this can be done already, by varying parameters or reordering sets of alternatives, etc., but for it to be done in any more flexible way, in particular in ways unforeseen by the human designer, advances in artificial intelligence on the lines discussed in Chapter 3 would be necessary. The other technical development would be to link all educational computer systems into a single network, which would have advantages if only to allow all of them access to a single central information bank. Others would be that every system could have access to a given pupil's educational record without the need for any special action, and that advances in teaching technique could be made instantly available to every system in the network. It would be as if every teacher in a country could learn continuously from the experience of his colleagues. Needless to say, the problems of organisation and control of the flood of data would be immense.

While the impact of computers on teaching methods is the most obvious and most dramatic of the interactions between computers and education, there are a number of others. Clearly, for example, the actual content of education, what is taught, has already changed as a result of the advent of computers, and this process can be expected to continue as their use becomes more widespread. The effects can be broadly divided into changes in general education — i.e. the basic education which every child receives — changes in particular areas of study, and the introduction of new fields of study.

As far as general education is concerned, it is already (at least in developed countries) a desirable and will increasingly become a necessary part of a citizen's equipment to know something about computers, what they are, what they do and (perhaps as important) what they cannot do. Obviously treatment in any depth of how computers work is impossible with small children, but the application of computers, and their limitations, can be introduced quite early, just as a child can be made aware of, say, the uses and limitations of electricity as a power source, or of cars as a transport system, long before it is possible to discuss in any detail how electricity can be generated or how an internal combustion engine works. There is, in fact, as we shall see, quite a strong case for at least a minimal introduction along these lines before a child is introduced to CAI techniques.

The importance of computers to the most advanced countries is already such that there is at this moment a problem facing their educational decisionmakers — how to retrain teachers (not just science teachers) and how to revise curricula in institutions concerned with training new teachers, in order to cope with this need. Awareness of this problem, at least in computing circles, is shown by the work done on this topic in recent years by a working group of IFIP, the International Federation for Information Processing.

Apart from this direct effect on general education, an indirect effect could well be an increasing need for education for leisure. As we shall be returning to this theme in Part Four we shall not pursue it further here.

Next, considering particular subject areas, it is clear that the content and treatment of many courses have already and will continue to be affected as a result of computer applications, in proportion to the impact which such applications have. In some the changes may be negligible, in others revolutionary. We have already mentioned in the last chapter the way in which computer techniques might encourage a more algorithmic way of thinking in medicine, and this can clearly apply to other fields, e.g. engineering or accountancy. Likely general educational trends would include more emphasis on principles and less on acquiring facility and practice in processes which are normally done by computer; more emphasis on the analysis of problems, processes and structures; and a less specialist approach, with more emphasis on adaptability and flexibility.

As well as such direct effects, there may be side effects, such as a shift in the pattern of studies, as with education for leisure mentioned above, but more generally because of differences in effects of computers in different areas.

One overall shift in the pattern, though independent of the relative importance of the various areas of conventional study, is that generated by the existence and needs of computing itself. This is what (sometimes confusingly) is known as "computer education" — i.e. education about computers, rather than by or with the aid of computers about other things. We have already mentioned this when dealing with general education, but "computer science" also exists as a specialist academic study, and in addition vocational courses for those intending to work with computers are spreading. The great majority of people working with computers today have been recruited from other areas — programmers, academic computer scientists, etc., started life as mathematicians, physicists or accountants, and so on. Clearly the balance will shift, so that in due course the bulk of computer specialists will have been in computing from their earliest training. However, the spread of the use of computers may nevertheless mean that the bulk of computer education (in this restricted sense) will be to non-specialists, to teach them relevant techniques, so recruitment from outside could continue indefinitely.

If this is so, then one potential problem — the training of sufficient computer staff — which could face the educational decisionmakers may be minimal. More important might be the other side of the coin — that computing may be too narrow a field for someone working in an applications area, which may not matter when there is a strong leavening of people recruited from that area on the computer staff, but may matter when everyone is a computer specialist and trained as such. Buildings are designed which are not ideal for their purpose, by professional architects trained as architects, and the same can happen with computer systems. With the best architects and computer systems designers this is not the case, but it is naive to suppose that all will be the best, and it may be preferable to seed the specialist knowledge with knowledge of a particular applications area as a matter of policy.

Unfortunately, there seems a possibility that the academic world of computer science may concern itself more with a much more trivial problem. Academics in other disciplines are wont to complain from time to time that "computer science" (or "informatics", to anglicise a term used in some other languages) is not a precisely defined field. It is in fact true that, although most people who call themselves computer scientists have a feel for what the scope of the subject is, it is still in the process of definition — which is hardly surprising in an area so new and so rapidly expanding. However, some academic computer scientists have become rather sensitive on the matter and feel that efforts should be made to make the subject academically respectable, whatever that may mean. The danger in such an attitude is that it can easily degenerate into pedantry and scholastic snobbery in which the essential point becomes lost — the intellectual insight and rigour which the field demands, and the intellectual challenge and excitement it offers. It would be unfortunate if excessive preoccupation with such a problem were to cause educational problems to be overlooked, especially if the attitude falsely maintained by some in other academic fields, that any concern at all with social or vocational aspects necessarily means diluting the intellectual quality of the discipline, were to become prevalent.

Such worries will not trouble other parts of education already explicitly catering for vocational needs. However, plenty of decisions will have to be made here as elsewhere, in particular on how to cater for the demand for computer ancillary staff. One trend which could develop is for courses in typing and clerical skills of other kinds in time to become more general courses in the use of keyboard machines, including computer terminals.

Such a development would be in line with the need mentioned earlier for greater flexibility. The need for this in general and specialist education occurs within computing itself, for the power of the computer to render human skills redundant can be applied there as elsewhere. To take programming as an example, computers are such that, in principle, if a task has been programmed once there should be no need to do it again, except perhaps for minor revisions through changing circumstances unforeseeable by the original programmer. The fact that programmers are in the long run doing no more than working themselves out of a job has been obscured by the rapid advance of hardware technology and in programming techniques, problems of compatibility and communication, and the sheer number of tasks to be programmed. There may be no end in prospect to the need for programmers, but this limiting factor should not be altogether forgotten by those planning for the future. A more important factor, however, is the nature of programming itself. With the development of high-level programming languages it has already become a much more accessible skill, and while the effect so far has been mainly to allow programmers to deal with more complex problems, ultimately it could mean that learning to program a computer would be no more necessary than learning how to order a meal in a restaurant.

Similar arguments apply elsewhere in computing. Computer operators may become as unnecessary as people to turn on one's television set or dial one's telephone calls, while even the need for computer engineers could diminish with the development of mass-produced standard hardware modules and of self-diagnostic, fault-reporting computers, complete with CAI teaching packages on how to use them.

By the same token, even if the need for computer specialists continues, the sub-specialisms may well disappear except inside computer manufacturing firms and academic computer science. In the 1950s everyone using a computer had to be his own systems analyst, programmer and operator, and possibly to some extent engineer. The divisions which arose in the 1960s, which at least in part must have been in response to the need for computing sections in industry and commerce to gain recognition as something more than just another service like the typing pool or duplicating office, and for programmers to gain greater status than that of a mere machine minder, could be quite transient — something again which the educational decisionmakers will need to bear in mind when planning courses.

As well as affecting educational technology and content in the ways described so far, computers may also affect educational philosophy, methods, and organisation — "methods" here being methods in general, not simply technical means of communication such as CAI. These are related topics, in that organisation and methods to some extent reflect philosophy, while organisation also depends to some extent on available methods, whatever the philosophy. It is therefore convenient to consider these aspects together.

One has already been touched on, namely the need for retraining, both computer-related (i.e. introducing people to new, computer-based methods) and computer-unrelated (i.e. retraining in new skills because old skills have become redundant through the introduction of computers and automation). The existence of educational departments in the computer manufacturers' organisations, and the educational programmes put on in industry (usually with their aid) for the benefit of staff who will have to cope with the new techniques may have been marginal, in two senses, in its effect on the educational picture as a whole (marginal in that it has not been great, and in that it takes place at the edge of the formal educational system), but may be straws in a wind which is strengthening in intensity. One of the biggest immediate headaches of the educational planners of the advanced nations may well be here.

The reason for this is that educational systems tend to be based on the assumption that formal education is something for one's youth; having ceased it and started on a working career, the norm is to have no further formal education. It is clear that a move to a situation where continuing periods of formal education, whether part-time or full-time, would be the norm in a person's career rather than the exception would involve a considerable change in educational philosophy. Though this would be most obvious in vocational education, the growth of adult education from a minor to a major sector would have repercussions everywhere in education, and indeed beyond, as it would affect such matters as employment practices and conditions, career patterns, and through them people's ways of life. These wider aspects we shall return to later.

The necessary transitions in the attitudes of those involved and in the organisation of education will be far from easy. When, for example, the British educational planners notably failed to make adequate provision for increases in the school population, even when the children had signalled their needs by the mere fact of being born some years earlier, it does not offer much hope that there will be any planning at all for coping with this kind of need, let alone careful investigations of the likely magnitude of the problem, or discussions of whether it is better to accelerate the process or try to hold it back.

If computers are likely to affect the philosophy of education by altering, or at least bringing into question, what education is for, they could also do so by modifying the views of educationalists about the educational process itself — how people learn, and how people teach. As in medicine, using computers as a teaching aid means taking an algorithmic approach, and in particular the discipline imposed on a course designer when planning a CAI system tends to make him consciously think about the relative effectiveness of various approaches. Thus, as a by-product of the use of computers, teaching methods generally could be affected. With the development of techniques mentioned earlier to enable computers to learn how to teach better this perhaps marginal influence could become greater. This brings us to the edge of artificial intelligence, and it will be clear from the discussion in Chapter 3 that a breakthrough there could revolutionise present ideas about the nature of learning — with consequent effects throughout education. Such matters are so speculative in this context, however, that there is little to gain by pursuing them further here.

Most of the matters discussed so far, though they might influence the organisation of educational services to some extent, would not necessarily involve a complete restructuring; even the massive expansion in adult education might be coped with by means of reallocation of resources within an existing structure. The one exception is CAI. If CAI were to become at all widespread, it might produce strains within existing educational structures which could bring about enormous changes at many evels.

One example is the question of examinations. Examinations are the cornerstone — almost, it sometimes appears, the raison d'etre — of more than one education system, and many educationists are concerned about this. However, it is quite clear from the nature of CAI that it lends itself to the "continuous assessment" approach; indeed, unless one questions the validity of CAI itself it is difficult to avoid the conclusion that it renders formal examinations unnecessary.

Related to this is the problem of selection, both by the pupil of different areas of study, and of the pupil for different kinds of education. The first is straightforward; too often at present a pupil's choice is governed by the availability of teachers in given subjects, and the depth of their knowledge in them. Under CAI the choice will be much more that of the library —

i.e. governed by what has been published. Of course, the cost of providing that subject, even if published, will still be a factor (just as purchasing a given book for a library), but this is no more so than at present, where the cost involved is that of employing another teacher.

The second type of selection is much more controversial — witness, for example, the years of dispute in Britain about the selection of children at the age of eleven for different types of education, academic or otherwise. However, the individual attention of which CAI is capable disposes of the need for this kind of selection on *educational* grounds (though, of course, it does not affect *social* grounds) — or, if it is preferred to look at it in this way, selection is a continuous process, like assessment. CAI could greatly weaken any *educational* arguments for different kinds of school or other educational institution.

It is worth pointing out at this stage that this feature of a CAI system can be implemented independently of the instructional features. In systems of this kind, usually known as CMI (computer *managed* instruction) the computer is used as an organisational and planning tool, scheduling assignments and work programmes for pupils in accordance with progress and revealed aptitudes, without having any direct teaching function.

As well as weakening the case for different kinds of school, CAI also weakens the case for having schools at all. For a child under CAI, there is no need to attend a class in a particular classroom unless the instructional program is dependent on human teachers as back-up to help with unusual difficulties; if the program is wholly self-contained, any suitable terminal linked to the teaching computer will do. Hence someone who has the kind of injury or permanent disability which at present prevents attendance at school could continue his studies equally well at home or in hospital, at least in principle. Similar arguments apply to those with difficult travelling problems.

It is clear from this that the potential challenge to existing organisational structures in education is immense. If the provision of CAI is to become at all widespread, it is likely to begin, for reasons of cost, on the same lines as school television — i.e. as a central service networked to all institutions in a given educational area. This could be expected to grow, providing more and more facilities, and the crisis would be reached when suddenly it would be realised that the institutions, instead of being users of the computer and TV networks (which by then could well be effectively, if not formally, united), were merely their satellites, and the real educational decisions were being taken by the network organisers.

If CAI were to be exploited to this extent, not only would the overall organisational structure be affected, but also its fine structure within the institutions, in particular the role of the teacher. The crucial factor here is obviously the extent to which education can in principle and in practice be taken over by machines. It is difficult to see that this could have reached anything approaching completion in the thirty years we are discussing — but it may well be that the crucial decisions, if only decisions by default, will be taken during that period.

Even if the problem would never arise in its extreme form, which would mean the potential closure of all educational institutions apart from the CAI networks, there are two partial ways in which it could arise, and here both are certainly conceivable in thirty years. One is that some subject areas, though not all, would lend themselves to total CAI treatment, so that while schools would exist for instruction in the non-computerised areas (quite apart from other reasons, such as social ones, which might justify their continued existence) teachers would not be required at all in the computerised areas. At one level this is no more than an extension (albeit an important one) of that part of knowledge which does not require teaching by specialists; however, it is clear that if, say, the whole of school mathematics or history were to be moved into that realm there would be significant repercussions. The other possibility is that the role of teachers might be reduced to that of supervision, monitoring the progress of pupils through their CAI courses, seeing that they were actually keeping their minds on their work, helping out with their human, non-instructional problems, and perhaps intervening in the CAI course, very occasionally, in cases of special difficulty not allowed for in the CAI program.

Put this way, the problem is reasonably obvious. Is the teacher in such a system a mere routine machine-minder, with a boring job in which his talents are largely wasted apart from the very occasional bit of trouble-shooting; or, is he relieved of a lot of routine teaching, so that while keeping an eye on many pupils (perhaps many more than is possible at present) he can give individual attention to the ones that really need it, and so that he can concentrate on roles such as teaching children to live in society and understand the needs of others, or imparting moral or religious instruction, etc., depending on what the prevailing educational philosophy regards as important?

This is a good illustration of the double-edged nature of computer development in many areas, and education in particular; the case of medicine, where as we saw in the last chapter the blessing is reasonably unmixed, could be the exception rather than the rule. The problems facing decisionmakers tend to be two-edged in another respect — computers may affect educational philosophy but equally one's educational philosophy

affects computer developments in education. Thus, if one's view of education is child-centred, the problem of the role of the teacher just discussed
comes into some sort of perspective; if it is best for the child to exploit
CAI to the full, and the consequence is that teachers become machine
minders, then that consequence and the organisational problems it
entails have to be accepted.

Many of the other problems similarly have more than one face. That of
retraining discussed earlier is one such. One might say that automation
should not be brought in until it is possible to do the necessary retraining;
but then if the retraining is not possible, is this because of the nature of
the retraining problem, the kind of people to be retrained, or shortcomings
in the educational system responsible for it? In many cases, including
this one, when the problem is tackled may matter as much as how — in
particular, sufficient foresight is required that action can be taken in time.
Certainly in the case of the retraining problem there is no excuse for this
not to happen.

Another example of the effect of philosophy upon development is the
question of computer use in brainwashing techniques. The line between
"education" and "brainwashing" is at best a hazy one, and indeed today's
dropouts in the advanced western nations tend to regard (or purport to
regard) their educational systems as forms of deliberate brainwashing.
It is not necessary to discuss whether a given education is brainwashing,
and if so, whether deliberate, to recognise that more effective methods of
education can equally well be more effective methods of brainwashing,
and (perhaps, since that would be true of any educational advance, more
significant in this context) that computer-controlled education offers
undoubted advantages to the would-be brainwasher. The myth that the
computer is infallible, though becoming discredited, is still widespread —
there is still a tendency to accept as fact from a machine something which
would be questioned if it came from a human being. But far more significant is the control over the content and method of instruction which is
exercised by those in control of a CAI system. No amount of screening of
teachers could give the same power over the educational system to a
totalitarian regime. In a democratic society, careful monitoring of CAI
would obviously be essential if this were to become a substantial part of
education, and adequate safeguards would have to exist against the
erosion of the political independence of the educational system. The
responsibility of the computer and educational professionals in this
respect is clear.

Perhaps more dangerous, because more insidious, than the risks of
deliberate and overt manipulation are those of undesirable side-effects,

arising unnoticed and difficult to eradicate — the results of decision by default or decision through carelessness. The feature about CAI, for example, which makes it so attractive is the individual attention which each pupil gets; but the other face of this particular coin is that the advantages of group learning could be eroded, and one's education become a very lonely process. As mentioned earlier, there seems little reason to doubt that computer-guided group learning could become feasible — but this does not of itself guarantee that it will be exploited.

Another risk is that education could become too stereotyped and mechanical. This may seem strange when the individual nature of the instruction has been stressed, and the whole point about the computer is its flexibility, which reduces or eliminates the stereotyping which is otherwise a feature of the mechanical age, from plastic eggcups to saloon cars to networked television programmes. There are two factors at work here. One is the natural human inclination to take the easy way out, and in computerised systems of all kinds the easy way is often the stereotyped and mechanical way. There are many invoicing systems which testify to the truth of this. The other factor is that, in a new field of application where one is feeling one's way, it may be necessary to stick to what is straightforward and mechanical — only to find that, when one has learned to do things in a more sophisticated way, too much time and effort has gone into the design and use of the old, mechanistic system to make it easy to abandon. In this case testimony is provided by the world's most widely used scientific programming language. A further, related danger, is that only what is simple and mechanical to do is regarded as worth doing — the attitude that turns the study of history into the learning of dates or the study of a language into the learning of irregular verbs. Such dangers arise in another computer application in education, not so far mentioned because not very important in itself, namely the computerised marking of examinations.

A further possible risk is that of undesirable psychological effects on the pupils themselves. Professor Robert Hess, of Stanford University, where experimental CAI work has been pioneered for a number of years, has been reported as having found 13- to 15-year-olds exposed to CAI crediting the computer *in a non-metaphorical way* with qualities like trustworthiness, reliability, veracity and fairness. Quite what the psychological effects would be on pupils who from their earliest years had received most of their instruction from a machine rather than human beings may be difficult to estimate, but obviously this is another factor to be borne in mind together with the loneliness problem referred to earlier.

At least the previously mentioned idea of the earliest possible introduction to what computers are and can or cannot do would seem to be indicated.

It may appear from the foregoing that educational decisionmakers are faced with the prospect of traversing a veritable minefield of difficulties. Yet, if all these traps were avoided, a further one would remain: the possibility that experimental teaching might be squeezed out. The average teacher teaches in a routine way most of the time ("routine" here being used in the non-pejorative sense of using known and tried methods) but in the classroom situation there is always the chance for a particular individual teacher to devise experimental approaches, or to digress spontaneously to catch the mood of or a spark of interest in the class. The more teaching is automatic, the more it is likely to be predictable and (however imaginative) routine, the less likelihood there is of new departures. Of course, not all such experimentation is successful, so it might be considered a price worth paying. Further, a sufficiently sophisticated computerised system could conduct experiments, either fed in or, if it were a learning system of the kind described earlier, generated by the system itself. There are further dangers here, for the systems designers to guard against, of instability, and sudden and startling changes of approach.

For the educational decisionmakers the thirty years which is our time-scale will not be easy. Perhaps their greatest test will be in timing the decisions, so that no decision is made too soon, either consciously or by default. One of the factors influencing the adoption of computer methods in education, as in other fields, will be economic, both unit costs of teaching and the relative availability of teachers in different subjects. In subjects with severe shortages — but in which there is a strong demand, not just from potential students but from national or commercial sources — the pressures may be so great that systems will be produced, possibly prematurely as far as technical capability is concerned, almost certainly too quickly to do the job properly, to which the educational world will be committed since, as mentioned above, what is then done would be extremely difficult to undo. The next thirty years may not see machines totally supplant men in education, but foundations could be laid which will determine the shape of education in the next century.

8　International implications

So far we have been considering the impact of computers on government in a purely national context, except for the special case of the military uses. In this chapter we shall take an international view. The principal aspects to be covered are the differential effects of computing in different countries depending on their resources and needs, the effects of computing on international relations, and the growth of internationally organised systems, both by intergovernmental bodies and by multinational corporations.

During the earlier chapters of this part of the book, we have tended to concentrate mainly on what may become technically feasible over the next thirty years, and the possible implications of such developments. Inevitably this has meant that, in terms of actual implementation, we have been thinking principally of the most advanced nations of the world. In other countries the exploitation of computing is not only likely to lag behind, but follow a different pattern. For example, it seems probable that for some time to come many developing countries will have an abundant supply of cheap labour. A distinction therefore needs to be made between those computer applications that are merely labour-saving and those which would not otherwise be possible. Only the latter type will be valid in these circumstances and even then the low level of consumer demand may rule many possibilities out of court. One area which will remain is the use of computers at government level to guide and control the expansion of their economies while avoiding the penalties that this has so often involved in the past. For example, simulation of a national economy on a computer model will enable alternative strategies to be evaluated, so that mistakes and the waste of scarce resources can be avoided when planning future expansion, as discussed earlier, and both the simulations themselves and implementation of the resulting strategies are likely to be easier than in highly industrialised nations where the situation may be far more complex and have undergone developments which, though now seen to be clearly undesirable, may be difficult to alter.

One trouble here is the natural fear in developing countries of neo-colonialism expressed through technological domination. This fear could have its effect in many ways, from sticking too rigidly to the doctrine that "independence means being allowed to make your own mistakes", amounting to a refusal to take advice from anyone or even learn from their errors, to suspicion that the simulation itself was being rigged to preserve the domination of the industrialised nations. This could involve some tricky political decisionmaking on the part of the leaders of the developing countries. Tact and understanding will also be called for from the advanced nations, on the part both of governments and of the computer firms.

This is not to say that the dangers of technological domination should be discounted. The area of overlap with other forms of technological domination, and economic domination, is a large one, too large to be covered here, but a few points which particularly relate to computers should be mentioned. Although, as we have said, a developing country may well have an abundant supply of labour, this may not apply to skilled labour or educated people for key positions. (The existence of Third World countries with a graduate unemployment problem shows that one cannot consider developing countries as a homogeneous group, however.) Thus, even with an army of clerks available to do the routine paperwork done in advanced countries by computer, a developing country may feel the need of a computer system at a more highly skilled administrative level. In places where the political system, for good reasons or bad, is unstable, leaders uncertain of their position may even prefer this. However, the importation of a packaged bureaucratic system could conceivably become, and could certainly be regarded as, a form of technological domination.

Another, and possibly even more critical, area of potential domination is in education, for the same reason — shortage of people with the necessary skills, in this case of teachers. CAI packages could have a lot to offer a developing country with a shortage of specialists in a particular field. However, a certain fear of becoming too dependent is understandable, even if the long term effect of raising educational standards is to reduce the need for dependence.

However, as with many things, these problems are part of a wider international problem which would exist whether computers were there or not. Let us consider now what effects the spread of computer use might have on international relations in other ways. The main ones must surely come from the development of international computer systems, which will be our main concern, but before looking at that it is worth pointing out that there may be effects on the individual and social level, as well as the governmental and organisational level. In many respects "computer people" already form an international fraternity. The domination of one corporation's products has obviously been an important factor in bringing people together and establishing de facto standards and practices, but it has been by no means the only one. The International Federation for Information Processing (IFIP) has played its part with its triennial conferences, the development of the international programming languages ALGOL 60 and ALGOL 68, and other co-operative activities. Job mobility of computer personnel, often in organisations of multinational scope, is another factor, and while this has been (inevitably) most obvious in the context of a single country, international job mobility also exists and might well be expected to increase. One can hope that the growth of an internationally minded computing community may help in a small way to reduce national and racial prejudices. On a more mundane level, the existence of people used to communicating in rather precise terms, in areas which involve the taking of decisions, may in the long run help to reduce the risk of international misunderstandings; the problems, for example, of different interpretations of international agreements within different legal systems are unlikely to appear in any serious form when one is discussing algorithms to be implemented on computer systems. The main programming languages are in international use, and a further factor is that they are based on English, which is very much the *lingua franca* of ordinary communication in the computing world. Spread of computer use will spread the use not only of programming languages like FORTRAN, the ALGOLs and COBOL, but also English (though increased use can also lead to diversification — ALGOL 60 has, for example, been "translated" into French).

However, although such effects at the individual level are in principle independent of the growth of international computer systems, they are likely to be minimal unless such systems develop, for staff will be needed to run them, and this greatly increases the opportunities for contact at individual level.

Any international use of computers implies an international organisation to run the machines. In many cases the prime objective of this organisation may be quite unconnected with computers as such. Nevertheless, the organisation will depend on the computers for efficient operation or even for its entire existence. For example, the police forces of the world will need to make co-operative use of computers on an increasing scale. This will be necessary in order to combat big crime, which is rapidly becoming an international industry. There is already a rudimentary organisation for co-operation in Interpol, but it does not have the power or the money. Unless a suitable organisation exists the technical ability to use computers in the fight against crime will be wasted.

A similar situation will occur in many other areas. The establishment of the necessary international organisations will require both the political will and a lot of hard negotiations. It may be that these organisations should be set up as agencies of the UN, or under the aegis of existing agencies. Alternatively, they may start with just a few nations joining together in an ad hoc fashion with others entering later. Whatever the mechanism, if they are not truly international and effective then the power of the computer will be wasted; it may be that here is an opportunity for the UN secretariat to take a real initiative. For example, one gets the impression that, while many UN agencies do useful work, they are of limited effectiveness — partly through shortage of money, partly through lack of political will among UN member countries, but also through technical and administrative shortcomings. If computers can help to bridge the gap between the aims and achievements of the many dedicated (and internationally or even supranationally minded) people who run these international organisations, then they will have a profound effect on the world political scene, for if a body becomes more effective it becomes more important and more influential as a consequence.

Turning now to the use of computers as part of international networks, an example that is already in operation is a time-sharing system based on a large machine in America that also has terminals in Europe. The underlying concept of this type of system is the distribution of calculating power. It is this idea that has led to much of the discussion of computers being organised as a public utility, described in Chapter 9, where one central machine services many users. On an international scale, while this type of system will increase in the short term, it may be doubted whether it has much long-term validity. The main justification for such a system is to obtain maximum use of a very expensive resource — the central computer — by exploiting the difference in time zones between Europe and America. Thus the peak demand for use of the computer in Europe will help to fill the troughs in demand within the USA. However, the time differences between the East and West coasts of continental America are sufficient to make this apparently worthwhile, yet experience shows that in practice the networks make little use of this facility. In addition, we have earlier noted in Part One that the cost of central computer power has already been drastically reduced, and this trend will continue. It therefore seems likely that there will eventually be very little economic advantage in such a system. As the central computer gets cheaper there will be a strong tendency to supply the calculating power where it is to be used, even if this means the machine is not utilised at maximum efficiency.

There are, however, a few cases where a continuing need for this type of network can be foreseen. One is where the problems to be solved are so complex that only the most advanced computers can tackle them. At any one time there will exist only a few computers that represent the extreme limits of the state of the art and can therefore be used for these calculations. The demand for the services of such machines will be relatively small but globally distributed. Another possible situation is where the demand for computer services in an underdeveloped nation is so small that it would not be worth setting up a separate organisation to deal with it. This could apply however cheap the actual computer becomes. In this case a nation may make international use of a service provided by a more industrialised neighbour that is primarily intended for its own internal purposes. Alternatively, a group of nations may operate a computing service on a regional basis. A further possibility, discussed again in Chapter 9, is the specialist large-scale databank.

A field that does demand extreme calculating power and which also depends on international co-operation is weather forecasting. The calculations involved in weather forecasting are so complex and voluminous that they will always need the biggest and fastest machines currently available. The data for these calculations must be gathered on a global scale and needs close international co-operation, while the results apply to geographical regions rather than countries. The weather does not recognise national boundaries — even in the English cricket season! Thus the World Weather Service may well be the prime example of this type of international computer usage where a few advanced machines supply calculating power for the whole world. The weather bureaux of individual countries will become increasingly subordinate to a single apolitical world-wide organisation providing a service to all nations, though, of course, some may set up parallel operations for military reasons.

A natural extension of this service will be to forecast the effects of weather conditions. For example, by linking knowledge of the amount of winds and rain to be expected with hydrographical data it should be possible to predict floods and tidal surges. A related topic that should also become amenable to increased knowledge and greater calculating power is the prediction of earthquakes. Thus even more types of natural disaster will be understood and occurrences forecast. This will allow precautions to be taken and relief operations planned in advance.

The international organisations responsible for such forecasting will face a major test when the advance of knowledge based on computers allows these natural phenomena to be controlled rather than merely forecast. For example, a weather pattern that would suit one country may involve a corresponding disadvantage for another. Unless some efficient political mechanism is evolved to arbitrate on these issues there will be great danger of international conflict. The determination of such cannot just be left to the scientists and technicians. However, this at least is unlikely to be a serious problem within our thirty years.

A more important aspect of the use of computers on an international scale will be to control communications. There will continue to be an explosive growth in the requirement for efficient communication between all parts of the world, and to satisfy this need there must be extensive use of computers in the communications network to control this vast increase in traffic. Computers are already being used to control telephone exchanges and message switching centres but this is only a small beginning; in future the whole communications network will depend on computers to achieve the maximum utilisation of the various communications media. This will be essential not only for inter-human messages of all kinds but also for the vast amount of inter-computer data that will be transmitted through the network.

As well as increasing the performance of the network, computers will be extensively used to preserve the integrity of the system. This will involve constant checking for any type of error and, in the event of a failure, automatically taking all necessary steps to remedy the matter. This may range from merely repeating part of a message in the case of an intermittent fault to reconfiguration of the network in the case of a more serious breakdown; in any event diagnostic routines will be applied to record and isolate the fault.

In the related field of transport a similar function will be performed, for example in air traffic control. Here the onset of bad weather or other hazards might cause aircraft to be automatically re-routed, possibly through another nation's air space, which must involve some diminution of the national sovereignty of the country being overflown. While this is easily seen in the case of a tangible object such as an aircraft, the same principle applies to any message. If the full flexibility and efficiency of the international communications network is to be achieved the computers must have the power to ignore national boundaries for some purposes. This is therefore another field where an international control body is required. The present arrangements for technical co-operation must be developed into political institutions to which countries will abdicate some of the powers that are currently reserved to individual sovereign states.

Another function performed by computers within the communications network will be that of security. Any form of censorship or monitoring of information by human methods will become quite impossible due to the sheer volume and rate of data flow. The implication is that any information that is stored in such a way as to be accessible from the communications network must be considered vulnerable to unauthorised enquiry and possible alteration. The prevention of such access will require extremely sophisticated use of computers.

The main international use of computers will be for the control of information. Earlier chapters have shown the ability of the computer to organise the storage of immense amounts of information, to correlate the various kinds of information stored and to retrieve particular information on a selective basis. This applies not just to an individual computer attached to a single database but even more to a network of computers and databases. The use of the ability on an international scale will place great demands on the communications network as already described. Far more important will be its effects on many aspects of social and political activity.

A very simple example of this type of system that is already in operation is the seat reservation system of an international airline. In such systems the reservation desks or travel agents in many countries can interrogate and amend a database held at the airline's headquarters. The sale of a seat at one terminal will immediately affect the sales situation at all terminals, wherever they may be.

One interesting application for international access to information is in the field of education. We have already mentioned in this chapter the potential value of CAI packages to developing countries, but clearly the kind of educational networks envisaged in Chapter 7 could be developed on an international scale. Possibly it is the communications aspect which would be most important here — but one can imagine the effects on the world's physicists if, for example, Einstein's early expositions of relativity had been broadcast on international educational channels, preceded and followed by CAI presentations of the necessary background material.

In the economic sphere one result that is already apparent is the trend to large multi-national companies. In the past the growth of a business beyond a certain size has been hindered by problems of control and communication. Thus as a firm grew larger the internal inefficiencies reduced its competitive edge, particularly so where the business was widely dispersed geographically. The information flow possible in a computer network will overcome this difficulty and the economics of size will be reasserted. The resultant multi-national companies will use their computers to maximise profit on a world-wide basis. Their headquarters will be situated in the country that offers the most advantageous tax and legal system, just as many shipping lines are nominally registered in Liberia; processes that are inherently labour intensive will be sited in countries where labour is cheap and plentiful. This can already be seen in the computer industry itself where components for American computers are made in Hong Kong or Taiwan. A similar situation can be seen in the European refrigerator market where most manufacture is in Italy, but there are already hints that this industry will move to even lower cost areas. This is only one aspect of the rationalisation of production on a global basis. It will give a powerful boost to world trade and will be of great benefit to those countries prepared to welcome such investment. However, it will hasten the decay of such industries in the more industrialised nations — the textile industry in Britain is only one example. There is a danger that this decay will lead to pressure to protect such industries by tariffs and quotas, and if this happens it will nullify the benefits to be gained from free world trade. To avoid this there must be wider appreciation of these benefits, together with greater investment in retraining for the employees of the declining industries.

If the multinational company is to gain full benefit from its world-wide activities it must have a most efficient distribution system; this will be another function of the computer controlled information network. The feedback of accurate and up-to-date sales data will be the basis for tight stock control. All this can be achieved by developments from current techniques and within the company's own computer system, but for its forward planning and market research it will wish to make use of information held in public networks where the issue of privacy, to be discussed in Chapter 20, becomes of prime concern.

The multinational manufacturing company will need to call on multi-national service companies to supply its specialised requirements — for example in banking and insurance. In banking this has so far been met by the formation of consortia of national banks. It seems very probable that this is at best an interim solution and that true multinational banks will emerge as soon as the problems imposed by differing national banking laws can be overcome. There will therefore be strong pressure for the harmonisation not only of banking laws but through the whole range of company law and taxation. Countries that persist in retaining an idio-syncratic attitude may find themselves missing out on the economic benefits to be gained from participation in these developments.

In a similar fashion the stock markets and money markets of the world will have to work closely together to provide the capital required by these multinational companies. This can already be seen in the growth of the Euromoney markets. In the future all international finance will be arranged via the various computer networks. Conversely, the existence of these networks will mean that flows of "hot" money will become steadily larger in magnitude and will take place more rapidly, not because speculators are trying to attack a currency but by the normal operation of business-men seeking the best place to invest their money. More and more firms will have the know-how and the means to do so on an international scale, and to counteract this will require either close co-operation in fiscal and monetary policy between all governments concerned on floating exchange rates that will adapt immediately to the currency flows.

The employee of a multinational company will be required to be far more mobile, especially in the management levels. This is evidenced by the great oil firms, where candidates for high office must have had experience in many aspects of the companies' operations in different parts of the world. The natural desire of these employees to enjoy a similar standard of living wherever they may be will be reinforced by company-wide standards of pay and conditions; this will be yet another factor in the trend towards a more homogeneous international culture.

One reaction to the growth of the multinational company will be the formation of international trades unions to represent their employees. If industrial relations are not to descend to the level of the jungle this will require more international regulations. It seems only a matter of time before this in turn leads to international political parties (other than the Communist party) pursuing similar aims in many countries. The end result might be some form of federalisation. It is to be hoped that the international culture postulated here must be one under which all men are willing to live; the dangers range from the use of computers to enforce a totalitarian society to a backlash of separatism and anarchy.

This brings us to the world of organisation and industry, which is our theme in Part Three. Many matters which will affect governments have still to be dealt with; however, it is clear already that it could easily happen that in the world to come the nation without a sophisticated computer system at a high administrative level will be at a severe disadvantage. The impact of all the developments we have been discussing in the diplomatic sphere will be to cause a change in the nature, and a great increase in the complexity, of international negotiations. The establishment of common company laws, to take one example, will require years of hard bargaining. The negotiations will be based on much greater knowledge of the importance of the various details due to computer information. It is certain that each delegate will have immediate access to his own computer network to determine the effect of each proposal and counter proposal on his country's position. This quantitative approach will, hopefully, reduce the importance of considerations of prestige and similar intangibles. The actual work needed to reach agreement will be much tougher and may involve a "neutral" computer to calculate solutions that would be reasonably fair and acceptable to all parties.

The country without the necessary information backup in such circumstances will clearly be handicapped; the value of international agencies with similar facilities will be proportionately enhanced. Possibly the development of neutral information systems at such centres as UN headquarters and the International Court of Justice may be the best hope that the defence systems described in Chapter 5 will never be used.

3 The world of industry and organisation

9 Computing as a public utility

Outside the world of government, many organisations already use computers. Since almost any organisation has to store and process information for operational or planning reasons, this is hardly surprising. In this part of the book we shall be looking at some of the implications of this, even though it will be impossible to survey all the myriad applications of computer techniques which are possible in commercial and other organisations. However, quite clearly, both the quantity and type of computer use which organisations need depends greatly on their size and purpose, and until recent years the use of computers has been confined to those wealthy enough and with sufficient need to enable them to purchase their own systems. The growth of hiring and bureau services has of late started to change this. In this chapter we shall look in more detail at the logical development of this kind of service, the concept which has already been mentioned once or twice before, the computer network. For the development of networks could change the pattern of computer use dramatically; rather than having to make a positive decision to "go computer", any organisation which wishes to use computing power will have it as much on tap as electricity, the telephone or, what is literally on tap, running water.

The example of electricity is perhaps a good one with which to introduce the idea of a computing utility. First, those organisations with the resources and need for that kind of power might obtain their own generators; then, as generative capacity increases and costs drop, some may sell excess capacity to those unable or unwilling to obtain their own generators; then organisations come into being simply to generate power for use by others as they require it; then, as really large-scale generation and power transmission becomes technically feasible, the fourth stage is reached, a grid system supplying power to all where and when they need it is developed; and finally one reaches a situation where even the large organisations capable of running generators instead rely on the grid system, unless they have special requirements, and electricity becomes so cheaply and widely available that it is used almost universally, in every home and office, and its cheapness, convenience and versatility means that it is used in many contexts for which that kind of power is by no means essential.

In computing we are in the third and at the verge of the fourth stage. We have already indicated in Chapter 2 the increase in power and capacity and drop in cost of actual computing which make feasible the large-scale provision of facilities needed for a grid system, the developments in interactive and multiaccess systems which make the necessary organisation possible, and the concepts of data transmission which bring computing power to the user even though the source of the power, the actual computer processor, may be as physically remote from him as the power station which provides the electricity for his terminal.

Thus a picture of a computer network emerges where, in a country the size of Britain, some fifty to a hundred large computer installations are connected to, and interconnected through, smaller exchange computers to which are connected millions of business and private subscribers, forming a national grid. As well as simple keyboard and display (by printing or cathode ray tube) terminals, which will certainly be almost universal to begin with and are likely to remain the most common, in due course there are, as mentioned in Chapter 2, likely to be all kinds of devices plugged into the grid — not as many as are plugged into the electricity mains, but considerably more than the few kinds of device using the telephone voice communications network.

The design and implementation of a data transmission network is a major national exercise currently being undertaken by the British Post Office, the telecommunications authority in the UK. At the moment, data transmission uses the switched telephone network for slow speed and dedicated private lines for faster transmission, but in either case it is more expensive than it would be when a network dedicated to data transmission, of the kind mentioned in Chapter 2, is used. It is obviously sensible to make use of the massive capital investment in the existing telephone network to begin with, but the dedicated network planned by the Post Office for the late 1970s will pay off in the long run, achieving the speed of the private line with the economy of the switched public network. Even more economy can be achieved by the use of the "store and forward" method of transmission. The simple transmission method dedicates the line for the whole period of a transmission, and much of this time may well be idle; in the "store and forward" system exchange computers build up messages, coming in at much slower speeds (e.g. the speed of a human typist) than the lines can handle, into packages, and then transmits these at maximum speed in short, sharp burst of a few milliseconds at a time. By using exchange computers to pack, route, switch and unpack messages in this way the major part of the transmission line — effectively all except the parts between the exchange computers and the users' terminals — can be shared among many users and used with much higher efficiency. Finally, yet more economy is likely in trunk transmission in due course by various advances in telecommunications such as multiplexing, pulse code modulation, microwave and laser beams and waveguides, leading, as again we mentioned in Chapter 2, to a vast increase in channel capacity for information transmission of all kinds — voice, television and data.

Probably in most countries the necessary planning and decisions for the provision of computing as a public utility along these lines will be taken by the responsible government department or public authority, and the necessary finance will be found from taxation, although there is no reason in principle why it should not be provided commercially, like the early telephone and electricity services; probably, because of the enormous capital investment, by a consortium. Ultimately, as we saw in the last chapter, international co-operation will be needed, e.g. through the International Telecommunications Union.

The availability of computing as a utility would have a profound effect both on private individuals and on organisations. The effects on the lives of individuals of this and other developments in computing are dealt with in Part Four, so we shall here consider mainly the effects on organisations. Clearly these may be of two kinds, depending on whether it is offering a new facility not previously available, or replacing an earlier facility or enabling it to be improved.

An example of a new facility would be a program available to individual subscribers to help them work out their personal income tax, by means of a simple conversational system which would question the caller and from his answers advise him on his liabilities and allowances. This could be provided whether or not it was linked with a government system for actual on-line tax assessment, as discussed in Chapter 4. The effect on existing commercial organisations would be minimal as this would not be competing directly against any service at present in existence. Although tax consultants might at first regard it as some kind of competition, in fact it would probably be used by people who at present do not use their services. Indeed they could probably extend and improve their services by offering a similar program themselves through the public network, for in this kind of system there is no reason why facilities need be provided only centrally. As well as providing subscribers with computing power and facilities, the network could simply connect those with special services to offer with those who want to use them, as indeed the telephone networks do now.

The example of an income tax program is typical of a wide class of applications suitable for network provision, which are characterised by the following features: frequent alterations in the basic information, here the rates of tax and rules for its assessment, quickly making handbooks, printed tables, etc., obsolete, necessitating regular reprinting at considerable trouble and expense; the fact that much of the information is irrelevant to a particular individual, so that finding one's way through a maze of alternatives can be confusing to the uninitiated; and the usefulness of such a facility to very large numbers of people. Other areas in which new facilities could be offered, either to organisations or to individuals, are in matching people's requirements for homes with properties on the market, where the turnover in what is available is high; similarly trying to match jobs with vacancies, mentioned in Part Two in connection with government employment and social security policies, but equally possible commercially; and theatre and ticket agencies of all kinds. Firms in these sorts of businesses will need to consider very carefully, as the computer utility approaches, how to deal with such challenges.

It will be clear from the foregoing and from the discussion of education in Chapter 7 that computer-aided instruction could be provided through the public network, rather as the broadcasting channels are used already for educational purposes. The three criteria are not met so strongly in this case: in most cases the instructional material does not change often, there is a maze of alternatives but this is difficult for the teacher/programmer to determine, leading to extremely complex programs, and any given CAI program will be used by far fewer people than, say, the income tax program. Thus the cost of such a facility would be high in comparison — though also, of course, the reward. Again, this has implications especially for such organisations as correspondence colleges or secretarial schools.

It is, in fact, the information industry in general on which the impact will be greatest. Consider, for example, a news service as a possible facility provided by the computer utility. One could connect to this service, and request the latest news headlines, or the news in the last few days or weeks, as required, on any specified topic, or the latest share prices on the stock market, or sports fixtures, results, scores, and tables. All of these share our three criteria: the items change frequently, any individual has to select from a mass of information (e.g. printed in a newspaper) what interests him, and large numbers of people would be interested in using such a service. The challenge is not so much to the telecommunications services already in existence, already on tap, able in due course (as we have seen) to merge with the new service, but to the older news media such as newspapers. However, people buy papers and magazines not just for such items, but for many reasons — to skim through the minor news items for anything of interest or amusement, for reviews, feature articles, editorials and comment, or pictures of pop stars or girls. One can imagine a subscriber using a news service from home or office to obtain up-to-date information on a particular topic, as English cricket enthusiasts telephone now for the latest Test match score, but the need for something to read on a bus or train, or relaxed in an armchair, will surely continue.

Nevertheless, the prime purpose of newspapers is to provide news, and the newspaper industry could well use a computer utility in two ways — first to improve its own news-gathering and news-collating capacity, and second to get this to its public with maximum speed. In the long run it could be the production and distribution side of newspapers which would be most seriously affected, perhaps with the evening newspapers leading the way, since it is there where the pressures and rewards of getting the news onto the streets first are greatest. Given facsimile copying terminals, it would be possible to obtain the latest edition of any desired newspaper — "latest" meaning only minutes old. Such terminals might well be specialised, so that newsagents and vendors would not altogether disappear, but turn into owners of such terminals obtaining copies of papers for their customers. In such circumstances the concept of the "edition" of a paper would be replaced by a timecheck of the latest update; the distinction between morning and evening papers would vanish, leading to the concept of the continuous newspaper. Papers could also be sectionalised, so that those who did not want the racing pages or business news would not need to have them.

Should such developments come about, the rest of the publishing industry, in books and magazines, will have to decide whether and how to react. The need for speed is missing, so conventional printing and distribution are fast enough; on the other hand, if an alternative distribution system exists anyway one should at least consider whether to use it. In addition, retail outlets for books and magazines always have a problem as to which titles to stock and in what numbers, whether to accept orders for out of stock items, etc. A development of a simple facsimile terminal to a full colour facsimile terminal with binding facilities would enable retail booksellers to stock a quite narrow range of bestsellers and popular magazines, but reproduce on demand any given item in one of a narrow range of standard formats. Specialist magazines with limited circulation might appear only in facsimile format, others in both, books might be published in facsimile from author's typescript only, facsimile from typeset only, or facsimile and conventional, depending on whether it was likely to sell in hundreds, thousands, or tens of thousands. The industry itself would have to decide whether it was worth developing such terminals and the means of keeping the publications on file. One side advantage of the facsimile method, of course, is ease of correcting errors without having to wait for a full reprint.

However, the information industry consists not only of making information available, but enabling people to find out what is available. A bookseller using a system on the lines just described would need to be able to find out at once what was available through his terminal — but this is a problem which exists already. How to cope with the "information explosion" and keep track of titles (and preferably also obtain abstracts) of papers, articles and books published in, say, a given branch of learning, or available in a given library or group of libraries, is something which has been tackled for a few subjects only, and only on a very small scale. If we apply our three criteria, it can be seen that in this aspect of the information industry the frequency of changes is important — new items are added every day. The second criterion, having to search through a maze of alternatives, certainly applies, as anyone who has searched through a library catalogue will know. However, although if the ideal of a universal retrieval system could be realised it would be helpful to large numbers of people, the frequency with which they would use it, particularly if related to the amount of information stored, is low, and the cost of designing, setting up and maintaining such a system even in a limited field is very large. To make it economically justifiable it certainly appears that such a service could only be maintained on a national or even international basis (for example by maintaining the system in one centre in one country and sending updated copies or additions periodically to others, as is already done in the commercial Scisearch system which covers titles in a range of scientific journals).

The implications for libraries and users of libraries are obvious, and the impact on modern industries, which are so information-dependent, would be considerable, particularly if, e.g. patent information were to be available through the network. However, there are other areas of activity in which much depends on simply knowing where relevant information is to be had and where to find it. To take one example: people go to lawyers as much as anything because they know the law, and how to find out what their legal position is in a given situation. A routine task like transferring title to a property could in principle be done through inter-active programs, the necessary searches into such things as local authority development plans which might affect the land, being done automatically through connection with the government network, contracts being exchanged simultaneously, and even the necessary mortgage arrangements and payments being carried through by connection with the financial network to be looked at in the next chapter. Lawyers, and others who similarly obtain part of their livelihood simply through selling specialised knowledge to the layman, might therefore well regard a computer utility as a threat. On the other hand, law involves interpretation as well as sheer factual knowledge, and a great deal of routine scanning of statute or case law — of complete texts as well as, in the general system described earlier, simply titles and abstracts — could be done more cheaply and conveniently for the lawyers if (say through their professional associations) a specialised information system were to be available to them through the network.

Hence those both directly and indirectly involved in the information industry will see in the computer utility both a challenge and an opportunity, and in each area the response to both will have to be carefully assessed. Most of the techniques are already possible or almost possible, involving the storage, processing and transmission of textual information in moderate quantities, at moderate speeds, both of which existing equipment is capable of dealing with. For the facsimile printing mentioned as a later possibility in the publishing field, or for even more demanding facilities, such as being able to request the display of a given film or tele-recording on one's display screen, much more powerful and expensive transmission, terminal, storage and retrieval facilities would be required. A whole new industry in computer information services may spring up exploiting typewriter or display screen terminals and operated by or through the public network, but merely overlapping slightly, not replacing, present services; those responsible for the present services should certainly be thinking about getting in on the ground floor of such new services, but there should be ample time for them to decide their longer term policies. For many of our thirty years people will be watching normal television transmissions, reading normal books, buying normal newspapers.

Outside the information services, the great value of a computer utility to the average organisation will be to provide special-purpose programs to help it in its work. Already the working engineer, scientist, statistician or designer can call on any of thousands of different programs to aid him in various standard computations; similarly administrators will be able to call upon business data processing packages, e.g. small businesses will be able to get their payrolls, accounts, etc., routinely processed. However, the larger firm might well wish to develop (or have developed before the grid was inaugurated) a complex system specific to the firm incorporating accounts, payroll, stock control, invoicing, production planning, etc. Similar facilities may not be obtainable by or through the public utility, and in any case the organisation may wish for many reasons, including privacy, to continue with its own system. Nevertheless, the private computer could be connected to the public network for the special services such as external information which it could provide, and effectively become a satellite to the system.

For most organisations, then, the problem of the computer utility will resolve itself into whether to continue with one's own private computing system, to link into the network, or to rely solely on the network. The problem for those planning the utility will be the balance between public and private ownership and control. As we have seen, many of the services which a computer utility could provide could be offered by private organisations using the utility as a medium, even if the utility itself were to be run by a government agency; and the necessary accounting could be done automatically by linking the network with, or using it for, credit-debit financial transaction facilities. However, the success of the network might then depend on the willingness of organisations to offer their services through it. Other services would in any case depend on the active co-operation of firms, libraries and institutions, including their willingness to use the services offered.

In order to realise the benefits of a public computer utility there are many technical difficulties to overcome, mainly concerned with the design and implementation of efficient and secure information systems. Although these problems are far from solved, it is possible to visualise their solution, though a fair amount of effort and resources will have to be devoted to bring this about. The real problems will, as in many areas of computer development, not be technical at all, but social, educational, economic, organisational and managerial.

10
Banking and finance

Of the many possible applications of computer techniques in the world of business and industry, probably the most important and fundamental is in finance. This chapter is devoted to this topic. Much of the illustration and detailed discussion will be taken from the British banking system, but the arguments and conclusions will, it is hoped, have a general validity.

The most routine and mundane operation common to all financial institutions is the keeping of accounts. A significant proportion of the labour and resources employed is engaged in accounting, which remains secondary to the prime functions of every business excepting, possibly, that of banking. In some firms a consequential or closely related operation is the issue, handling or receipt of large numbers of paper monetary instruments of one kind or another. These operations had been mechanised extensively in advanced European nations in the decade before 1939 and this process continued with renewed impetus after 1945 because of greater competing demands for labour.

Larger organisations everywhere were already looking into the possibilities of using the new "data processing" computers in the mid-1950s to assist them in handling an ever-rising tide of transactions whilst coping with the increasing scarcity and mounting cost of labour. Progress was at first slow, but as the cost of storage tumbled and experience in method study accumulated the computer was applied more frequently and more confidently.

Within the United Kingdom, several otherwise unrelated factors have come together to precipitate in the last few years a massive investment in or commitment to computers and their ancillary equipment, which makes the situation there particularly interesting to study. First and most important the British Government had decided, at long last, to move from the traditional sterling system to decimal currency based on the pound as the major unit; secondly some satisfactory remote access teleprocessing techniques had been developed by users; thirdly, computers of much greater speed, capacity and cost-effectiveness were coming on the market; and fourthly, the spiralling costs of labour and of floor-space were becoming an acute problem, particularly in London, the centre of the sterling area.

As a result, almost all the larger financial organisations planned to transfer rapidly to computers before decimalisation a good proportion if not all of their accounting, and the preparation of much of the paper they issue. But in those parts of the financial world where small firms predominate, the advance of computers has been much slower and patchy. As an example, the 220-odd firms comprising the London Stock Exchange were using between them only thirty central processors early in 1970, and many of those for the processing of valuations and other statistical investment work rather than for accounting.

In general, by Decimalisation Day, computers had taken over much of the work done formerly on accounting machines. Their use had usually been justified by potential staff savings, and although these savings have rarely been as large as was hoped for there has probably been an increase in performance. Whilst development costs have been high, much has been learned which will be of greater benefit in the years ahead.

As for the immediate future, broadly speaking, organisations had either rushed to complete the introduction of computer accounting before decimalisation or had converted or renewed their accounting machines. The former had gained computer systems which ranked for improvement and consolidation before new developments were undertaken, and the latter would have no need to consider computers again as an alternative for some years to come.

This is not to say that the 1970s will be a period of stagnation. Among developments now likely the emphasis will lie away from the mass processing of straightforward accounting. In some cases efforts will be made to create useful secondary work to take up unused time on computers already justified for other purposes. In others they will be directed towards improving methods of input or output, particularly where newer devices show promise for integrating the computer with normal day-to-day business functions. In yet others they will be concerned with making greater effective use of data already available from the accounting operation for statistical and other management purposes.

In some of these researches the way will be laid for further changes when the next purchase of computing equipment becomes due: increasing numbers of replacement machines will be required after 1975. It is probable that these will be of greater power and that teleprocessing will be introduced where it has not previously been used. Direct input through simple terminals or over display screens, coupled with enquiry facilities to reduce the demand for printed daily output, may reduce computer centre costs sufficiently to cover the line costs involved.

As far as the smaller organisation is concerned, the increasing and improving range of visible-record or unit computers is likely to attract many of these more than the larger and more complicated machines. They are much more precisely related to present clerical or machine tasks; the capital outlay they require is usually lower; they present fewer premises problems than a major computer installation; and much of the systems work and all programming may be done by the installers. The segregation of software from hardware costs (known as "unbundling") which is now the policy of IBM and other manufacturers providing equipment for the commercial market in the USA and Europe is beginning to bring home to such organisations the high cost of systems study and of programming the larger computer configurations.

Alternatively, some small firms could opt to hire computing services from computer service bureaux, which offer access to greater computing power and expertise and more opportunity to modify and subsequently to develop the tasks undertaken. However, the high initial costs of devising and establishing open-ended systems and the lack of control over continuing or urgent tasks performed in bureaux make minicomputers more attractive to many small users. It could well be that only when a computer utility of the kind described in the last chapter is generally available that such firms will move towards that solution.

This brings us to the banks' own plans for teleprocessing systems. All the major British banks are currently involved in installing multiterminal systems which should, by 1974/75, link all their 10,000 or more branch offices with their central computing facilities. By then, the early terminals which were used simply for transmitting data read from punched paper tape should have been replaced by interactive keyboard/display terminals, or programmed small computers as satellites, able to be used for printing urgent output in the branch, and for enquiries, as well as for transmitting directly input data keyed in on them.

The development of newer and interchangeable classes of terminal should make for a widening use of the networks created, such as for the control of cash dispensing machines and the acceptance and control of varied clerical input outside the immediate accounting range, like stock and share deals and instructions to make payments overseas.

Advanced work-study and cheaper computing power could enable many clerical routines to be applied to computer terminals in such a way that the logic of each operation can be controlled and verified. As a bonus for terminal applications of this kind accounting data can be gratuitously collected and the workload of the accounting input section correspondingly reduced.

Ultimately, such services could become part of the wider range of services offered by a national utility. We have already mentioned this in relation to payments made automatically for the use of services obtained through the utility. At some point decisions will have to be made, probably at a very high level, as to whether the banks' networks should be wound down as their services are progressively transferred to the utility, merged in with the utility to form an integral part of it, or kept in parallel existence with necessary cross-connections. Such decisions will depend, *inter alia,* on technical questions of compatibility.

By this time it should be possible to link their customers' systems to any bank's equipment for such time as is necessary to receive input direct or to transmit appropriate output for printing or filming in the customers' own premises. Apart from the transmission of bulk work, the opportunity to link "point-of-sale" terminals in retail shops not only with the retailer's own stock control and financial computer but also with the banking system would presage direct payment from purchaser's to vendor's accounts without the use of paper dockets.

Now let us turn to the banks' money transfer services. Central to the financial world is a need for simply but efficiently transferring money, which itself is the means of exchanging goods and services in a modern society. Cash is the oldest, simplest, most straightforward and universal means of exchange, but when it exists in quantity in any one place it presents problems of control, security and mobility. Over the years the cheque has come into use as a more efficient means of settling accounts at a distance or for larger amounts. In recent years its use has increased sharply — by 7-10% a year in Britain since 1945 — as more and more individuals have opened bank accounts and have elected to make some payments by cheque. Some four to five million a day now pass through the banks' central clearings in London: this in spite of the reasonable suspicion of private cheques among many traders because a few may be returned unpaid.

To assist their paper to become more generally acceptable in place of cash the banks have issued many of their established or creditworthy customers with plastic cards to identify them and to guarantee the cheques which they issue. To enable them to handle the paper involved they have installed computer-controlled reading and sorting machinery which allows them to capture, as a byproduct, some 50-60% of the input data arising from each branch. This has beneficially and significantly reduced the branch effort required in using their computer accounting systems.

Following criticism by their government that the general public in the UK lacked a satisfactory money-transfer service, the British banks began their "Credit Clearing" (later called "Bank Giro Credit") system in the early 1960s. The automation techniques then being introduced in the cheque clearings were of little practical assistance here, and it still remains a clerical system. These two privately operated services were more recently joined by the National Giro Service which has used computer accounting and other advanced techniques, such as the optical reading of data, right from the outset.

Although the rate of growth in the Cheque Clearings has steadied, the volume of transactions passing through these three transfer services combined is rising faster than ever. And, in spite of much automation, all three handle millions of pieces of paper a year and experience the attendant problems of controlling, transporting and eventually storing them. In the same way as the banks now effect most of the payments they make under standing orders merely by showing automated debit and credit entries on the payers' and recipients' accounts, means will eventually be found to avoid moving, or even creating, much of the paper which today passes through the normal transfer services.

Let us consider, then, the prospects for moving away from paper and cash. Their own automation programmes are now sufficiently advanced to enable many banks to accept input from or create output for certain large customers or organisations in machine-readable form, thus pioneering methods which could combat the problems arising from ever increasing volumes of paper documents. An Inter-bank computer bureau has been established in the UK as a clearing house for data of this kind.

Towards the end of the century the development of a national message-switching network and the common use of computer terminals in business may make it possible to widen such a service so that businesses could initiate transfers from their own accounts over their own terminals. However, this would neither be universal nor supplant entirely the present services: it would merely cream off some of the continuing rise in the number of transactions handled. Any system of this kind may present serious and difficult problems in the event of disputes arising either from discord between the parties involved or, per misadventure, through wrongly transmitted data.

If the problem of identifying an unknown destination account could be solved and the recipient of funds could be advised quickly without producing and sending paper, then the days of the cheque would be numbered. But at present and for the foreseeable future it remains the most convenient instrument for settling accounts or making payments in a large variety of circumstances. Research is being done in Europe and in the United States into a system which may be satisfactory in the retail trade or where the debtor wishes to settle a debt in person. A specially encoded plastic card provided by the intending purchaser, perhaps one of the cheque or credit cards in use today, would be inserted into a sensitive and identifiable terminal: after verification an immediate transfer of funds would be made and a receipt provided for the payer.

It is sometimes said that we shall soon become a "cashless society". Whilst the number of paper transactions does rise, it is not necessarily correct to assume that the proportion of transactions being settled in cash is falling. For large volumes of small payments for goods or services there is, as yet, no better, simpler or cheaper method of settlement than the tendering of cash. This fact is unaffected by the increasing use of vending and similar machinery. Only political decisions, it seems, could reduce the volume of cash settlements by such methods as making all public transport free of charge.

It is possible, however, that the nature and composition of token coinage could change by the end of the century. Such change is likely to make it lighter in weight and more positively recognised by machines: plastic coins bearing an implanted electronic device would achieve both objectives. It must be remembered that the increasing relative cost of labour should cause more coin-operated and note-operated machines to be introduced: even many bank cashiers may have been replaced by paying-in, encashing and change-giving machines in twenty or thirty years' time.

The current principal alternative to cash for everyday transactions is the charge card, like the Diner's Club card. These are commonplace in the USA — so much so that it is said that some traders are suspicious of those tendering cash since this implies their credit must be bad — but less prevalent in the UK and Europe, though their use is growing. They are currently attractive to travellers and as an easy, if expensive, means of gaining credit. But some retailers resist them, maintaining that cash is simpler and cheaper to handle, regardless of the risks involved. The creation of a network with cheap terminal facilities as already described would add immeasurably to the appeal of these cards to consumer and trader alike. Their ability to be used in cash dispensing machines would complete their usefulness and acceptability.

Mention of the different pattern of use of credit cards between Britain and the United States demonstrates that problems do vary from country to country, though usually the differences are in the relative importance of different aspects of banking, rather than differences in kind — even in decimalisation the UK was preceded in recent years by other countries, e.g. Australia and New Zealand. However, it is worth looking at some of the most marked differences.

In the USA there are hundreds of banks and most have no more than one or two offices. These offices may be very large by UK standards, but only on the West Coast is there to be found a bank with a branch network resembling those common in Europe. Whilst the cheque is used extensively there is no centralised cheque clearing facility and the several credit cards in issue have penetrated deeply, to provide an alternative simple means of paying for goods and services. Banking methods in many fields, such as lending and credit rating, are more formalised, and thereby lend themselves more readily to a computer application. These distinctions have led to a minimal use of terminals and teleprocessing and a greater reliance on magnetic ink encoding and input from document readers and sorters.

In Western Europe the principal banks have branch networks, but the cheque is comparatively uncommon and many trade settlements are still effected by drawing Bills of Exchange on debtors. The alternative facility for remitting monies by Giro transfer has been established longer and is used for a far greater proportion of settlements than in Britain. Considerable and varied routine use is made of computers although the focal features experienced in the UK — the automation of cheque clearings; decimalisation; and the collection of mass transactions input from widely spread branch networks — have been absent. Many future developments run parallel to those discussed above in relation to the UK banking system (e.g. Sweden is further advanced towards an integrated banking network) but deeper interest is currently being shown in matters such as international payments which, particularly within the EEC, represent a greater proportion of total activity.

In recent years the customary method of paying executive staff in Britain — by credit to a bank account — has been gradually extended to many monthly paid employees. Nevertheless, the repeal of the Truck Acts did not cause a sudden switch away from paying labour in cash, although it allowed this method to be extended to weekly wage earners. The security problems associated with the collection and paying out of large sums of cash are leading more and more employers to encourage the acceptance of this method among lower paid staff by subsidising the running of their pre-requisite bank accounts. As more employers handle their payroll on a computer they may even be able to benefit further by passing the credits in the form of magnetic tape.

For their part, whilst the banks have generally welcomed the accounts of executive and senior staff, they are finding that those of the greater volumes of lower paid staff now coming to them are far less remunerative. Computer accounting has eased the clerical problem of maintaining and controlling them, especially during periods of peak activity, but the resulting aggregate balances are often too fleeting and too small to make a commensurate contribution to their costs. There is little doubt that banks would not wish to contemplate an account for every employed person, let alone for every adult member of the population. This would only serve to transfer to their counters problems such as the paying of cash to employees. It would aggravate their premises and labour costs and would divert expensive managerial effort towards controlling or preventing small irregular overdrafts.

In Britain, whilst present habits and customs prevail among the mass of industrial labour the National Giro would probably be equally as reluctant to accept the challenge of an account for every worker: their paying agent, the Post Office, already has enough problems in manning its counters.

Yet at root a considerable reduction in the handling of cash and many other national benefits could be realised if account-holding were universal. Wages, salaries, pensions and social security benefits could all be credited under advice direct to beneficiaries. Regular outgoings like gas, electricity and water bills, rent and rates, mortgage and other nationally agreed payments could be debited, again under direct advice where the amount is not fixed. Such a system need not, and probably should not, be loaded entirely onto one agency — government and private banks, Giro, etc., could each take a share.

To prepare for this trend, education in the later school years should already be laying emphasis on budgeting, household management, savings and investment; and not just in sixth forms and colleges, but more particularly among the less articulate early-leavers. Similarly with adults, the public campaign needed to introduce any scheme of this nature would make the one which heralded Britain's decimalisation seem insignificant: the handling of coin was not alien to the traditions and inclinations of that still massive section of the general public which has no need for and some suspicion of accounting; which transacts its business entirely in cash.

Organisational and economic benefits would accrue from more general public acceptance of fortnightly or monthly pay and greater variation in the times when pay is passed. Considerable progress towards these aims has been made in recent years indirectly because of three other trends:

(a) a rising proportion of the population is employed in "white-collar" jobs;

(b) an increasing percentage are owner-occupiers or intending owner-occupiers, who tend to learn more about finance; and

(c) increasing numbers are or were students receiving grants through an account.

Universal accounting would facilitate the introduction of other equitable measures, some of which are already under public discussion: better means of ensuring collection and payment of maintenance or alimony; of automatically recovering judgment debts; and of recompensing injured parties in criminal proceedings. Even the handling of the affairs of bankrupts and similar special cases could be better controlled if their income and the bulk of their necessary outgoings had to pass through, say, an account in a closely surveyed section of a government bank or Giro system.

This brings us to two further matters for discussion: the provision of credit, and the relationship between banking and government activity. First, the question of credit.

In the immediate post-war years the relative importance of the UK banks as suppliers of credit diminished as other institutions such as finance houses mushroomed around them. Although the restrictions placed on lending from time to time by British governments were often blamed for this, the banks eventually realised that, in spite of the apparent increase in their business shown by increasing turnover and the growth of the Cheque Clearings, they were failing to attract their fair share of available deposits. To combat these trends without departing from their cherished views of proper banking business, they have each acquired varying interests in some hire purchase companies, finance houses and merchant banks, and have consolidated their interests in certain foreign banks: they have also widened the range of sundry services offered. The growth of American banking offices in London in recent years has created a very competitive market in which the domestic Clearing Banks have now to earn their deposits. Monies deposited have been easily and profitably lent as the demand for and the price of credit have both been buoyant and at a high level for some years.

Whilst the standard method of lending to companies and other businesses in Britain is still by way of overdraft, more and more private bank lending is arranged on separate loan account and is repaid in fixed instalments in the same way as hire purchase financing. Increasing volumes of private lending and the high cost of the trained managerial staff needed to arrange and control private overdrafts or loans might well lead to the development and use of credit ratings as is done in the United States. Only a step removed from this would be comprehensive records of bad payers, such as is already available in the hire purchase industry. The collection and retention of relevant data and the assessment of a rating from the data available are obvious computer applications.

It is at this point that the concern of those who are worried about the prospect of "the databank society" become acute. We have discussed in Chapter 4 the government use of computers, in particular in relation to taxation and welfare benefits; we have discussed in Chapter 9 the concept of a public computing utility, much of whose traffic would involve financial transactions; we have discussed in this chapter the already developing banking networks. Clearly each network could remain totally separated; each could remain under separate control but be linked; or any two or all three could be merged. There are important implications for all in each of these possibilities. Some of the political aspects, and the implications for individual freedom, will be discussed in more detail later; as far as the financial aspects are concerned there are points to be made on each side. If one considers the possibility of the total merger, the government may wish to keep some of its traffic off the public network if this were thought (despite whatever safeguards were built into the system) to be the only certain way of ensuring complete security; banks may wish to be free of potential government monitoring, and be seen by their customers to keep their records secure from interference or scrutiny; commercial organisations and private individuals may wish neither government nor banks to become omniscient about their financial affairs. On the other hand, a unified accounting system could greatly ease the problems of government in collecting taxation and disbursing benefits, simplify business transactions, and make life much easier for the individual citizen.

The crucial questions are those of the technical safeguards which can be built in to ensure confidentiality; the amount of confidence in those safeguards; and who has overall control of the management of the system. One of the strongest arguments for the involvement of private banks in a universal accounting system is that they could be seen to be protecting not only their own interests, but those of private organisations and individuals, through insisting on adequate safeguards and exercising their share of the control of the system on behalf of their customers.

Outside the banks there are other organisations whose business is money, and some mention of these is warranted. We have already mentioned briefly hire purchase and finance houses, and in any case they could be regarded as bank-like organisations specialising in one kind of activity. The two major sectors remaining are the stock market industry, and insurance.

As far as some of the business houses, e.g. in the City of London, are concerned, a surprising number of these are quite small as organisations go, and a considerable proportion of their business is done by personal contact with the minimum of labour and paperwork. These are much more likely to be interested in other communications developments such as multiway videophones, though they might well be prolific users of specialised information services. Similarly many stockbroking firms are small; but here, of course, the need for up-to-the-minute information and rapid computation is obvious, and applies to the one-man office as well as to the large firm. Specialised services are already available, and their use and services will certainly grow. Stock exchanges themselves will almost inevitably become almost completely automated, if at a slower-than-feasible speed in some cases because of the conservatism of members. One implication is that the subprofession of stockjobbing (i.e. dealing only with other stock exchange members, not with external investors) could disappear altogether. Larger firms of stockbrokers will, of course, increasingly come to depend on computing facilities — both in-house and networked — for investment research, portfolio analysis and so on, as well as for routine transactions.

As in a good proportion of their smaller transactions brokers are already instructed through the agencies of branch banks, the development of national message-handling facilities might lead to the automatic passage of orders from outside the City indirectly to the market over the banks' teleprocessing networks. The significance of this would rise as the numbers of private small investors increase.

Stockbrokers, merchant bankers, company auditors and registrars are all likely to develop, to a greater or lesser extent, systems to assist them in advising their clients. They will be concerned about such matters as the relative profitability of a company, its placing in a takeover or merger, its value to a bidder, or the effect on its finances of further capital. Some of them, as well as companies themselves, might wish to assess the effects of new products or of variations in a product mix, and to forecast cash flows, market trends and other aids to decisionmaking. Computers could not only enable them to digest and analyse a mass of statistics but also, by using constructed financial models, enable them to project the effect of their recommendations or decisions in a more scientific and, hopefully, more accurate manner than is presently possible.

The changes which computers bring about in the overseas offices of banks of all countries are likely to be very varied. Much will depend on their size, the nature of their business and the extent to which computers are used elsewhere in their bank. The passage of data over international telephone or telex lines presents more problems than are met with in a national system, quite apart from possibly higher costs. Thought is, nevertheless, being given already in Europe to international links and the expansion of the EEC should deepen the interest in and widen the influence of such a scheme. The considerable Eurodollar market and the special position of the United States dollar in world settlements should demand the inclusion of North America at the earliest stage. An interesting recent development here is the founding of SWIFT, the Society for Worldwide Interbank Financial Telecommunications, with the aim of establishing a network linking some seventy European (including British) and American banks.

Internally the major banks may well move towards using their networks to transmit foreign payment instructions between their specialist overseas offices and their domestic branches, regardless of the method of inter-national transmission in use.

In the insurance industry, as in other sections of commerce where the maintenance of account records has assumed massive proportions, many computers have first been introduced as advanced accounting machines. The reduction of problems in this area and a greater realisation of the potential of the newer, more powerful machines could now lead to their use as management and actuarial tools. The accumulation and analysis of statistics and the estimation of risks and probabilities is work to which computers are ideally suited. Similarly, in the particular field of life assurance, computers have an important part to play in calculating terms tailored more closely to the individual case, and in subsequent maintenance of records. Life offices are, of course, specially concerned with the management of massive investment portfolios, and here, clearly, computers can be used by them in the same way as stockbrokers and investment managers generally.

To sum up, one can expect the next thirty years to see progressive changes in the use of computer techniques in the world of finance generally, and consequent changes in banking, accounting and investment practices. In some cases these changes will be prompted by the demands of the banks' commercial and individual customers, or of governmental policies; in others the banks themselves may give a lead. To predict the details of these changes, or the speed or order of their arrival would be hazardous in the extreme; such matters are much more likely to depend on economic considerations and on the labour market than on the available level of technical achievement. A high level of interest rates has persisted for some years throughout the world as well as in Britain. In this technological age the thirst for capital will tend to remain unquenched: no long-term reduction in rates therefore seems likely so long as business activity and confidence remain high.

Correspondingly, investment in equipment is expected to give a high immediate return: in much of the financial world the best direct returns by far on investment in computers have arisen and may continue to arise from the accounting application where relatively large workforces may be effectively reduced. Many future applications should enhance the service given by, or the bargaining power of their promoters rather than reduce costs from present levels. Their commissioning and the speed of their development is likely to depend on competition and economic confidence reflected in such indicators as stock market trends, the percentage of unemployed and wage and price indices, as much as in the current costs of computer hardware and software. Perhaps the most difficult decisions which the banking decisionmakers will have to make will be about when to lead, and when to wait for a lead from others.

11 Computers in the manufacturing and process industries

The field of industrial applications of computer techniques is so vast that books can (and have) been written on single industries or on single types of application. All that can be done here is to look at the more important kinds of application in quite general terms, at the trends which might appear in industry as a whole, and at the kinds of problems, again in general terms, which those in industry responsible for relevant decisions might be expected to have to face. In this chapter we shall consider in some detail what the various activities are that go on in the manufacturing and process industries, and how current computer developments relate to them. Then, in Chapter 12, we shall consider the implications of these and other developments for the people working in such industries and in commerce generally. We do not attempt to distinguish between private or state-owned enterprises, or to any great extent between different types of manufacture or process, although obviously there will be variations in the impact of computers resulting from these differences.

In considering the constituent activities of manufacturing and processing industry, it is necessary, for each one, to give both a name and a definition. The reason for this is that the name used varies from one firm to another, even within one industry, while some functions are so vestigial in certain industries that their presence is often not recognised.

We begin with design. This, fairly obviously, is the process of deciding, in full detail, what is to be produced. It normally starts with a concept which is first developed theoretically, and then further developed using models or laboratory tests, by a professional engineer. The resulting design, in the form of sketches and notes, is passed to draughtsmen who complete the detailed design in consultation with the design engineer and a production engineer (whose prime responsibility is to ensure that the designed product can be manufactured economically). The final result of the design process is a set of detailed drawings and items lists.

The terms "computer-aided design" or "design automation" are normally reserved today for the use of large software packages, frequently in association with interactive graphic displays, light pens, etc. The practical application of this sort of computer usage in British industry is negligible at present, although one or two firms are doing some good work. There is enormous potential for development of this kind, with particularly great benefits in terms of the time taken from producing a design to selling reliable hardware.

Large stand-alone packages of this kind can be expected to continue being developed slowly during the next five years or so. The rate of development is slow, partly because of the present high cost of the special hardware and partly because managements in general, and design engineering managements in particular, do not yet realise what are the potential benefits. In addition, in some companies which do have some idea of what might be done, design engineering managements are repeating the mistake made some years ago by other areas of management in many firms, in underestimating the manpower required to unlock the power of the computer.

The reduction in hardware costs discussed earlier, and the profitability demonstrated by the pioneers in the field during the next few years, should be sufficient to increase the demand and hence the relevant software and application development rates. In large firms one can expect by the end of this decade to find common use of integrated packages, leading directly from one design stage to the next, and ending with the direct production of paper tapes (or whatever is then the normal medium) ready for input to numerically controlled machine tools in appropriate industries. Other outputs from the integrated design package will be items lists on direct access computer files. Such files, which contain the necessary links to reveal the complete (multi-level) structure of a product, are already used by many firms, using manual loading procedures, as an output from the drawing office; they then serve as the main means of communication between design-oriented and production-oriented departments.

The difficulties described below of putting the main planning functions on the computer are likely to delay the full integration of computer-aided design systems with production control systems until the 1980s. However, even before this time, it is likely that the jump will be made to integrate automated design with automated inspection and testing. In so far as drawings are still needed, they will also be produced automatically, using hardware such as that already being used in a few industries.

Turning, then, to planning, we can define this, rather narrowly, as the job of deciding, in the light of the drawings and items lists (or their computerised equivalents), what is the sequence of operations needed to make each part, sub-assembly and assembly and what manpower/machine time is needed for each operation.

Except in a few industries where the planning function is unusually simple, it seems quite likely that the use of computers to help in the fundamental functions of planning will be in the form of extensions to the computer production of control tapes for numerically controlled machines. The complexity of the problem is such, however, that progress is likely to be insignificant until towards the end of this decade, by which time the use of new manufacturing materials and machines may well have simplified the problem to some extent in most industries, while both computer hardware and software will be better able to tackle the rather difficult decisionmaking problems involved.

Once major parts of the planning function can be performed effectively by computers, it will be possible to bridge the gap which will by then exist between computer-aided design systems on the one hand and production control systems on the other. As indicated above, this is not likely to happen before the early part of the next decade.

The planning of production programmes is usually regarded as the first function of production control, but is sometimes carried out by the Planning Department. It consists of deciding, in the light of a known sales programme, production resource limitations and finished parts storage costs (which consists largely of interest on the tied-up capital), what quantities of goods should be produced (i.e. completed) at what times. It is frequently, especially for products which do not involve complex assembly processes, merged with the order control function to be discussed shortly.

Where complex assemblies are involved, the product structure files mentioned above are often used, in conjunction with the sales programme, to establish the gross requirements for components and sub-assemblies, and hence the future demands on financial and other resources. Together with actual resources expected to be available, this is an estimate of the information needed for decisionmaking in this area.

The middle of this decade should see the successful implementation of fully effective systems for establishing net requirements (i.e. gross requirements less those parts already available) by computer, with automatic feed through to computer scheduling systems, following a manual decision as to the actual programme to be followed. Such systems will be complex because of their intimate links with shop loading procedures and work in progress, purchased parts and finished parts stores. In order to run with reasonable efficiency on the computer they will need to use more sophisticated file organisation techniques than those currently available.

Following the integration of computer-aided production planning with computer scheduling, to be discussed shortly, and the rest of production control, there will almost certainly be a period when the emphasis will be on improving the efficiency of the later parts of production control, and integrating it with stock control, cost accounting and financial accounting. Attempts then to automate the basic production programme decision are still likely to fail until detailed computer maintained personnel records have also been integrated with the production control systems. This is likely to be achieved during the 1980s.

A completely computer-performed production programme planning system is therefore feasible, and is likely to begin coming into use in a decade or so, by which time the hardware and software needed to make such a system operate with reasonable efficiency in terms of computer usage should also be available.

The next activity to discuss is order control. The order controller uses the production programme, the drawings and items lists and the planned operation sequences to determine the required timing and batch quantities (or flow rates) for production of all the required piece parts, sub-assemblies and assemblies, and places the appropriate orders on the works and on sub-contractors. In parallel with this activity and very closely related to it (indeed, often merged with it), the material controller determines the required purchases of raw materials and other items obtained from outside, and places the necessary orders on the buying department. In both cases appropriate scrap rates must be allowed for, and further orders placed if actual scrap is excessive.

In a batch production situation a problem arises when more than one product has to be made using the same machine or manpower resources (especially when the machines or men have specialised abilities, which is normal). Because different products have different manufacturing times, a queueing problem will arise, with batch A waiting for batch B to complete a particular operation before batch A can progress. The result of this situation is, of course, a build up of "work-in-progress"; this represents tied up capital and is therefore a cost which should be reduced if possible. The production controller therefore has to reconcile three not entirely compatible objectives:

(a) to minimise capital tied up in work-in-progress;

(b) to ensure that resources are fully utilised;

(c) to ensure that products are completed in time to keep customers satisfied.

Even if only one of these objectives had to be achieved the problem is impossibly complex for complete solution, even for relatively small numbers of jobs and machines, in a jobbing machine shop. It is even worse when the same problem arises in multi-level assembly work, and one has to add to all this that some products are wanted more urgently than others, some resources are more expensive to leave under-used than others, and some batches involve greater work-in-progress costs than others.

The decisions to be taken in this context are:

(a) which batch should be loaded onto a resource first, when there is a queue?

(b) when should new batches be loaded on the works in order to have them completed on time, bearing in mind likely queueing delays?

In the absence of a computer, a very crude rule of thumb is all that is possible in both cases; a number of such rules are known which give tolerable results.

Computer "solutions" fall into two classes at present — academic attempts to achieve a perfect solution, which invariably need far more computer time than is available, and more sophisticated rules of thumb which fall short of perfection but can be considerably superior to manual methods. This problem is not likely to be finally solved until artificial intelligence methods are applied to it, but, nevertheless, computer scheduling methods are already rapidly replacing manual ones.

The equivalent problem in flow-line assembly production (e.g. the motor industry) is "balancing" an assembly line, that is, ensuring that the resources are shared between points along the assembly line so that the rate of flow of assemblies is the same at each point. The problem is a little simpler than scheduling batch production, but, nevertheless, a perfect solution has not been found.

In both cases the systems normally operate in isolation (so far as the computer is concerned) from other computer systems, but they will lead fairly readily to the extraction of progress information, as described below.

As the scheduling and monitoring becomes more efficient, the progress data extracted will become more reliable.

A major development to be expected during the first half of this decade is the extension of computer scheduling to batch assembly shops, together with the integration of computer scheduling with production planning of net requirements by computer mentioned above and with work-in-progress stock control. This will lead immediately to better priority information for progress purposes, for machine shop scheduling and for purchasing. Under these circumstances the computer can monitor scrap rates and draw attention to the need for additional scrap replacement when scrap rates are excessive, or to impending surpluses if scrap rates are lower than expected.

The middle part of this decade will probably see priority being given to refining systems of this kind, in particular by integrating them with accounting, stock control and progressing systems, until the order control function as such will, towards the end of the decade, dwindle to disappearing point as a manual operation in large firms.

The remaining major production control function is to progress the actual production work: that is, "progress chasers" monitor the activities of the works and take corrective action as necessary (setting priorities, taking exceptional measures to obtain parts, etc.), so as to ensure that the plans for production set by order control are achieved.

The only common use of computers in this area as yet is to provide progress chasers with information as to what progress has actually been made or occasionally, in better systems, to report failure to achieve planned progress. The data on actual progress is in a few cases collected by the use of on-line computer terminals in the works area, but more frequently by off-line data collection systems into which data is entered through a combination of punched card readers, plastic badge readers and simplified keyboards. By far the most common method, however, is by the use of documents filled in in the works and sent to a data preparation section for coding into punched cards, paper tape or magnetic tape.

An indication of impending changes for the progress function has been given above. When both work-in-progress stocks and job loading are monitored accurately and scheduling is done efficiently and adequately by computer, the progress function will be reduced to taking action to correct computer-reported deficiencies and to carry out short-term monitoring of critical areas for which computer turnround times are inadequate.

The return of routine shop floor progress data by written documents will almost certainly be replaced to a large extent over the next few years by off-line data collection equipment, which has already been proved to be a valuable aid in some firms. This will speed up the monitoring done through the computer, so reducing that needed to be done by progress chasers. Over the same period, similar systems are likely to begin to be introduced to assist the monitoring of stores transactions and goods-receiving operations, although in this area the ability of the computer to check the accuracy of the transaction data will often lead firms to go directly to on-line computer terminals.

Later in the decade, as management reaction times are reduced, on-line data collection will start to replace the off-line systems on the shop floor, and those few firms who are already using on-line data collection will begin to reap real advantages from their early experience in the field. On-line systems will rarely be economic, however, until the hardware developments we have discussed, notably cheap high speed store and faster and greater capacity mass storage, become available.

With on-line monitoring of the movement of goods, manual monitoring by progress chasers will become unnecessary, but will be replaced by a need to give them the processed data to act on quickly. Initially, overnight printouts from computer files may be adequate, but the next step, to be expected around the end of the decade, is the use of on-line terminals to give progress chasers the information they need when they need it and for them to report back on their actions.

Thus, in about ten years' time, we can expect to see progress chasers in large firms reduced to accepting information about delays from the computer, interpreting it into instructions to storemen and shop floor operators, and reporting back to the computer. Since storemen and shop floor operators are likely to have on-line computer terminals themselves by then, for routine reporting of transactions, it will be a relatively small extra step to eliminate the progress chaser entirely by using the shop floor and stores terminals to give instructions directly. This can be expected to follow during the 1980s.

In some industries, notably in process control applications, computers directly control all, or more usually some part, of production, but there are immense difficulties in trying to apply this approach to batch production work.

When the jobs in a production area are scheduled, as described above, at a sufficiently detailed level the results can be used to instruct a foreman or chargehand as to the sequence in which he should take jobs queueing for his attention. This is only rarely achieved at present, but much more frequently a list of this kind is used as a guide, since it indicates the relative priorities of the jobs.

Computer instructions are likely to remain at the "guidance only" level, and to be directed to foremen/chargehands rather than to the operators themselves, where the work is done by skilled men using conventional tools, until highly sophisticated personnel files are available on the computer for use in this kind of decisionmaking. This is because in this environment the individual skills of the operators are as important as the capabilities of tools and machines. However, this development may be overtaken by the increasing use of numerically controlled (NC) machines.

The use of NC machines is restricted at present both by their capital cost and by the cost of programming them. Computer assistance with the programming is possible, but is limited by the fact that very large computers are needed. It is possible that the programming may become easier and that the capital cost may come down as plastics and similarly formed materials replace machined metals, which seems likely to happen over a very wide field during this decade. The expected advent of cheap high-speed computer store is certain to make computer assistance with the programming more readily available, so NC methods of production can be expected to be normal by around 1980.

The extent to which numerical control will be used for assembly operations is impossible to predict, because of the enormous variations in the nature of the task between different industries. For most such operations, the equivalent of the conventional general purpose metal-cutting machine tool has yet to be invented.

On-line control of production machines looks economically unattractive (except in process control industries) until it can be integrated with computer-aided design and integrated production control systems. One can therefore expect the first few success stories in the early 1980s and a rapid spread during 1985-90.

Finished goods are inspected and tested (sometimes all, sometimes only samples) to ensure that they meet the required standards. Work-in-progress is usually also inspected by one of a number of possible procedures.

Many attempts at fully automatic, computer-controlled testing have failed as a result of the great difficulties involved in coping with what appear at the outset to be minor details. This is an area which superficially looks ideal for direct computer control, but in which successful applications are so far extremely rare (except possibly in the process control industries).

However, a few fairly general purpose inspection machines are now available, and special-purpose computers are used to test some particular products, such as certain aircraft and rockets, although even these are more usually used for relatively limited field testing of in-service equipment than on the end of a production line.

A more modest assistance is sometimes given to inspection in the form of a printout from the product structure file described earlier. This can help, for example, to determine whether the correct components have been used in assembling an electronic circuit.

It can be expected that experience with special-purpose computers for particular kinds of automatic testing together with the gradual development of equipment to aid inspection and testing in most other areas will make possible numerically controlled inspecting and testing machines for many industries by the end of the decade. This should correspond conveniently with the maturation of major computer aided design systems capable of producing the necessary control tapes for these machines.

A later development, which will become economic when the speed of decisionmaking has been raised considerably by the integrated production control systems described above, will be to put the inspection and testing machines on-line to the computer, allowing two distinct benefits:

(a) feedback of failure rates for use in "order control" functions of deciding future production quantities;

(b) automatic adjustment by the computer of the tolerances to be applied during testing, so as to give a pre-specified statistical distribution of performance of items which pass the tests, independently of the distribution of performance of items as produced. This development is likely to coincide with, or perhaps follow, on-line control of production machines (except in batch assembly production).

It can be seen from the above survey that we have hardly begun to witness the massive changes in working conditions and industrial practices which automation can be expected to bring about. In particular, as well as changing the nature of industrial work, like other kinds of mechanisation it tends to reduce manpower needs for a given level of production. Computer systems of the kind now being implemented tend to reduce the need for clerical workers by around 10%; the earlier stages of integration of the various production control functions, can be expected during the first half of this decade to raise this figure to about 50%. In large and medium size firms further integration during the second half of the decade, together with a growing amount of computer decision making, could virtually eliminate order control and progress departments by around 1980, and the latter part of the decade is likely to see a rapid reduction of about 30% in the need for middle management as well. During that same period the growth of computer-aided design and its integration with NC machines could well mean a drop of around 90% in the need for draughts-men, mainly occurring towards the end of the decade. The development of NC machines at this time may well also lead to a reduction in the need for machine operators of around 60%, this figure increasing to about 90% in the late 1980s under the impact of on-line computer control of the machines.

This brings us, then, to one of the major themes of the next chapter.

12 Manpower and management in a computer-based society

One of the most significant trends which can be detected in the developed countries as a result of advancing technology and, as we saw at the end of the last chapter, of automation in particular, is in employment. For example, in the UK over the last two decades there have been decreases of a quarter of a million or more in agriculture, in mining, on the railways and in the armed forces; these decreases have been offset and an additional two million absorbed into the working population almost entirely by the service industries, including distribution, education, medical services, banking, insurance and catering. Employment in manufacturing industries accounts for only a quarter of this increase of over three million. This shift of emphasis clearly has more to do with mechanisation than with automation, but it is the background against which the introduction of computers has to be considered. Between 1966 and 1969 the greatest reductions, apart from and in any case exceeding those in the categories mentioned above, were in retail distribution, in building and in textiles and clothing. The last is another example of the move away from low technology industry but the first reflects the rapid growth of self-service. Further examples of this were reductions of 25% in employment in laundering and dry cleaning and of 6% in garages and filling stations. This is self-service of a simple kind, but within the next few years we can expect to see it in a much more sophisticated form, as we have already shown in earlier chapters, in fields such as banking and education, essentially as a result of the use of computers; in the same three years in those particular fields there were increases of 9% and 15% respectively in the numbers of people providing these services.

161

Another area of expanding employment is in medical services, which in the UK now employ over a million people. This illustrates the need to look at employment from a completely different viewpoint to that of the familiar job classifications if the extent to which automatic processes will replace human effort economically is to be assessed. It is of little help to know how many doctors, nurses, teachers, miners, bricklayers and shop assistants there are in the community. Rather, one needs to know the type of work which each is doing at different times. In a hospital, for example, one would find time spent on making decisions about treatment, retrieving information about patients' histories and comparable cases, manipulative skill, operation of complex instruments, preparation and administration of food and drugs, personal comforting of patients, waiting for intermittent signals requiring responses, physical effort, allocation of available beds to patients, clerical calculations and political arguments aimed at securing better facilities. This list is probably far from exhaustive, but clearly it is more directly related to the ways in which computers could replace human work than a list of staff categories: surgeon, physician, matron, sister, staff nurse, radiologist, physiotherapist, cook, receptionist, porter.

The types of work that are most readily displaced by computers are often the skilled as well as the semi-skilled ones which have been introduced by automation. Not only will the operatives on mass-production lines be made redundant when these are fully automated but the specialist craftsmen will not be needed when numerical control tools can do their work more perfectly and consistently than any human being can. Already the demand for the manufacture and operation of accounting machines and of card punches has been greatly diminished by the spread of computers and of terminals reading printed, typed or magnetically encoded characters. Before long we can expect that fewer programmers will be needed because computers will themselves be used more to generate new programs once the logic has been defined. Those who have progressed from working on the shop floor to quality control, inspecting goods produced by others to check that they are satisfactory, will find that computer-controlled systems can detect any errors they make much more reliably and can correct most of them without human intervention.

Another mode of work that is readily automated is the storage and retrieval of materials and information. This includes not only obvious examples like office filing systems and libraries but also the provisioning of a warehouse or of a retail shop, the maintenance of contribution records and payment of claims in insurance schemes, and writing legal textbooks and searching them for precedents.

In offices a good deal of time is spent transcribing information from one form to another. When one dictates a letter, either the sound waves one produces are converted into a pattern of magnetic polarisation on a tape or a secretary listens and writes in shorthand the equivalent of what is said. In either case, she then has to type the letter and, after the recipient has read it, perhaps he gives it with others to a clerk who transcribes the essential information from them on to a sheet of paper which is given to a punched card operator. Finally, the punched card contents are converted by another machine to a record on magnetic tape which is used by a computer to complete the process begun by the dictation of the original letter. In 1900 one would have dipped a quill pen in the ink well on the desk, written out what was wanted and sent the office boy to fetch it. Commerce is on too extensive a scale for this to be practicable any longer, but increasingly, as already for travel reservations, one may expect to dial up the supplier's office, send a message (initially via keyboard, but ultimately, perhaps, by a spoken message recorded at once in a form which can be processed by computer) and within seconds receive a reply indicating what action is being taken. Thus the amount of transcription necessary in present-day commerce can be reduced, by developing such means of responding to enquiries.

We noted in the last chapter the trend towards the progressive transfer of most forms of manufacturing and processing in industrialised nations to automated machinery controlled by computers which are programmed to schedule production according to input data, also obtained automatically, such as the quality and composition of the raw materials, the functioning of the equipment, relevant environmental factors such as humidity or temperature, and so on. Such process control computers will in due course be able to run for twenty-four hours a day, every day, and will not require anyone to operate them. Most computer operating today is concerned either with handling peripheral devices (information storage devices like magnetic tapes or disks, or input-output devices like printers, typewriters, or card readers or punches), or with resetting the computer itself to run a different set of programs. Some people will still be needed for this kind of work at computer installations offering bureau services, e.g. through a computing utility, to users whose data needs to be made available, processed and stored separately, whether or not they are using a standard program or other facility; however, when computers are dedicated to a particular automatic process in a single organisation, such attention would be unnecessary, given mass storage, if required, compact and cheap enough for physical changes to be rarely needed and the use of display screens to make other forms of reading information superfluous.

An important function of these control computers will be to keep themselves working correctly. Most faults only occur intermittently at first but, if nothing is done about them, they recur more often and in time are likely to stop the machine altogether. Each time that an intermittent error occurs, the computer will repeat the operation that has failed until it is successful and then it will record details of where and when the failure occurred. This accumulation of errors can be examined periodically by a special program occupying some of the computer's storage space, and multiprogrammed to take corrective action to prevent the repetition of such faults, while other parts of the system continue in use. A similar program could also carry out precautionary servicing periodically of parts of the system which are susceptible to developing faults.

Sometimes human intervention may be necessary to cause the machines to work properly again. A fault may persist, so that the whole or part of the system is prevented from functioning. If there were any risk of explosion or overheating, for example, or if traffic were being controlled, there would then need to be a duplicate system that could take over the job within a fraction of a second. There would probably also be an alternative system if a service were being provided to the public, such as banking or booking hotel rooms, but it would not be economically justified if the purpose were production for future sale, when a few hours' interruption would not have major consequences. Though a fault may be bypassed, its cure may require removal of the defective part and its replacement. Circumstances may arise which were not foreseen when the computer program was written or there may be logical errors. This could cause a message to be displayed indicating a halt in the program or that it is in a loop of operations from which it cannot break out. There may be faults in the power supplies or on the telephone lines used for transmitting data. The machines may shut themselves down when they sense, by smoke detection, for example, that a fire has broken out in their vicinity.

Computers are, short of the development of artificial intelligence, necessarily limited by the scope of their programs so that, as well as operating faults, there will be shortcomings in meeting the desired objectives of their owners which will constantly require the development of extensions to the programs. There will also be complaints by consumers, some of which will draw attention to faults in the hardware or in the programs or, more frequently, in the data used not having been subjected to tests sophisticated enough to detect some invalidity. Similarly, some consumers will raise objections to the charges made or will request a special product or service which is outside the scope of all programmed possibilities. These can be treated in the same way as if they were system faults, and the manager concerned then has to decide whether or not it is economically justifiable to respond to them. In principle, an enormous variety of possible results can be programmed to satisfy personal choice, in contrast to the constraints imposed by mechanisation without the benefits of computer control.

There will be continuing correction of computer faults and extension of their applications. However, in practically every situation which can be envisaged, computers can continue working normally, isolating the fault for subsequent correction while productive work continues, or they can switch to a degraded or alternative mode of operation and signal the need for remedial action, or they can shut themselves off safely until someone comes to put them right. Only sabotage and theft are likely to be outside the scope of this self-protection. Short, again, of highly-developed artificial intelligence, human beings with sufficient intelligence will be able to frustrate any automatic protection and can only be prevented from planting bombs or from stealing confidential information, for example, by physical security. The seriousness of this threat may well be the principal factor determining the way in which a lot of people will work by the end of the century. If it is too grave, many people will have to spend hours at a time close to geographical concentrations of computers in order to guard them. Otherwise they will be able to spend most of their working time in their own homes.

Current trends suggest that, typically, a quite large assemblage of automated machines and its controlling computer system would only experience about one fault per day which would need human attention. Many of these would be programming errors whose circumstances could be transmitted to the worker's home through the public network or by dedicated private line, and displayed on his terminal screen. Through direct connection with the computer system he could investigate the fault and find out enough to decide what should be done to make the program start running again. Only in about half or fewer of the fault situations might it be necessary for the worker to leave home. Generally this would be for an hour or two to collect an identified part from a depot, then go to the computer installation and replace the faulty part there, afterwards returning the latter to the depot for any necessary further examination and for possible repair and re-use. In a few cases, the fault might be so complicated or obscure that he would have to spend several hours at the installation diagnosing it. On this basis it is possible to do some rough calculations. Such a worker might spend six periods of eight hours each or four of twelve hours each during a week, some in the daytime and some at night, at home or at some other notified place equipped with a computer terminal, with the job of looking after five computerised systems. Most of the time he could occupy himself as he chose. That would include sleeping because the terminal would be fitted with an audible alarm. On average, he would need to leave home about five times during the week, spending about fifteen hours working or travelling, and he would also spend about an hour at home putting right another five faults from there. He would also need to spend some time learning new techniques, a matter to which we shall return later. Thus ten people could provide maintenance for ten computer systems, with seven of them working in any particular week; the 30% margin would allow for illness but otherwise represent time totally free of all commitments. The number of computer engineers would therefore roughly equal the number of such computer systems (e.g. perhaps a few hundred thousand eventually in British industry). Even allowing for covering for sick colleagues, each would work less than forty weeks in the year, during each of which they would have to be on call for forty-eight hours a week, but actually be engaged on work, or travelling to and from their site on business, for a third of that time. Such calculations are, of course, very rough and ready, but may serve to bring home the magnitude of the changes in work patterns — and hence the organisation and management of industry — which are possible and whose consequences will have to be considered.

This mode of work need not be limited to automated industrial activities. Most of us in the affluent West have a lot of electrical machinery in our homes now — television sets, telephones, washing machines, cookers, dishwashers, refrigerators, record players and so on — and by the end of the century these will be still more widespread. These machines generally work for months at a time perfectly or with minor faults which we tolerate. Yet there is a general attitude of dissatisfaction with them, certainly in Britain. This is not because they are poorly made but because it is so difficult to have them repaired when they go wrong. Those who repair them generally work only from 9 a.m. to 5 p.m., when there is often no-one in the house they are to visit. Many seem incapable of predicting when they will arrive, so that one can make special arrangements to let them in and still achieve nothing. When they do appear, they often lack the skill or the tools to repair the machine or find they need a part, which they have not brought or which is out of stock or obsolete.

This problem could be solved by the same call dispatching system as previously described for computers themselves. They would have a program to store the addresses of the engineers on duty for each period and to transmit to one an alarm and information about any irrecoverable fault which occurred. Similarly, servicing agents could use a computer to record the addresses of each type of engineer and to assign to them messages from householders which would include as much detail as possible so that the right tools and parts could be brought. Definite appointments could be made, usually within a few hours of the incident occurring. This call dispatching procedure for both computer and household appliance maintenance would include reserve addresses to call in case the worker primarily responsible was already attending to some other fault. Provided that the planned working time was no more than about 60% of the standby time, it would not be long before someone was found at home in the list of possible addresses.

A considerable number of service industries could be organised in this way. It could apply to the whole of the building repair trade, to all forms of central heating and ventilation systems, to gas appliances. Before very long, we are likely to be using battery-powered cars in towns. Whether these are individually or communally owned, they could be serviced on the same basis.

Thus computer techniques could bring about changes in modes of employment in areas which might at first sight appear to be relatively immune from their influence. No doubt there will continue indefinitely to be scope for the individual craftsman who does a superior job, but the incompetent plumbers, carpenters, television repairmen and the like who nevertheless at present seem to find employment will find it hard to face the competition of the large computer-based organisation which can send the man with the right skill at the right time.

The overall effects on employment of these various developments in industrial automation and computer-based organisation will, of course, depend on other factors also. The economic factor will be an important one; some industrial processes are easier to automate than others and this will produce a differential effect across industry; much will depend on how much the potential for increased production which the use of computers offers is matched by a demand for greater affluence and by the practicability of distributing the extra wealth. This last point is often taken up by those who refuse to accept that automation may have substantial effects upon employment; they give as an analogy the prediction that the invention of the loom would destroy the weaving industry, whereas it led to a massive boom and increased employment opportunities.

This argument is, however, too facile: it overlooks both the largely untapped demand for cloth and the largely untapped natural resources at the time the loom was invented. Now, many industries keep up demand artificially by built-in obsolescence and encouraging evanescent fashions, and we are also in many areas approaching a resources crisis; more important in our present context, this argument ignores the fact that the changes which computers are bringing about are of kind as well as of scale.

However, supposing that the trends already discussed can be projected for as long as thirty years without being significantly affected by these economic factors, we can conveniently conclude this part of the chapter by summarising the types of *industrial* work which will probably remain by the end of this century:

— a small number of people engaged in discovering radically new concepts and techniques;
— a considerably larger number responsible for filtering these innovations, identifying market needs and deciding which are economic — the suggestions these people would investigate would come not only from their organisation's inventors but also from the requests to satisfy the special needs of customers for variants of standard computer processes;
— appreciable numbers of highly qualified engineers and analysts engaged in design, program planning, testing and installation of the selected new and modified systems;
— a substantial number of maintenance engineers needed to interpret the faults recognised by computers and to correct them by program changes or by substituting new modules of machinery for those which are found to be defective;
— some administrative and operational functions will remain necessary, but these will be far fewer than at present;
— there will be a continuing need for managers to organise the gradual transition to more extensively computerised modes of operation, to communicate with employees, consumers, suppliers and society, and also to respond to that kind of fault signal caused by an exceptional combination of circumstances which has not been foreseen and whose resolution requires an unprogrammed decision.

Looking in more detail at the role of managers in computer-based industry, they remain ultimately responsible for the definition of the organisation's objectives, the selection of the information which they need the computer to collate, analyse and store, and the taking of decisions formulated by this computer processing. They have to provide the value judgments which enable the data processing system to be programmed so that the statement of problems to be solved can be deduced from the information available about the organisation's activities and environment. Many of the decisions to be taken will then be logically predictable but, when new initiatives are needed, managers will be presented with the range of choices, with indications of the consequences of each decision and of the constraints affecting each of them. At present, most computers are used piecemeal for individual applications like invoicing and receiving payments from customers, stock dispatch and control and job costing and payroll. Quite often, therefore, decisions are called for which are outside the scope of the computer program. As more integrated applications are developed, for example, linking the production process with the control of finished goods, parts and raw materials and all payments to and from employees, customers and suppliers, the level at which managers intervene to define information needs and to take unprogrammed decisions will gradually rise.

Managers will increasingly become technical advisers working within a structure of management services embracing information processing, operational research, organisation and methods and economic forecasting. They will obtain information and transmit instructions, giving them a role analogous to that of the central nervous system in relation to the executive directors as the brain of the body corporate. In some enlightened organisations the head of management services now ranks with the financial, production, marketing and personnel directors and this should become general practice. Incidentally, this should go a long way to encouraging computer specialists to develop similar allegiances to the entities for which they work as those which accountants, engineers and social workers have, without losing any sense of professional identity.

Present hierarchical structures of management are likely to give way during the rest of the century to specialised staff groups, for two reasons. Firstly, the numbers employed in large manufacturing firms will decline substantially and those displaced will tend to move, at least for a while, to service industries generally organised on a smaller scale. Secondly, more training and greater competence will be required by everyone because all the less demanding functions in present jobs will be computerised. Consequently, there will be less need for personnel supervision at levels below senior management. They will still have a considerable supervisory role, being especially responsible for the recognition and development of general management potential among the technically-oriented middle management. They will also have to decide on promotions and other rewards to acknowledge specially meritorious performance, on secondments and training as part of management development, and on incentives for particularly unpleasant or hazardous tasks which can neither be automated nor attract enough people to do them otherwise.

Computer programming will take care of the more straightforward personnel aspects of present-day management. It will apply salary policies and do all the necessary allocation of functions, taking account of pre-defined employee preferences, consequent on holidays, retraining, illness and giving effect to plans for standby and part-time working during the various hours of the day and days of the year. This would be derived from managerial decisions on the allocation of people and other resources between research, development, standard production and satisfying requests for variants. Although the arguments for and against a particular decision would be more clearly expressed, there would still be differences of opinion and interpretation. Thus senior managers will continue to have to spend an appreciable proportion of their time adjudicating disputes between subordinates.

Those most seriously affected will be the lower levels of management, such as factory foremen and heads of accounts departments. One of their main functions is to deal with the unusual circumstances unfamiliar to their operatives. For a time they will be invaluable in explaining to the systems analysts how they do this, but eventually all these exceptions will be handled by the computer programs. Many of them will be too old to learn the new skills of data processing adequately. In some cases there will be enough of their former work which cannot be expressed in logic and arithmetic for their experience to remain essential to the system, so they have then only to adjust to the transfer from line to staff management. Often, however, even this will not be required so that, although they may lose no pay, it will be very difficult for them to retain their self-respect when they have lost both functions and subordinates. In these cases, early retirement may be the only answer, but this can be foreseen and planned for years in advance because of the time which it takes to introduce data processing systems.

The most characteristic effect of the introduction of computers and of automation generally is that this takes away the boring parts of people's work which require no intelligence precisely because they can therefore be done by a machine which has no intelligence, only an ability to follow instructions very rapidly and reliably. This means that human beings are left with those aspects of their present jobs which are the more interesting but also are the more responsible and so most likely to cause stress. This will be true of both technicians and managers. Apart from some difficulties when computers are badly designed, built or programmed and suffer from unidentified faults, usually occurring only intermittently so that they are not easily reproduced, there will be many problems due to people working under strain and therefore behaving unpredictably and disrupting systems. There are two main ways to combat this. One is better education, and the other is greater opportunity to work in relatively short bursts and to have opportunities in between for leisure activities unrelated to work instead of this relaxation of pressure being provided by the more boring parts of the job as they generally are now in a normal working day. For professionals this will tend to be the pattern of work anyway, but for managers it may have to be deliberately contrived.

Despite the increasing technical content of his work, the manager will fundamentally remain someone concerned with personal relations whatever his environment. He has to motivate his subordinates but, as they will be more techically proficient and intelligent than the typical worker now, the manager will need more expertise in order to earn and to retain their respect. He should also be prepared to discuss with them the broader business context of the work. He will need to resolve the problems which arise from stress and from human error in ways satisfactory both to the individuals concerned and to corporate objectives. He will have to work with colleagues and superiors to agree on courses of action within the organisation, and with consumers, suppliers and authorities to harmonise those actions with the needs of the community as a whole. All this will demand, in 2000 just as much as now, education in personal relations and in communications as the primary attributes of managers. In addition, it will be vital for all managers to be numerate and to appreciate current technology; they will need training for this and to develop analytical skills for forward thinking and planning. Top management must recognise the importance, not least for themselves, of such education on a recurrent basis to keep pace with new inventions and concepts and provide opportunities and positive encouragement.

Not only is education important, but there must be an environment receptive to new ideas so that managers can apply what they have learnt to their daily work. The transition to progressively more automated work will cause many economic, technical and human problems which would be examined as far as possible in case studies during training sessions. The right balance has to be found between the speed of technological change and the ability of workers and managers to acclimatise themselves to it. Management must have clear objectives and the ultimate authority to enforce decisions to prevent atrophy and extinction if technological change is resisted, for redundancy is more likely to affect those firms which do not use computers and therefore cannot compete, than those which introduce them in time and reduce the labour required for a given volume of production. However, full consultation is essential on the successive steps of selection of those to develop and introduce new systems, retraining of them and then of others when the current operations are displaced, and reassignment or redundancy of any who are no longer needed. This means that everyone in a factory or office where computers are to be introduced or used more widely should have the plans explained fully as soon as they are formulated. Then they can understand how they will be affected personally, even if they have only a vague idea of national plans, and can propose changes to the scheme to ease the transitional problems and to increase the long-term benefits.

Currently the overwhelming pressure of immediate problems to be resolved prevents most managers from giving adequate attention to planning more durable policies. A frequent by-product of this is the patching of existing systems and the diversion of effort to expediting interim solutions, so that there are too few designers left to work out, test and implement comprehensive solutions of all these current short-comings within a reasonable time. This arises partly from impatience, but also from lack of confidence in taking risks when in the past these were based largely on hunches. Now the construction of mathematical models of the economy and the use of computers to analyse them enables calcu-lated risks to be taken by providing facilities for anticipating trends and consequences and for planning in more detail with greater accuracy and flexibility. Parameters can be revised frequently enough to respond promptly to changes in the situation. Thus problems can be resolved before they reach a climax and cause panic reactions as to a fire; it will be possible to alleviate the perennial preoccupation with comparative trivia of immediate importance which is the besetting sin of industrial management and of national government alike.

It can be seen that, while industrial decisionmakers will have many problems to face, not least those of labour relations, the main ones arising from the industrial use of computers may well be political and socio-economic in nature. A major preoccupation of governments will have to be the method and pace of transition to a society in which computers are fully exploited. This cannot occur in isolation in any one country and it will be vital to see, as already considered in Chapter 8, when and how it can come about in the tropical and semi-tropical countries as well as in the more developed parts of the world. It involves a social as well as a technological revolution. We are going to have to adopt a different attitude towards employment, but it will not be a simple transition from the ethical link between income and work. This can be traced back to puritan-ism but really became established during the industrial revolution. Although there was still a leisured class, those who belonged had to justify themselves by having retired from a successful business career or by having borne the white man's burden in the tropical colonies. During the twentieth century, retirement pensions and unemployment benefits have been introduced in many countries but they have never kept pace with inflation, so that those who depend on them have had both the privations and the reputation of second-class citizens. In rare instances when a man with a large family can receive slightly larger benefits by not working than he can earn in unskilled employment, this often provokes criticism for evading his obligations to society.

In future we have to accustom ourselves to the possibility of producing and distributing enough food and sufficient goods and services of all other kinds to all without everyone having to work what we now regard as full-time. On the other hand, we cannot achieve this without any organised effort at all and assume that whatever is required will be done in return for a comfortable existence without any incentive. In industrialised countries, there has been a steady reduction in the number of hours worked each week, but it will not be meaningful to continue much further in that direction. In tropical countries, the much lower standards have been supported by long hours of inefficient work by people exhausted by endemic disease and malnutrition.

In the UK about half of our food is produced by $1\frac{1}{2}\%$ of the population. One would not expect to have achieved this degree of specialisation everywhere by the end of the century, but it seems reasonable that the cultivation of the land and of the sea-bed need not fully occupy more than about 10% of the world's population. (This would still be supplemented by many others growing a few vegetables, keeping a few hens and so on.) About 40% of the population are under 15 or over 65; the increase among the latter resulting from medical advances will be offset by more widespread planning of smaller families, so we shall assume that this proportion will not change much. Most of the remainder will need to work in one of three ways. Some will respond to needs to rectify or to develop the functions of computer-based machinery in the manufacturing, process and mining industries. Some will similarly respond to the needs of young children and of those too elderly to look after themselves and keep homes comfortable for everyone else. These two will both be intermittent types of work at all hours of the day and night.

The third type of work is the movement of goods, which seems bound to continue largely unaffected by the spread of computing. It will frequently involve fairly protracted exertion, in contrast to the response to automatic or human signals which characterise the other types. A lot of effort is at present spent on transporting information in the form of letters, newspapers and books. As explained elsewhere, this will soon become unnecessary because information can be stored in computer files for reference when required. But we cannot do the same with food and drink, clothing, furniture and household appliances. Over 40% of those employed in retail distribution deal with food and all but a few of the others in durable goods of some sort. In Britain, these people are about 10% of the working population.

Within a factory automated transfer lines can be built to minimise the amount of materials moved by men. In city centres some tramways for automatic goods vehicles may also be used, and similar techniques might be economic on some inter-city motorways in densely populated countries. Mostly, however, this will make little difference to the total function of transferring goods from a few factories and ports to millions of households dispersed all over the country (and also taking away the residual waste to prevent pollution). The growth of supermarkets and the decline of door-to-door delivery will rationalise the requirement, but the retail and wholesale trades and the road haulage industry will continue to need nearly as many workers as today.

This is just as valid world-wide as it is in any particular country. It is a truism that feeding the world's growing population is limited not so much by inability to produce enough food as by the problems of distributing it from where it can be grown to where most of the people live, even to the extent that surplus harvests are destroyed in some temperate lands while hundreds of millions starve. Air and sea transport are more readily controlled by computer than road traffic, because there is more freedom of movement (we shall return to this in Chapter 16); even so, human supervisors are still needed to accompany air or sea vehicles in order to reduce, further than is possible by automatic remote control, the risks of death, destruction or pollution from an air or sea accident.

A situation in which the reduced amount of work which has to be done is unevenly allocated clearly contains some potential social and political instability, or at least possible features (such as many people leading essentially empty lives) which many would regard as undesirable. Something can be done at industrial level to help to avoid this. One can begin by replacing by an annual salary all types of payment related to the length of time worked or to the amount produced, eliminating therefore hourly wage payments, overtime, shift allowances, piecework and payment by commission. Instead, each individual would have planned working periods or (where appropriate) periods on call — generally less over the year than current working hours — with the understanding (perhaps by means of a national "on call" system for all) that in exceptional situations (illness of colleagues, natural disasters, etc.) additional hours would be worked without extra payment.

The justification for this is that the quality of the work done would be (as it is in some walks of life already) far more important than the quantity. The quality would depend very largely on how recent and how extensive was the training a person had received, so that an incomes policy reflecting this would be needed. An adequate basic income would have to be established which would be paid to those who had retired and to those from the age of eighteen devoting all their working time to education, not only students in the conventional sense but all those who were re-training so that they could use a newer technology in their work. The parents or guardians of children under eighteen would receive appropriate lesser payments on their behalf related according to age to the adult basic income. Most of those working in automated industry, in house-keeping, in agriculture and in the movement of goods would receive an income slightly greater than the basic amount. About 10% of the population would be likely to belong to each of these four categories. If the second is extended to all those performing intermittent personal services in homes, catering establishments, hospitals and elsewhere, they would total about 20%, mostly women. The allocation of work would be pro-grammed in such a way that it was as evenly distributed as possible, taking account of individual preferences and ensuring that those who received salaries as workers did not evade their share of the responsibilities. By means of wage agreements and good price policies, adjusted by national and international taxation, similar levels of income could be set for all. In recognition of the need for quality, rather than by any disproportionate allocation of the work to be done, there would be groups who would be able to earn larger salaries because of the greater efficiency of their factories, farms or depots. There would also be individuals who would supplement their standard incomes by receiving payments from others for such personal services as creative art, entertainment, taxi operation, interior decoration and hairdressing. Opportunities would continue for those who wished to earn more from investment and from gambling to do so to whatever extent taxation policies allowed. A few people would opt out of the community system of work and rewards altogether, except for a national insurance type of payment, so that they could devote themselves entirely to these personal services if they were so proficient that they could earn a better income that way.

Given an industrial incomes policy of this kind, there would be left a small minority of the population, probably between 5% and 10%, comprising the scientists, technologists, educators, managers and planners upon whom the smooth working of a society based on the extensive use of computers would depend. If this is regarded as arguing in favour of a meritocracy, then all that can be said is that the facts of computer development inexorably lead to the conclusion that, in our timescale if not in a more utopian age, such an elite will both exist and be essential. These people would clearly need a great deal of education, both initially and at frequent intervals later to keep them aware of the latest developments; both their employers, and the nations of which they are citizens, need to recognise the importance to them of seeing that this education is of the highest possible quality, and would ensure that those whose functions are primarily technological are aware of the purposes to which their work is directed and that those primarily concerned with administration understand why scientific developments are relevant and important to their work. The policy which would apply to remuneration of this elite obviously depends upon political ideology, but the attitudes which apply throughout the Western world and indeed many Communist states also would mean that they would receive very much higher salaries than the basic income mentioned above, justified by the relatively higher strain under which they would work and the responsibilities which they would carry.

It is very difficult to foresee how supply and demand will compare for this elite. In the past, even in times of high unemployment there have generally been too few people qualified to fill all the vacancies for highly skilled work. However, this could very well be due to shortcomings in the educational system rather than to lack of talent or of willingness to accept responsibility. One such defect is illustrated by the chronic graduate unemployment in India, resulting from a bias towards law and arts courses for whose products there is little demand, whereas a severe shortage of scientists, engineers and doctors persists. On the other hand, the recent increased unemployment among graduates in Britain is almost certainly due to temporary economic conditions rather than to any long-term effects such as those of the introduction of computers. The recent recession has caused many employers in science-based industries to cease practically all recruiting for a year or two in order to protect the jobs of those already engaged, at the same time as the uniquely rapid growth of higher education in the 1960s has ended, reducing the number of academic opportunities available. Very soon both industrial and teaching posts are likely to be in greater supply again.

In the advanced nations of the world there has been in recent years a general and considerable increase in the numbers of university students, both absolutely and as a proportion of the age group. Some "more means worse" dissentients notwithstanding, the general opinion has been that this has not meant a lowering of standards, which gives hope that there will not be too limited a pool of ability to staff the upper echelons of our technological societies adequately. Nevertheless, it is very likely that in spite of and partly because of the transition to greater leisure for the majority of the population, the leaders will have to work as hard as or even harder than they do now and will only gradually be able to delegate some of their functions to others. In the longer run, they ought to be able to enjoy more leisure like everyone else, but it is very unlikely that anyone with the ability and the desire to belong to the higher income group would be denied the opportunity.

The changes in employment resulting from the wider use of computers are likely to have transformed the way in which most people work by the end of the century but this will be a gradual, not a revolutionary, process. The introduction of any particular computer system may take up to four years to plan and to implement. During this period more people, or at least more man-hours of work, are invariably required. Whether the number of employees then declines depends on whether or not there is enough demand for the product concerned to absorb the increased output that is possible. This in turn is affected by whether this particular firm is pioneering more efficient production or is catching up with developments elsewhere in order to survive. In the latter case, it would be a question of some of the original work-force remaining after computerisation instead of all becoming redundant. This could be phased gradually as a continuation of retraining, which would have to be on a much more extensive scale than now both for changed occupations within any particular industry and for progress from less to more technologically advanced employment for everyone, outdating skills acquired in formal education and at the beginning of working life.

As already explained, it is essential to look at the kinds of work people do instead of at conventional job classifications. Some work types that can readily be taken over by computers and automated equipment have previously been discussed. These were:

— calculation and statistical analysis
— assembly of parts
— inspection to establish whether quality is satisfactory
— storage and retrieval of materials and information
— transcription of information between media and its transfer between locations.

A tentative list of others follows, making twenty categories of work, which will doubtless need amending and extending, but could form a basis for further investigation and planning. The next few have been or could quite readily be automated also, but those later in the list will probably need specifically human skills as far ahead as we can foresee. They are:

— sensing and interpreting physical characteristics (brightness, loudness, temperature, acidity, etc.)
— performance of prescribed series of adjustments
— recording and reporting events and decisions
— response to random enquiries
— learning and memorising facts, techniques and experiences
— movement of people and goods
— planning, allocation and control of the achievement of stated objectives
— diagnosis of faults and decisions on action to be taken
— persuasion of others to accept one's interpretation or recommendations (These last three comprise a large part, though by no means all, of jobs which are generally described as managerial or professional.)
— interpreting and providing for undefined individual requirements
— adjudication of disputes between people
— discovery of new concepts and techniques
— assessment of personality
— concrete expression of abstract ideas
— relief of the pain, sorrow or anxiety of others.

The arguments we have considered suggest the need for a major research project by technologists, economists and sociologists into the nature, purpose and motivation of work, which could be started by examining the modes of work done by a sufficiently representative sample Government, industry and the universities would all contribute to such research, which might well justify the endowment of foundations specifically concerned with it on a continuing basis. Essentially linked with such investigations would need to be research into how people spend their leisure, why they spend it as they do and what further opportunities they seek. Then economic planning could be based on a clear understanding of the practicable scope and rate of application of computers. Within this framework, long-range plans could be developed for each workplace, with full consultation between management and trades unions, which would define the modes of work currently being performed, those which would be eliminated, reduced or increased by the use of computers and the timescale on which this would occur. The age and educational potential of each employee would then be analysed so that a career plan could be devised for each which would identify those who could continue doing similar work until retirement, the type and duration of retraining needed by others, those who would become redundant according to present concepts of employment and the extra workers who would need to be recruited from schools and universities or from other jobs. These local detailed plans should then be merged by regional planning authorities so as to achieve an orderly transition from the sort of nearly full employment we now have to the pattern anticipated for the future. This pattern might be established in manufacturing industries before it became possible to extend it to service industries, which could in some cases absorb more people for a while before computers came into wider use there.

Thus computers will, as they are more and more fully exploited, lead to greater and greater changes in the internal organisation of and practices within industries, and in patterns of employment within and between industries. If we have not mentioned matters such as ownership and control of industry, it is because there seems no reason why computers should have any direct effect on this at all; computers are willing slaves and work as well for any master. And if we have tended to concentrate on employment it is because, as so often, it is on people that the main effects of the changes will fall. What this could mean to people's lives we shall discuss further in Part Four; for the moment, we shall simply stress one potential danger implicit in what has gone before, namely that of creating a class of permanently unemployables. Without care, and probably deliberate policy, a class could develop of people hereditarily condemned to the sort of vicious circle which much of the black population of the USA has experienced — educated in inferior schools, lacking technical qualifications, therefore only able to do jobs which are increasingly becoming superfluous, therefore forced in unemployment to live in a squalid environment which stifles any expression of talent in the next generation. Greater educational opportunities form part of the answer, but in the long run only a fundamental reappraisal of the concept of employment and "working for a living" is going to suffice.

13 The computer industry itself

At the end of the last chapter we said that there seemed no reason why the development of computer use should have any direct effect on matters such as ownership and control of industry. There is one important and obvious exception to this general statement: the computer industry itself. The development of computer use, and social and political effects of and attitudes towards computers may clearly have direct and profound effects upon the structure, control and policies of the industry which manufactures them. That industry therefore deserves separate study in rather more detail.

"Prophecy is the most gratuitous form of error." So said George Eliot in Middlemarch, and as we explained in the Introduction our intention throughout is to keep the element of prediction to the essential minimum necessary for there to be any meaningful discussion at all of what the future may have in store, but otherwise to deal in possibilities rather than probabilities. If there is a greater predictive content here than in earlier chapters it is partly because the subject is more specific, partly because we have a longer history to guide us. After all, the computer industry must necessarily have been involved with computers from the earliest days. Some of the patterns have already been set. Or so it appears. To prophesy about the development of the industry is still a dangerous business, even if it is to be hoped that errors of the magnitude of the early prediction that the entire needs of Britain for computing could be met by one giant machine will be avoided. In fact, as the title of this chapter implies, we shall simplify matters somewhat by concentrating mainly on the hardware side of the industry. In particular, in order to try to see how the pattern and organisation of computer manufacturing might develop, we shall take up again the example of the British industry, already discussed at the beginning of the book as a case of special interest.

We have already in Chapter 1 sketched the early days of computing, from the time of Babbage onwards. We may note, incidentally, that the first example of government support goes back to Babbage; £17,000 was injected into his Difference Engine project over a period of twenty years. We saw how early pioneering work was done in British and American universities and research establishments, leading to the commercial exploitation of the new machines. Most of the firms entering the computer manufacturing business were already manufacturers in related areas — electrical and electronic equipment, or business equipment. It is instructive to look in turn at the main firms which became interested in computers, and what happened to them.

IBM, before entering the computer field, was already a large manufacturer of business equipment. Although, as we saw in Chapter 1, it was rather slower off the mark than some other firms, the massive resources which it put into computer development, and its existing sales network and large number of customers for conventional business equipment meant that it went from strength to strength. Even today its non-computer interests would make it a large firm; but today computing dominates, and IBM is the principal supplier of computers virtually everywhere in the world outside the communist bloc, with the exception of the UK. One of its earliest successes, the IBM 650 which was the first computer to sell in hundreds rather than tens or twos, was due to IBM's realisation that what computer purchasers, particularly in the business field, would want above all was reliability.

Ferranti's, a British pioneer, were manufacturers of electrical equipment. Computing did not come to dominate the firm and it dropped out of the field when ICT (International Computers and Tabulators) took over its computing interests.

Lyons, another British pioneer, was as we have seen unusual since it was a catering firm for which this was a totally new development. In 1963 it dropped out of the field when it sold its computer subsidiary to English Electric, a further British firm early in the computer field.

Univac, on the other hand, was the first firm explicitly founded on computers; we have described in Chapter 1 how this enabled Remington Rand to become, in further contrast, the first firm to buy its way into the computer field by taking over a smaller company.

Two British punched-card firms, Powers-Samas and British Tabulating Machines (Hollerith) independently entered the computer field; the computer interests inevitably dominated and in 1959 they merged to form ICT, which later took over the computing interests of Ferranti as already mentioned, and of two other British electrical firms, General Electric and EMI (Electrical and Musical Industries). Two further British electrical firms, Marconi and Elliotts, had their computer interests taken over by English Electric.

Meanwhile, further firms were entering the market, notably in the United States, Western Europe and Japan — business equipment firms like Burroughs and National Cash Registers (USA), electrical firms like Telefunken and Siemens (Germany), Philips (Holland), American General Electric and RCA, the Radio Corporation of America. Further, by the middle 1960's new firms, purely in the computing industry, had appeared, firms like Control Data and Digital Equipment in the USA and Computer Technology in Britain.

The year 1964 is a convenient date to begin recounting the more recent history of the industry. IBM announced its 360 series; ICT announced its 1900 series; English Electric-Leo-Marconi had been formed the previous year and was actively bringing its plans to completion for its System 4 range, an improved version of RCA's Spectra 70 which was actually announced the following year; and in Britain the new Labour government took office with a firm commitment to "the white heat of the technological revolution" (in the new Prime Minister's phrase) and set up the new Ministry of Technology. The "third generation" of computers had arrived, and computers had entered the political arena.

The "third generation" was a natural progression from an increasing tendency in the early 1960s towards overall sophistication of existing equipment and systems, rather than simply technical innovation. This tendency was in turn due to the fact that the market rather than the manufacturer began to dictate the policy for development. There had been a tremendous increase in the commercial use and application of computers, and commercial users were more interested in continuity, reliability, and the means of planning ahead, rather than keeping up with each new technical advance and having to rewrite all their programs and change their systems with each new computer they bought. The significance of the 360 and 1900 announcements was that each company announced not just a single machine, but a "family" of machines, from small to large, with each configuration individually compatible to its neighbour in the series. This was achieved by rigorous standardisation, so that any of the peripherals could be attached to any of the processors, further storage or input-output devices could be added at will up to the capacity of the processors and, if necessary, a larger and more powerful processor could replace the existing one if the user needed more powerful facilities as his use of computer techniques increased. This is what the commercial users, now beginning to plan ahead seriously for computer development, were looking for. The IBM 360 series was an immediate success, while the 1900 series became IBM's major challenge in the UK and began to win export orders also.

The battle for success, or in some cases survival, in the computer industry was becoming more intense. Essentially it was IBM versus the rest; it was viewed differently in America and the rest of the world, but in both it became rather more contentious than merely competing for sales. In America there was little if any political element to this — American world dominance was taken for granted, though it was notoriously difficult for foreign firms to break into the US market even with highly competitive tenders — and the battle was rather on the legal front, with IBM's competitors seeking, eventually with a modicum of success, to limit its dominance by invoking the anti-trust laws. Elsewhere, however, the problem was seen as one of domination by American industry, as in so many other fields, and whether the domination was by IBM or by some other American firm was a secondary matter — even if IBM's world turnover was by now greater than the gross national products of many states.

Nowhere was this more acutely felt than in the United Kingdom, the one nation which, as we described in Chapter 1, might have been able to stand up against the Americans, and which was still the one Western nation in which IBM did not have the lion's share of the market. Before the 1964 Labour government came to power, a senior member of the previous Conservative administration had said that the sooner the British industry sank beneath the waves and allowed the Americans to get on with the job, the better. Not surprisingly, the British industry did not agree, and approached the new government at many levels to make its views known.

The argument, expressed briefly (which it rarely was), ran on the following lines. The computer was rapidly becoming the nucleus of all successful organisations; industrial, commercial, governmental, academic. The supply of such a vital element could not be left purely in foreign hands, however competent or friendly the supplier. External supply meant an abandonment of sovereignty and control. Secondly, the pattern of overall management would in future be more and more dictated by the use of computers and their allied management programs. If these were developed mainly outside Britain then management patterns would be dictated from outside and the creative function of British management could become atrophied. Thirdly, a nation needs science-based industries so that the country as a whole can benefit from the fall-out of new techniques. The greatest amount of such fall-out is generated by the computer industry. Fourthly, a native industry would help correct the imbalance in the balance of payments situation created by excessive imports of computer equipment.

These arguments were accepted by the then Minister of Technology, Mr. Frank Cousins, and support for a viable, indigenous British computer industry became official government policy. This having been decided, the British industry was examined in the light of its position vis-à-vis the rest of the world. The American industry dominated the world, having some 75% of the world market. As we said, only in Britain did it not have the lion's share. It was decided that to have two British computer companies in the face of such competition was not commercially sensible so action was begun to bring E-E-L-M and ICT together.

In March 1968 the two groups were brought together to form International Computers Limited (ICL). In addition to the two major companies, Plessey and the government were both shareholders, holding 18% and 10·5% respectively. The government, through the Industrial Expansion Bill, provided £13,500,000 towards the future R&D and subscribed a further £3,500,000 for £1 shares at par. Although a representative government director was appointed to the IC (Holdings) Board, the government gave assurances that they would in no way interfere in the day-to-day management of the company. They have been as good as their word. Since 1968 ICL has prospered in the highly competitive world of business and scientific computers, in every way surpassing the forecasts of progress made to the British government at the time of the merger. Today it is a company with a turnover of £150 million, employing some 28,000 people, trading in over seventy countries, exporting some 40% of its total output and is profitable.

The computer business never stands still, however. In America the high cost of trying to build and market better IBM-type systems than IBM has driven RCA out of the computer business. This has had a catalytic effect on the European computer scene where Siemens had been developing the RCA systems under licence most successfully and had captured some 15% of the German home market. Deprived of RCA's continuing support, Siemens quickly sought new partners with a similar design philosophy. It found these in CII in France and Philips in Holland. Government backing in varying degrees is given to all three companies, particularly in the area of preferential purchasing for government systems. Because of IBM's historical dominance of the market, existing government installations in Europe are largely IBM systems and governments are anxious to replace them with IBM-type systems locally manufactured. The new grouping of Siemens/CII/Philips is likely, therefore, to adopt the policy that proved so expensive to RCA, but it is hoped that government support will enable them to pursue it more successfully. In Germany AEG-Telefunken have decided to merge their scientific and commercial computing interests with those of Nixdorf AG, a remarkably successful manufacturer of peripheral equipment and intelligent terminals with a strong European marketing force.

However, the competition remains intense and the pace of development swift throughout the industry. There is no time for the British or the European computer industry to pause for a period of self-congratulation, or for their governments, if they are really determined to become less dependent on American technology, to sit back. The technical and commercial successes achieved so far, such as ICL's equal market share with IBM in the UK, increasing sales in other countries such as Sweden, France, Holland, Switzerland, South Africa, Australia and New Zealand, even £2,000,000 sales of peripheral equipment to the United States itself, are satisfactory, but no more than a base on which to build.

On the political side there have been uncertainties in the recent past because of a number of factors — economic difficulties, unease on the world's money markets, the long drawn out negotiations for the expansion of the European Economic Community and the political battles inside the countries involved which resulted. However, by 1972 some at least of these had clarified sufficiently to make it possible to look ahead with more certainty. The keys as far as Britain was concerned were the extent of government support, and the accession of Britain to the EEC, and by mid-1972 the British government had in the latter case got its legislation through Parliament, and in the former case had made its long-awaited announcements, the run-up to which we described in Chapter 1.

The first government announcement was of £14·2 million of support for ICL for the period up to September 1973; this was followed a little later by a second announcement of 3 million for smaller firms, particularly software contracts. As this book goes to press it is still uncertain whether any further announcements are to come, but it is clear that the sum committed so far is well below the level recommended by the House of Commons select committee report. As a result, much criticism has followed, both inside and outside the computing world, of the amount of money committed, of the lack of indication of any longer term plans and of the relatively low level of support for smaller British firms marketing minicomputers, peripherals, and software. On the other hand, the sum provided for ICL was in fact what the firm had asked for, the plans it had made on that basis could go ahead, and there was obviously the hope that the commitment would in fact be a continuing one and that longer term plans would be announced during the coming year. Further, the renewed pressure by those in the political world and outside it for greater government support for the British computer industry generally might lead ultimately to an increased commitment not only to the smaller firms which were the critics' immediate cause for concern, but to ICL itself.

Meanwhile, it could look to the future as part of an enlarged EEC. The European computing industry, in turn, long used to being part of a Community, one of whose aims was to become an economic bloc capable of challenging the Americans on a world scale, could only welcome the accession of Britain and the strongest indigenous computing industry outside the USA.

In fact, that the EEC authorities already regarded ICL as part of Europe was demonstrated by the early invitation from the Commission to join with the other native European computer manufacturers in submitting proposals for the joint design and manufacture of a very powerful computer for the Europe of 1980. This invitation was extended before Britain made her last application to become a member of the EEC and was the only official approach to Britain made at that time. Since then, ICL has been a full member of the European study group, meeting regularly with the other manufacturers to discuss how to provide European solutions to European problems. After rationalising the European situation, then it will be necessary to find an opening into the US market, one of the richest marketing territories in the world.

During bilateral discussions with the various European companies ICL discovered that CII, the French national computer company, was having technical discussions on common standards and interfaces with the Control Data Corporation (CDC) of America in much the same areas as was ICL itself. Further three-way discussions produced the rational solution of the forming of a joint study company, Multinational Data, in Brussels to continue the work for the three companies and to arrive at basic standards for both hardware and software. Through CII, both Philips and Siemens will now have the work of Multinational Data available to them and it is possible also that other European manufacturers, perhaps Telefunken/Nixdorf, after observing the progress of Multinational Data, will wish to be associated with it and to adopt the agreed common standards and interfaces. In this way progress can be made to extend the European industry's R&D capacity and to open up still further the market areas of the USA and Europe.

Such arrangements and alliances will probably be effective up until 1980, and maybe beyond, because computer systems have a five to seven year life and development cycle. It is likely that systems under development now will be marketed in 1973/74 and the range of systems to come after that will possibly be introduced in 1980/81 and may well last for seven to eight years; possibly longer.

The same sort of timescale, say ten years, will also probably be needed for the enlarged EEC to settle down, find its feet, and determine its role in the world; but to try to project beyond that, to the end of our thirty years, is necessarily far more speculative. Certainly — short of startling changes in the direction of political evolution — there will be no "British" or other national computer industries left in Europe in any narrow sense; rather will there be a European group or partnership, marketing world-wide and, if current trends continue, with strong links inside North America. The dominant position of the manufacturer will probably have changed and the likely structure of any computer group will be that of a holding company containing elements of manufacturing, a software house, computer bureaux, management and staff training businesses and, most important, a business that deals effectively with the interface between man and machine. Currently, computer systems are generally inadequately utilised, partly because of lack of experience, staffing shortages and slow acceptance by middle and senior management of modern management techniques. A very significant factor slowing down their economic use, however, is fear and resistance to change as such. In a largely godless society the computer has replaced the Divinity as the unknown, all-powerful and mysterious force that human nature seems to require. The coming of a computer into an organisation sparks off countless fears in people at every level. Such fears breed resistance to everything to do with the new systems of work brought about by the computer. Some of the resistance will be conscious, much of it will be uncon-scious. Both, combined at all levels of the organisation, can do an enormous amount to undermine the effectiveness of the system that has been introduced.

It will be necessary, therefore, for as much attention to be given by the computer industry, as a result of the trends in retraining, and employment patterns generally, discussed in Chapter 7 and again in Chapter 12, to explanation, education and assurance of staff at every level, as is given to achieving technical excellence; the computer industry will not be able to afford to stand aside from the social effects of the use of its products. This will bring into the computer industry new skills and intellectual disciplines that will undoubtedly change it, almost certainly for the better.

Finally, we need to look at the development of new power bases in the world of the future. Dr. Herman Kahn, that most distinguished futurologist, has predicted that the major power in the year 2000 will be Japan. Certainly the Japanese computer industry is powerful and expanding. Of the five companies currently manufacturing computers in Japan, four have links with American manufacturers. The Japanese government is applying pressure for these links to be broken. A government body has been established to provide finance to the home industry. Japanese computers are being marketed effectively in Eastern Europe. There are many parallels between the situation of Japanese industry now and that of Britain and Europe six years ago. In thirty years' time the Japanese industry may well have rationalised itself further and will certainly be marketing in Europe and the developing countries. The British industry by the end of this century may be looking as eagerly for a Japanese partner as it has done for a European and American partner.

It is likely, however, that by the end of this century large companies will not be seen primarily as American, British or Japanese. By then they will be as large and as powerful as many nation states but much more international in outlook. A new form of political pattern will have to develop to deal with the interaction of vast industrial combines and the power blocks of America, Russia, Europe and Japan. Diplomacy as well as trade will be the business of every element of the world computer industry.

In any event, by the year 2000 government involvement in private business management will have grown substantially in all sectors, but particularly so in the computer business, an area too vital to national, and international, security to be left to the private sector alone. Increasingly it can be expected that governments will dictate what shall be produced, where, how and at what price.

All of these coming changes, and the effects of present change, spell out a clear message to the manager concerned with the future of the computer industry. He must cease to be parochial and fixed in his ways; instead he must be international and highly flexible and he must ensure that his company is also. The multinational companies are growing in number, the successful ones are rapidly expanding their hold on markets. It has been predicted that by the year 2000 a mere 200-300 multinational corporations will be responsible for 60%-75% of the world's industrial production. To be amongst that number, a computer services corporation will have to make use of the most advanced forms of scientific management to ensure that its resources are economically allocated on a world-wide basis, regardless of the historical accident of its country of incorporation.

Some of the things that any successful corporation must do if it is to be in the top 300 can be listed. They may seem obvious, but there will be comparatively few corporations doing them all today.

1. Creation of medium- (three-to-seven year) and long- (ten-to-twenty year) term plans that treat the entire world as one market and eliminate "domestic" and "foreign" differentiations.

2. Inclusion in such plans of major international mergers and acquisitions. Few, if any, corporations will be able to maintain a pace of expansion on a global basis commensurate with the imperatives cited earlier purely through internal corporate growth.

3. Inclusion in such plans of a scheme to find and develop the kind and number of managers required to make the company truly global.

4. Modernisation of criteria for measuring investment and performance. Years-old, domestically orientated standards are of progressively less help in meeting current and prospective challenges and opportunities; at the very least, greater flexibility is required in respect of pay-out periods, particularly in the light of the long-term market potential in the less-developed areas.

5. Adoption of a planned evolution of the company's organisational structure. Steps should be taken to prepare the entire top management for phased assumption of world-wide responsibilities, since, in the final analysis, a company's total resources will be most wisely allocated and most effectively utilized on a global scale when one management team is responsible for them. All too often, in the absence of a plan to effect this preparation, a company will rush headlong into the so-called "world corporation" form of organisation — and fall flat on its face.

6. Creation of a concept or philosophy of ownership and a plan to carry it out. Again, lacking such a plan, companies stumble into a structure of ownership of world-wide facilities that neither furnishes highly desirable management control nor satisfies the justifiable yearning of peoples throughout the world for industrial ownership.

7. Introduction of a formal, scientifically organised and operated management information activity. Keeping executives alert to upcoming revolutionary changes in markets, consumption habits, laws, trade patterns, corporate practices, financial sources, and the like, can no longer be left to chance or the individual whim of

each manager. For efficiency and reliability central co-ordination is needed — especially at headquarters — covering world-wide environmental surveillance, inter-company communications and the technology of information collection, storage, retrieval, and dissemination.

In Chapter 2 we looked at the kind of technical developments needed for the systems of the future — devices for on-line collection and validation of data replacing conventional methods of input by punched cards or paper tape in most situations, more flexible visual and printing output devices, larger, faster and cheaper means of immediate and direct access storage, and so on. This discussion, as we said at the start, was firmly rooted in what is now being done; the computer industry is well aware of these needs and is actively working on them. We also mentioned the problem areas of software reliability and man-machine communication. One of the recent developments in the industry has been the growth on the software side, sometimes offshoots of existing hardware manufacturers, sometimes new specialist firms such as consultancies set up by programming experts turning freelance, or computer service bureaux buying computing equipment and selling its time, and their supporting services of standard or custom-built programs. A restructuring of the software industry could well play its part in solving the problems of systems design described in Chapter 2, in alliance with general improvements in programming technology and a basic rethinking inside the industry's research organisations, academic institutions and elsewhere of the basic problems of instructing and communicating with a logical machine. The growth of professional software organisations should bring improvements also in the management of projects, the degree of quality control and the rigorous testing of the end product.

As we have seen, and have still to see in later chapters, by the end of this century the pattern of our society, whatever it may be, will be greatly dependent on and influenced by computer exploitation; that is, dependent on and influenced by the products of the computer industry. The challenge and the responsibility are equally great.

14   Computers and opinion forming

In a book about the making of decisions, one kind of organisation which certainly deserves special consideration is that which is concerned with the influencing of decisions. A variety of organisations of this type exist — advertising and marketing organisations, political parties, pressure groups of all kinds, bodies which exist to represent the organised opinion of specific groups of people like trades unions, residents' associations, and so on. With these we can associate peripheral organisations which exist to ascertain opinions rather than influence them — market research organisations, opinion polls, election organisations, etc. These often exist to serve, or in the case of election organisations are served by, bodies of the opinion-forming type. Computer techniques are potentially of great importance to all of these.

For the purpose of this chapter we can ignore the standard commercial computer applications, such as payroll, which these organisations, like any other, can employ. What we shall be concerned with are the integral activities of ascertaining and influencing opinions. If we begin with the advertising and marketing of a commercial product, among the main activities are determining who are the potential purchasers, what their needs are, what their prejudices are, how their interest can be aroused, and then contacting them. There are various levels at which computers can be used in these activities.

One thing which computers can certainly do is enable existing methods of ascertaining customer habits to be applied far more efficiently, because of their capacity to deal with large amounts of information. Analyses of consumer preferences, loyalty to brand names, reactions to different kinds of marketing, can be carried out in far greater detail, with greater precision, over larger numbers of people than is possible without their aid.

All this can have its effect on mass marketing techniques such as television or radio advertising, newspaper and magazine advertising (particularly if allied to more precise information about the kind of viewer/listener/reader it will be reaching), packaging, special shop displays, promotion offers of all kinds (specially reduced prices, giveaways, bargain offers on other goods, vouchers, etc.) and competitions. The effect on individual marketing techniques, at present mainly by mailing and door-to-door selling, though some use of telephone selling is also made, is potentially of a different order of magnitude. The case of mailing is perhaps the best to consider in detail.

The most obvious starting place is the use of the computer to store and keep up-to-date lists of names and addresses to whom material is sent; this can be used in conjunction with other automatic equipment actually to produce and mail the promotional material. The next step could be the use of the names to produce individually addressed letters, beginning "Dear Mr. Smith" rather than "Dear Sir or Madam". Then other information contained in the address list can be used to "personalise" the letter further: "Dear Mr. Smith, I am pleased to invite you to take part as a representative of Muddlecombe in a nationwide survey. All you have to do is . . . " In parenthesis it can be noted that this kind of promotion may be counter-productive, in that such crude psuedo-personal correspondence causes irritation to some. This can be reinforced if the main content is of low quality or less than honest, as in "I thought I would write to you personally to tell you . . . " when the signature is printed and the letter is going out in thousands, or "You have been specially selected as the only person in Lower Upham to be offered this opportunity . . . " when the recipient finds that half of his neighbours are on the same mailing list. If this kind of promotion is associated with computerised mailings, it is contrasted unfavourably with the reverse situation which can arise when, say, trying to get a personal answer from a computerised invoicing system if an account is incorrect. It is hardly surprising that people are suspicious of computers when obviously impersonal material is pseudo-personalised whereas obviously individual material is impersonalised ("Please quote computer number 00095732225080012 on all correspondence") and it appears impossible to get personal problems dealt with.

In fact, this kind of promotion is likely to spread, with the result that the public will gradually become more sophisticated; when one receives something of this kind once every few weeks they have some chance of being looked at, but when they come in by every post only the ones which are of most appeal will have a chance of being taken seriously. In managers in the business world, already subjected to a flood of "junk" mailings, calls by salesmen and promotional telephone calls, the advertising industry has a guineapig population for developing these techniques; however, the behavioural pattern of this population differs from that to be expected from the general population because many managers retreat from the onslaught behind a barricade of personal secretaries, not available to the ordinary citizen.

There are a number of possible extensions to the crude techniques described so far. Firstly, additional information available from the mailing list can be used in order to vary the approach to the recipient. For example, usually the sex of the addressee is known, and differences in approach could be used accordingly ("Dear Mrs. Jones, as a woman you will know that . . . ") or regional variations could be built into the way the letter was phrased if market research showed that these were distinct enough to have an effect. If, for example, it was known that in one part of the country strong coffee was favoured more than elsewhere, the promotion (for the same coffee) could refer to the strength of the new blend, or alternatively to its delicate flavour, depending on the address to which the mailing was being sent. Statistically this might pay off, the increased cost of regionalising the mailing being more than paid for by resulting increases in sales.

The weakness of this technique is precisely because it is for the most part based on statistical evidence; an ardent advocate of women's rights might well be insulted by a letter beginning "As a woman . . . ", while a Scot living in Leeds might not take kindly to being treated as a typical Yorkshireman. Ideally (from the advertiser's point of view) the approach should be specific to the individual. The advantage of doorstep selling, and to a lesser extent telephone selling, is that the salesman can tailor his presentation to the individual he is addressing, and the most successful doorstep salesman is the one who can quickly "size up" his victim and invent the necessary approach to gain his interest. The salesman is, of course, in an interactive situation and can modify his prepared line, unlike the television advertisement or the circular letter, however personalised. We shall come back to the interactive aspect shortly.

The information about the sex of the addressee can, to a limited extent, be used directly, e.g. so that products specifically for women are only advertised to them and not to men, as well as statistically. If other information is available to the advertiser this could similarly be used either directly or statistically. Such information might include age, occupation, whether or not a car owner, number of children, and so on. A promotion might be specifically of a product for the motorist; on the other hand, it might be of a superficially unrelated product but slanted in a particular way because statistically motorists are known to have certain attitudes. Almost any such information might be of potential value to an advertiser.

A surprising amount of such information can be gleaned by collating existing information, using lists of membership of societies, professional registers, telephone directories and the like. The address itself may yield information about whether the addressee owns or rents his home, and if he rents it whether from a public authority or private landlord. A decision by the advertising and marketing world to extend this individual-ised method of promotion could lead to secondary businesses spreading which specialise in obtaining and selling such information — the credit rating agencies are examples of existing organisations of this type, and they could well diversify their activities into this area, effectively compiling dossiers on individuals. Already there is a ready market for mailing lists of people who are likely to be interested in specific types of goods, and another indication of the same trend is the willingness of organisations to buy information (albeit only statistical) derived from the British national census of 1971.

All this is information which might be regarded as being to some extent in the public domain, with the exception of credit rating. Some people prefer to conceal their age; if they are ashamed of their occupation or it is a criminal one they may wish not to reveal that; they may prefer not to confess to owning a car or a television set if they are running them without licences; but most people are on the whole quite open about these matters. Obviously a lot depends on social organisation and custom, but very often the required information could be obtained simply by asking the person concerned, whether or not the asker had any legal right to the information. Credit ratings, however, are based on information of a different kind, namely the observed behaviour of the individual in certain situations. Similar information can be obtained by advertisers by observing the responses of their addressees to a succession of mailings. Any advertiser does this now at least to the extent of dropping people off the list who show no response over a given period, but clearly this could be made much more sophisticated. "Whether or not you wish to take up this remarkable offer, please return the reply-paid card with the YES or NO stamp attached" is a primitive example of trying to rate an individual's responsive-ness to circular letters.

An advertiser with such a system would clearly be extremely interested in the responsiveness of those on his mailing list to the circulations of others. Except in the case of direct rivals, exchanges of information for mutual benefit would certainly take place; one possibility might be the growth of advertising agencies specialising not in selling particular products like soap or birdseed but to selling to the people on its files. Ultimately this could mean approaches not only being made solely to those with a given minimum likelihood of responding positively (the minimum depending on the target success rate) but individually tailored to that individual. As well as the obvious advantages to the advertiser there would be advantages to both advertisers and recipients in reducing the incidence of unwanted or objectionable (to the individual) mailings, such as offering a central heating system to someone who has just installed one, or a book of nude pictures to an elderly lady of conventional views, or an atheist tract to a devout Christian. On the other hand, many people would certainly object to the existence of such a dossier on their lives, habits and inclinations, while others who did not object to the existence of a dossier *per se* might dislike the thought of being manipulated. On the other hand, still others might positively welcome the certainty of hearing about the latest books of nude pictures or atheist tracts. These aspects will be considered further in Part Four, but clearly the level of acceptability of such techniques will have to be considered by decisionmakers both in the advertising and marketing industry, and in the government departments and other bodies responsible for regulating activities in that area.

The measurement of responsiveness is the nearest approach to the interactive situation that can be reached in mailing. However, such individual dossiers could clearly also be used to brief doorstep or telephone salesmen, and information gleaned by them as to individuals' preferences entered into the dossier. A further extension of these advertising methods is possible through the use of the national computer grid. Individual transmissions could be used as an alternative to doorstep selling, yet would be interactive, and make possible an instant sale and transfer of the necessary funds; general advertising transmissions through a television channel could be accompanied by an appeal to viewers for an immediate response through their terminals, the results of which could be used both as data for evaluation of the success of the chosen approach, and an item to be added to the dossiers of the individuals who do, in fact, respond. Again, the ultimate development of the use of public utility information networks would be the tailoring of every promotional transmission to the characteristics of the response from each terminal. As before, whether such individualised advertising ever comes about depends on the costs and returns of such methods compared with others available, and, of course, on what the rules of the utility authority permit.

In many respects the potential of computer techniques for political parties and opinion pressure groups is similar to that already discussed. Similar techniques can be and are used for political propaganda as for commercial advertising. What differences there are arise from the differences in organisation and motivation. Political parties in most countries have fewer resources than commercial advertisers, and rely heavily on voluntary labour. Further, they can usually expect more coverage and direct support or hostility from commentaries in mass media. Thus political parties, to make full use of the kind of techniques discussed earlier, have not just one class of individual to deal with, the potential customers in the case of a commercial advertiser, but several overlapping ones. They have to keep up the morale of their party activists, to keep them working for the party and, if possible, working harder; they have to retain the confidence and support of their rank and file followers; they have to retain the interest of the media and convince them they are worth supporting; they have to identify and try to appeal to the opinion leaders which exist in any community who are not already committed to themselves or another party; and finally, they have to appeal to the voters. The problem is complicated by the intricacies of the political structure in different countries; one can cite the American primary elections, where candidates have first to be elected as such by registered voters, or safe seats in countries with simple-majority voting systems, where the effective election of a representative takes place not at the polls but at the meetings of the selection committee of the dominant party.

The serious exploitation of computer techniques by political parties will depend principally on the twin factors of cost and effort. Democratic political parties are notoriously short of money, and until costs of computing come down dramatically only those with wealthy backers or, as in Sweden, subsidised from public funds and hence more certain of a regular income can be expected to be able to consider obtaining their own systems. In the immediate future the chief hopes of parties in obtaining computer facilities lie in the possibility of support from friendly organisations like businesses or trade unions; in due course they can be expected to make use of public utility facilities. In fact, the main needs of political parties for computing facilities lie in organising (often in a very short time as an election is called) a mass of voluntary amateur workers, keeping track of supporters, particularly those who respond to appeals for funds, and maintaining an information service to aid its propaganda. Maintaining a file of political attitudes for every voter is hardly a feasible proposition in the foreseeable future.

Pressure groups may be of the form of factions within political parties, such as the Monday Club or Pressure for Economic and Social Toryism within the British Conservative Party, or supporters of primary candidates in the United States, or exist outside or across them, such as penal reformers, civil rights movements, and so on. Within parties it is probably only where factions are fighting for control through internal elections that computer techniques might be of substantial value, to organise and keep track of support, and probably only where this occurs on the largest scale that it becomes feasible. The most obvious example is in the American Presidential race, in primary elections, selection of delegates to the nominating conventions in non-primary states, and keeping track of and influencing delegates at the convention itself. Millions of dollars are commonly spent on behalf of leading contenders for nomination, and so it is hardly surprising that computer techniques have already started to be used there. However, this is in a contest where the ultimate prize is the most powerful job in the free world, one to which many people give much money and effort. Not only will computing have to come down dramatically in cost to become at all widespread in lesser contests, it will also have to become simpler and more familiar. There are many cheap means of increasing efficiency in organisations which are not used by political groups simply because those concerned are not sufficiently motivated or knowledgeable to implement them.

In the case of other pressure groups or special-interest organisations it is again the financial and informational facilities which will be of most interest. Many pressure groups rely on donations for their existence, whereas mass representational organisations like trades unions have membership record problems which can be, and in numerous cases already have been, solved by computerisation. But the use of computer techniques to help in marshalling facts in support of arguments or campaigns is potentially of greater significance, especially if the group wishes to be taken seriously by and exert influence on those with much greater fact-gathering and -collating capacity such as the press, broadcasting authorities, or government departments, all of whom would by then be using similar techniques. This is reinforced still further when the organisation is in a bargaining position, as in the case of a trade union seeking a new wage agreement. The same arguments then apply as to the case of international diplomacy mentioned in Chapter 8 — he who enters the negotiating chamber without the support of a database will be naked indeed.

Finally, we come to opinion-collection. Much of what computers can do in this area is apparent from what has gone before, and need not be laboured, the chief factors being the increased speed, accuracy and detail which become possible. This is true even if the raw information is obtained by conventional means such as questionnaire or interview and only afterwards input to the machine. Speed can be increased still further, however, by using network techniques for direct input by the interviewer of the data he is collecting; it is possible that such techniques would have meant that the political polls could have avoided their humiliation at the British General Election of 1970. All but one forecast a Labour victory, and afterwards suggested that the reason for the failure was the delay between interviews and results, which meant that a last-minute swing to the Conservatives was not detected. On-line input of responses would have meant that this swing would have been detected, if it actually occured, or alternatively, that the poll organisations would have had to have found a different excuse. The development of a public utility, of course, would mean that the pollsters' sample could be contacted and questioned through their terminals directly, giving the possibility of virtually instant collection of opinion on, say, the current position in a rapidly-changing situation, of a far more useful kind than sending out an interviewer for spot interviews. There would be dangers of sampling error arising from who owns or is accessible through a terminal, but this is something which these organisations are already aware of and used to allowing for.

This brings us to the possibility of voting by computer. In complex elections in the United States, where many contests and issues are voted on simultaneously, mechanisation and, latterly, computer counting have been used for many years, since its cost is much below that of counting by hand. As computing costs drop and labour costs rise this could become true of much simpler elections, even the single-contest simple-majority type. One side-effect of this would be that one of the strongest arguments for that type of election — its simplicity and ease of counting — would no longer apply, as a computer can cope equally easily with proportional or preferential systems which many regard as being fairer.

Computerised voting systems at present in use, in America and elsewhere, such as in student or trade union elections in the U.K., rely on indirect entry of votes using punched cards, special ballot papers or the like. The possibility exists, however, of direct input of votes — either through special devices in polling booths which are connected to a remote computer (e.g. belonging to the local authority) or through terminals of the public utility. For example, a former British Minister of Technology, Mr. Wedgwood Benn, has advocated the use of such methods for push-button referenda on issues of the day, quite apart from actual elections. It is very easy to become enthusiastic about such possibilities and make glib statements about "participatory democracy", but there are very severe difficulties about such systems which those involved — which ultimately means all citizens — need to consider very carefully. There is the question of security, what happens if a system failure causes a vote to be lost. There is the question of the secrecy of the ballot, and whether this can be maintained — and, at least as important, can be seen to be maintained — when votes are input from identifiable terminals. There are the dangers of voting under intimidation at a private terminal rather than secretly and free from intimidation in a public booth. There is the question of ensuring that everyone has an equal chance of participating, and has the necessary information to enable him to do so. There are the dangers of decision by the instant panic or euphoric reaction. The whole recurrent argument about the nature and purpose of representative government becomes involved.

Yet the attractions of the idea are undeniable, and if a public computing utility comes about pressure for something along these lines may well increase; it is, after all, the other side of the argument that a computing utility puts far more potential power in the hands of government. It shows how the computer revolution may make it necessary to rethink from the beginning the whole complex of relationships between government, society and the individual.

4 The world of human values

15

The quality of life

We live in a world of change. This is such a commonplace in this technological age that it is easy to overlook both the scale and the pace of change to which modern man in the industrialised states of the world is subjected. The impact of computers is only part of that which has occurred and will continue from the motor car, television, plastics, aviation, nuclear weapons, the contraceptive pill, and so on. If the eventual effect is greater than any of these on the way that we live, it is because computers have, as we have seen, applications in so many areas of human activity.

Most people's lives can be split into a number of aspects — as part of a general culture, as part of a local community, at work, domestically — interacting to a greater or lesser extent depending on the individual and his situation. Technological change can have differential effects on these aspects. Aviation may affect an individual's life hardly at all, except deterioration of his environment through noise, television may bring him entertainment and instruction in his home, yet reduce community life around him, the contraceptive pill may have a profound effect on his family life, and have its effect on the general culture of society, the motor car may give him freedom to travel for pleasure, have a wider choice of jobs, yet severely harm the quality of his life in other ways through noise, fumes, congestion and the building of ever more roads.

The example of the car illustrates how difficult it is to talk too freely about "the quality of life". For many, life would be wholly drab and humdrum without the car as an interest and a means of escape; for others it is an abomination. It is not simply that technical progress can be used for good or ill; it may genuinely be difficult or impossible to enhance the quality of life for some without depressing that of others. Where the pleasure or comfort of a few is dependent on the annoyance or discomfort of the many the choice may be easy, but this is not always the case. Even where someone is engaged in some quite harmless occupation, like quietly watching television in private, it is difficult to be too dogmatic, since it could be argued that his quality of life would, on balance, be enhanced if television were not available and he had to make his own entertainment. In discussing the effects of computers on individual lives we shall, therefore, not attempt to give definitive answers to such questions. We shall rather point to possibilities, and try to show the choices which may be open to individuals and to society as a whole.

In later chapters of Part Four we shall be looking further at the way in which computers can help in planning the environment, which has become recognised in recent years as being of central importance to the quality of human life, and then their impact on the everyday world of work, home and recreation. We shall also look at intellectual and cultural development, and two important aspects of the relation between the individual and society — the problem of crime, and the problem of individual privacy. For the moment we shall consider briefly how human attitudes to life generally might be affected by the spread of computers. Of course, it will take many more than thirty years for any changes to become deeply embedded in human culture, but trends of greater significance than the transient fad should have started appearing by then. Computers will have been with us for some fifty years, and the same kinds of differences in attitudes to personal transport that occurred in industrial nations between 1900 and 1950 may perhaps be looked for.

We have already touched upon the main likely difference in Chapter 12 — the attitude to work. Over the years mechanisation has come to have some effect on attitudes; certain kinds of work are now regarded as being for machines to do rather than men, and gradually there has been a move towards shorter working lives. Retirement before it is forced on one through illhealth or other incapacity is regarded as not only socially acceptable, but a right; a man is not regarded as lazy if his working week is thirty-five hours and his annual holidays four weeks. Nevertheless, the general underlying feeling remains that of the sanctity of toil, the dignity of labour, and the right to work. As we saw in Chapter 12, the long-term effect of computer techniques may be to shift this position into one where work is increasingly regarded as a privilege rather than a right, where it is remembered that toil was the curse which God placed upon Adam, not a blessing. The question then arises, what will replace work? Lives without work could be dedicated to hedonistic emptiness, or to intellectual and cultural stimulation and creativity. If "the right to work" is replaced merely by "the right to entertainment", it may be doubted if any significant advance in the quality of life will have been achieved. "The right to occupation" might offer greater hope.

As well as a more general attitude that work is for machines rather than men, the growth can be expected of the attitude that routine decisions are for computers rather than men to take. The wild swings in recent attitudes to computers, from total faith in everything that comes out of them in the first flush of enthusiasm when little matters like the accuracy of the input data, the competence of the programmer and the correctness of the underlying analysis are ignored, to utter scepticism and distrust, may well continue for some time, but finally settle down into a matter-of-fact acceptance of reliable systems — or a sullen acceptance of "them", the systems that tell us what is good for us and what to do and are difficult to catch out, bamboozle or fault. As a result the general feeling might become that what humans should do is concern themselves about the really important and interesting decisions — or that all decisions can be left to "them" and that intellectual work is no more for humans than physical work.

As well as attitudes to machines and humans and the relationship between them, we have to consider other attitudes which computer techniques might indirectly affect. One pervasive modern attitude is that the big organisation is necessarily impersonal, that large-scale operation is necessary for efficiency and that the human beings involved must mould themselves to fit the requirements of the system — the conveyor belt society. It is quite apparent that the further spread and entrenchment of bad computer systems could reinforce this feeling and turn every individual into a computerised statistic, with less and less scope for individuality. On the other hand, the capacity for computers in dealing with information at individual level could, given good computer systems, enable everyone to have both the feeling and the actuality of individual treatment and consideration from any organisation, from government bureaucracy downwards. What depresses the quality of human life is making uniform what should be diverse, and making diverse what should be uniform. The benefits which human organisations tend to bring are those of uniformity — equal treatment under the law, and the like — at the price of stifling diversity; computers can cope both with uniformity where it is needed, and diversity where it is needed.

The computer can be used to enslave human lives, or to enrich them. Its power, like that of any other technological device, resides not only in itself but in the minds of those who decide where and when and in what manner to use it.

Nor, despite its power, is it all-powerful. It can enrich human lives, as we hope to show in this part of the book, but it is not a panacea, it will not bring utopia. The final trap, when all others have been avoided, is in thinking that having solved these problems, we have solved everything, as many societies and individuals have discovered in chasing after material affluence or emotional gratification. A computer may help us to plan our cities so that people may move easily and freely across it; it will not tell us that, if there is a garden in its centre through which people can stroll, it will make their journey seem shorter. We might say, to the world thirty or three hundred years ahead, as Flecker did to his poet a thousand years hence:

> "I care not if you bridge the seas,
>   Or ride secure the cruel sky,
>   Or build consummate palaces
>   Of metal or of masonry.
>
>   But have you wine and music still,
>   And statues, and a bright-eyed love,
>   And foolish thoughts of good and ill
>   And prayers to those that sit above?"

16 Planning the environment

Nevertheless, it is with computers that we are concerned, and it is with metal and masonry, among other things, which computers can help us deal. In this chapter we shall be concerned with ways in which computers can assist in the physical environment in which we spend our lives.

Much has been written and spoken on this general subject in recent years, mainly because at long last it is beginning to be brought home to people, in particular to politicians, that unplanned use of physical resources, or isolated planning in specific areas or for specific purposes, is no longer a rational procedure, at least in heavily populated areas. It has been the increasing pressures of population, plus in the developed countries increasing expectations due to material affluence (e.g. for a home and a car), plus cumulative effects of pollution due to industrialisation, plus increasing traffic congestion, which has brought this about. The topic is again an enormous one, so once more it will only be possible to look briefly at some of the main areas where computers can play an important role. Communications is one in which computers have already been extensively used, both in the regulation of traffic in congested conditions, and in the planning of new transport systems, so these aspects will be considered first; then we shall consider urban planning, and finally problems of conservation.

In order to provide for the rising demand for road traffic, counteract the effects of increasing congestion and delays, and reduce the terrible toll of accidents, traffic authorities in several countries have come to regard it as more and more necessary to apply the principles of computing and automatic control to the operation of road transport systems. Work has been in progress for some years on a whole range of these possibilities, starting with computer control of traffic lights in urban street networks, and proceeding to complete automation of the driving of road vehicles, which has so far been tested only on prototype installations.

Though it is in road transport that the problems are most acute, and so it is on the control of freely moving road traffic that we shall concentrate, there are also, as we shall see, some important actual and potential applications of control technology and computing to other modes of transport.

Computers have been applied to traffic signal control systems in several cities; well-known installations of this sort are in Toronto, London, Liverpool and Glasgow, where the results have been notably successful. Similar systems have also been introduced in several West European cities, and are now beginning to appear in the USA and the USSR. Experience suggests that savings of over 10% in journey times are typical and that similar reductions in accident rates occur. These promising results have usually occurred in spite of overall increases in traffic flow since the systems were started, and they have usually been maintained over rush-hour as well as slack periods. The resulting equivalent financial savings have been many times as great as the costs of installation.

Computers are already beginning to be used for the automatic control of road signs, providing information and guidance for drivers. For example, on British motorways, computer-controlled signals have been placed about one to two miles apart, on the central reservation between the two carriageways. Under normal conditions, the signals show no symbol but, in bad weather or near an accident or roadworks or other hazard, they indicate either a recommended speed or a lane closure. In principle, it should be possible to devise considerably more advanced systems, with computers working out optimum traffic flow plans in the light of up-to-date information on traffic conditions, collected from vehicle-detectors in the system, and then sending to roadside displays appropriate recommendations for route and driving speed at a given time and place.

General Motors has developed the DAIR (Driver Aid, Information and Routing) communications system, which automatically gives route instructions, communicates traffic signs and roadside messages, and provides a radio link to the driver to call for emergency help or information if necessary. This system is part of a more general concept of Electronic Route-Guidance System (ERGS), being developed under the sponsorship of the Office of Research and Development, Bureau of Roads, USA. The driver enters a codeword, representing his intended destination, into the appropriate equipment in his vehicle, and is sent back appropriate route-guidance information as he passes each major intersection or turning in the system. Such a system would not only relieve the driver of much of the effort of route finding, but would also reduce congestion and delays by achieving more uniform distribution of traffic through the road network.

Research and development of automatic guidance and control of road vehicles was pioneered, about ten years ago, by General Motors, RCA, and Ohio State University in the USA, and by the Road Research Laboratory in the UK. Their approach was to use a limited access road, under which a guide cable and detector loops are laid. The guidance system ensures that the vehicles are driven straight, at suitable speeds and spacings. Preliminary tests showed promising results; since then, both theoretical and practical studies have continued in the USA, especially at Ohio State University, and they have recently been resumed at the Transport and Road Research Laboratory.

There seems to be little doubt that automatic guidance and control of road vehicles, though it is difficult and though some traffic experts are sceptical about it, is feasible in principle, if not with existing technologies, then at least with those likely to be developed in the near future. However, a very large research and development effort will be needed, to fill in all the details necessary to implement a satisfactory automated system. The trend of American thought on these systems is that they are most likely to be achieved in the USA through an evolutionary approach, moving through several successive stages, each of which would be compatible with existing traffic at that stage, with the whole process envisaged as taking several decades. This system would apply to limited-access roads only, mainly to motorways and major city streets, and it would be used by individual vehicles which would be driven manually on the rest of the road network. In Europe at least, it may be possible to introduce an alternative to the evolutionary approach, namely the direct development of fully automated specially reserved roads, for example for buses and heavy goods vehicles, perhaps before the end of the 1970s.

The full assessment of the feasibility and desirability of automated road systems needs consideration of reliability, where many further improvements need to be made; of safety, which would be vastly improved by the introduction of full vehicle control, with consequent drastic reduction of road accidents; and of costs, which — preliminary analyses suggest — are very roughly of order £10,000 to £100,000 per mile of lane and £10 to £100 for the adaptation of each vehicle using the system, giving an extra running cost perhaps about 1p per vehicle-mile at most.

We shall only mention briefly equivalent developments in other forms of transport. Automatic control of tracked vehicles is already in being on certain railways, for example the Victoria Line in London, and it has been operated successfully there. Several teams of investigators of possible new urban transport systems have considered the possibility of using similar techniques for more individualised public transport systems inside large cities and conurbations, for example the Cabtrack system and various auto-taxi systems. Computer control of the navigation of ships seems to be feasible in principle, though it will have a rather different nature from control of other transport modes, because of special problems such as accurate location and identification of vessels and the much longer times needed to complete braking and steering operations. Very surprisingly, hardly any research and development seems to have been carried out in this area, but it is becoming urgent in view of the increasingly disastrous, toll of collisions at sea. Lastly, computer aids to flight control have been very important for some time, and their extension and improvement could, for example, significantly reduce air accidents and shorten the delays due to circling round congested airports.

The next major area we shall consider is that of transport planning. This is concerned with the estimation of future demands for travel and of the degree to which these requirements are met by existing transport systems. In the light of this information, it considers how to contribute to the formulation of a series of alternative transport plans which meet this estimated demand, together with other community objectives, and considers how to compare and evaluate these plans, in both economic and social terms, in order to reach a satisfactory solution. Finally, it specifies methods of financing and implementing the chosen policy. Much of this process requires extensive calculations, which can readily be performed by computers; these calculations are relevant to time periods ranging from several years to about an hour.

The transport planning process can be subdivided into the following stages. Firstly, data are collected, largely by surveys, about current patterns of land use, population, economic factors, and journeys; these data are analysed with the aid of computers. Attempts are then made to establish quantitative relationships between all these variables, which are then used to predict their future values, especially future demands for journeys between given origins and destinations, using specific modes of transport. Further calculations can then be made to test the effects of alternative transport systems, to find out how far they improve traffic flow, reduce congestion, cut down accidents, shorten journey times, and allocate traffic more efficiently between different transport modes. Cost-benefit analyses can be carried out, to evaluate the effectiveness and economic value of proposed improvements to transport systems and alternative new systems.

Indeed, transport planning, with the aid of computers, can be applied to the integrated design of a balanced overall transport system which best meets the likely future needs of the community. For example, it can provide improved designs of road and rail networks, and better specifications for public transport services. It can help to co-ordinate different modes of transport and design more satisfactory interchanges between these modes. Its techniques can be used to indicate how to achieve a better balance between public and private transport, so that public transport can provide services of higher standard at lower cost, and so that there can be less congestion of the roads by private vehicles, at the expense of the general public.

Nowhere is this of greater importance than in planning the transport systems of urban areas. It has already been pointed out that computer-controlled traffic signal systems have been used successfully in several cities. These, together with other computing and control techniques, can be applied to help overcome congestion, reduce journey times, and cut down accidents. With the aid of special equipment in vehicles, it will also become possible to implement road-pricing techniques, which will discourage vehicles from using overcrowded urban areas, thus opening the way to freer flow of traffic and more effective use of public transport.

Computers are already beginning to be used to provide schedules for bus services, and they will be an important aid to the provision of the more individualised public transport systems of the future. One example of these, on which preliminary experiments have already been done with promising results, is the dial-a-bus type of system, where a passenger wishing to make a journey telephones a local centre, so that soon afterwards a minibus calls either outside his home or at a nearby stop. While this type of service is probably most appropriate for smaller towns and for scattered suburban areas and perhaps also nearby rural zones of large cities, several types of "auto-taxi" service have been proposed for the most heavily populated parts of conurbations, where they can cater for more special journeys of a kind which cannot so readily be covered by underground railways and normal bus routes. For all these systems, computers will be very helpful in determining the optimum paths and timings of journeys, to suit the public's travel demands best. Provision must be made, not only for transport inside cities, but also for interfaces between various parts of cities and terminals of long-distance rapid rail, road and air transport between cities.

Another important way to help overcome the transport crisis in cities is to provide radically improved road and street networks. The new techniques required here will become much more readily applicable with the aid of both numerical and graphical display computer methods. Existing street networks in cities and towns are often far from optimum, involving as they do indiscriminate mixing of different modes of road transport, many unnecessarily long and roundabout journeys, and all too often awkward access to public transport stations and stops. There is, therefore, much scope for provision of separate roads for different functions, and also for segregation of local traffic from roads catering for longer trips inside cities. Careful consideration should be given to appropriate geometrical design of street networks, and the computer can be specially useful here, both in tracing the routes and in evaluating overall network effectiveness in meeting likely transport needs.

This brings us to the whole field of urban planning. Housing in particular is an area where the computer's capacity to deal simultaneously with both individual and large-scale requirements has great potential. Computer-aided design techniques, which are already being developed and applied, can be used to design homes which are better and cheaper and provide a more pleasant environment for living; this sort of design can be tailor-made to fit the needs of individuals and families, and it can be adapted to allow for changes in these needs over the course of time. Visual displays can be used to provide pictures of provisional architectural plans, which can be modified step by step until the requirements of the customer are met; this process can include fitting the furniture into a convenient layout. The whole process can be carried out very rapidly, while, at the same time, the computer can calculate and record the cost of each successive design and the amounts of components and materials that it uses; thus designs can be chosen with reference to available budgets as well as to quality of home. With the aid of prefabrication techniques, it will become possible to design flexible homes, enabling a wide variety of interior layouts, with different partitioning into rooms, to be used inside the same dwelling, with the minimum of trouble; similarly, these techniques can be used to extend a home while the size of the family increases and to contract it after the children have grown up; here again, the computer can be used to map out the desired changes very quickly. The total costs of these new types of home will not be unduly large, and may soon drop below those of present-day housing, because computer-controlled machine tools will allow a very wide range of parts and structures, for use in prefabricated buildings, to be made remarkably cheaply. Indeed, the constructional costs of housing, though not, of course, land costs, may well fall rapidly as soon as these innovations are under way.

Computers can be used to design, not only better homes and buildings, but also more pleasant cities, with improved overall structures and better laid-out neighbourhoods, reflecting the true needs of the community. This would have to be done within the framework of a unified approach to town planning which would have to be developed and implemented. If the major challenge to architects is to grasp and exploit imaginatively the possibilities for building design just described, the major challenge to planners is to grasp the opportunity to move once and for all away from the haphazard and piecemeal kind of urban development or redevelopment which has been the rule in the past. Attempts have been made at integrated planning, keeping due balance between all aspects of city life, and maximising as far as possible, within physical limitations and the conflicting tastes of human beings, the quality of life for all of its citizens; however, these have been the exceptions, and have been mainly confined to totally new developments, such as Britain's "new towns", where the planners can start almost from scratch. They have been the exceptions simply because of the sheer complexity and size of the design problem; it is here that computers can lighten the load, leaving the human planners free to concentrate on the really creative and intuitive matters of what this town or city could and should be like. The excuse will no longer be able to be made that the task of unified planning is not feasible; failure to apply such methods will be a failure of will or imagination, not of technique.

Obviously such a new approach would need to be tried out first in developments such as new towns, where the constraints imposed by existing structures are less irksome; however, a new design system, once proved in this way, could be used on redevelopment projects in existing cities, planning not only the final shape of the city but the phased implementation of the plans, taking into account the preservation of existing structures of historical or aesthetic importance.

It is not intended by the foregoing to imply that planners are not already aware of the need for integrated planning; on the whole they are, and many attempt as far as they can to apply it. The trouble is that too often they must necessarily make simplifying assumptions and impose additional constraints (or accept those thrust upon them) simply to make the task practicable. What is needed is the realisation not only that unified planning is desirable, not only that the computer is a useful design tool, but that the computer has the potential for making unified planning possible on a scale and of a generality unachievable hitherto.

Besides providing adequate housing and transport and shopping and public utility services, appropriate to the varied needs of different sections of the population, truly integrated urban planning would have to ensure the provision of sufficient job opportunities, educational facilities, and cultural outlets in the city, and, above all, restore the sense of community, which is so sadly lacking today in too many places, not only at the urban but also at the suburban and neighbourhood levels. Thus the different needs of the citizens should be covered by a unified interlocking pattern of planning. Full advantage should be taken here of the new technologies. For example, the provision of more extensive and higher quality tele-communications in the future will drastically reduce the need for transport further afield, thus removing much of the present congestion and need for commuting, and counteracting the present trends towards a rat-race society; instead, more civilised local patterns of living in cities and towns would then have the opportunity to come once again into their own.

To these matters we shall return in the next chapter; meanwhile we shall conclude this discussion of computers and the environment by considering briefly how they can contribute in the two important problem areas of pollution and conservation.

Computers can help to protect the environment and conserve natural resources in a number of ways. They can be used to improve the planning of the environment as a whole, so that available resources are allocated as usefully and with as little waste as possible and so that damage to the environment and to the quality of life are minimised; in relation to planning, they can help in detecting and ascertaining what resources actually exist; they can help in monitoring for pollution or for unexpected or unscheduled use of or change in resources; and, finally, their effects on various aspects of life can lead directly to reductions in the demands for materials and in the levels of undesirable side-effects such as pollution and noise. We shall briefly discuss each of these possibilities.

We have already seen some of the ways in which computers can help in planning land resources, in the particular case of urban development; more generally, they can be used to optimise the use of available land for the various agricultural, industrial, transportation, housing and recreational needs of the community. This kind of optimisation can be done in all sorts of contexts, notably in process industries using material resources, for example, so that "waste" products and "waste" heat are salvaged and recycled more efficiently, not only saving materials but also considerably reducing pollution of all kinds.

More generally, in recent years attention has been devoted to the possibilities of developing mathematical models, based on a general systems approach, that will describe more or less accurately the interaction of resources with each other and with the environment. One of the best known examples of this trend is the series of "world dynamics" models developed at the Massachusetts Institute of Technology as part of the "Predicament of Man" project sponsored by the Club of Rome; similar programmes, on a smaller scale, have recently been started in the UK, for example, at the University of Sussex, and by SPUR (Study Panel for Unified Research); the Department of the Environment has started to assess some models of this type. Important work of this sort has also been done by Fremont Felix, who has considered the possible effects of gradual slowing down of economic growth rates. The models are still comparatively crude, representing only in broadest outline the multiplicity of factors that affect the evolution of planet Earth; however, they do seem to give some useful broad qualitative indications of the way in which the world situation might develop, if various types of policy are adopted during the coming years. Computer implementations of these models can show graphically, for example, the nature of the interactions between birth rate, death rate, population, capital investment, food per head, natural resources, pollution, material standards of living, and quality of life. These results seem to show that many, if not most, types of policy will lead to some sort of "ecological catastrophe" for the world, if not within a few decades, then within about a century. This disaster could result from overpopulation, pollution, depletion of resources, or some combination of these factors, for example. However, more stable solutions can arise under favourable conditions. This suggests that it is worthwhile carrying out extensive research on this kind of model to seek policies and plans which might offer some hope of avoiding the environmental crisis which threatens and, as we said in the introduction, must be borne in mind as a proviso whenever forward projections are made. As far as decisionmaking is concerned this is, of course, back in the sphere of national governments and international relations.

The next two uses of computers can both be seen as ancillary to the planning use, in different ways. Clearly, when one is planning the use of natural resources, it is helpful to have accurate and detailed knowledge of what resources are available. Computers have some role to play here, for example to assist in the analysis of geological surveys, the collection, monitoring and processing of data from measuring devices, and so on. This last merges into the third use, the continuous monitoring of the environment. The obvious case here is that of meteorological data collection and forecasting, not at present for control purposes but for contingency planning and the avoidance of unnecessary damage because of storms, etc. Other such applications would include monitoring of variable resources such as water — one possibility of great potential value to the world's food resources would be the automatic detection and monitoring of the movements of shoals of fish — and automatic checking of pollution hazards, e.g. in rivers downstream of industrial enterprises.

However, some of the most important effects of computing in this area may be indirect rather than direct. For example, although it is commonplace at present for computerisation to result in a vast increase in the paper consumption of an organisation, through the generation of printouts, in time there is hope that this will be reversed through the spread of on-line interactive systems and the instant availability of required information on a display screen. This could eventually lead to a great reduction in the demand for paper, which would in turn lead to reduced depletion of forest resources. Computers themselves are becoming progressively more compact, and thus they will themselves consume fewer materials and less fuel and power; though they are, of course, dependent for their manufacture on high-technology industries which do not necessarily share these characteristics, computers are in themselves extremely civilised devices compared with other machines such as cars and aeroplanes, clean, quiet and economical in their operation. Apart from indirect effects such as this arising from their own operation, there are others arising from side-effects of their use. In several ways, as indicated already, computers can cut down the need for travel, and therefore lessen the effects of noise and air pollution from land and air transport. The use of computers to prevent collisions at sea could in its turn avoid much pollution of the oceans that would otherwise occur. The applications of computers to industrial design, production engineering and management described in Chapters 11 and 12 will lead to much more efficient industrial and commercial practices, much less wasteful of materials and energy.

We have seen in this chapter that there are many opportunities for applying computer techniques to the many environmental problems which face the modern world. Given too conservative and shortsighted attitudes by the professional people concerned — architects, designers, planners of all kinds — or their employers — transport authorities, city authorities, government agencies and departments — these opportunities will not be taken up, at least with sufficient vigour for the outcome to be affected more than marginally. Given imagination and a high standard of computing expertise, computers could help to make the problems much more tractable. No-one could claim that computer techniques alone can solve these problems, or even guarantee their solution if combined with necessary measures in other directions; however, adequate commitment to computing techniques, including undertaking the necessary research, would surely increase mankind's chances of avoiding an environmental disaster. For all that anyone knows, it could make the difference between success and failure. The challenge for the decisionmakers is this: that time is running out on this planet, this may be the last chance that we have in a once-for-all process, and therefore any means as hopeful as this of avoiding an irretrievable crisis cannot be lightly dismissed.

17 Computers and everyday life

In earlier chapters we have come across numerous ways in which computers could affect our everyday lives. There are the implications of the changes in the pattern of education discussed in Chapter 7; the development of a public computing utility described in Chapter 9; the moves towards a cashless society outlined in Chapter 10; the changes in patterns and modes of employment which we saw in Chapter 12 as a major consequence of industrial and commercial automation; and the environmental implications just mentioned in Chapter 16. In a sense, therefore, this is a summary chapter, drawing together these threads, though moral and legal matters will be further dealt with later in Part Four.

Computers have so far had very little effect on the way that people in general live. Obviously those directly involved with computer operation in office or factory have been affected, likewise those made redundant through automation, but the lives of the great mass of people even in the most computerised nations have remained virtually untouched. Some will have had brushes with bad invoicing systems, or have been fobbed off with an excuse about inefficiency being due to a computer, but that is about all. In fact, really large-scale effects will have to await a public network, a financial system if not a comprehensive utility, but it is worth considering, before we come on to this, what possibilities exist, other than in the specific areas discussed earlier, short of such networks — specifically, the use of computers domestically.

To get the matter in perspective, let us consider a family wondering whether to purchase a second car. A small saloon would in 1972 cost about £800, say, and they might estimate it would be used for 500 road-hours at a total cost of £200 each year. For about the same capital cost they could buy a simple teleprinter and an acoustic coupler to enable them to use service bureau dial-up services through their telephone. However, even supposing it was in use no more than one hour per week, their total running costs might be three to four times that of the car, depending on how much advantage they took of the reduced off-peak rates habitually offered by these services. Similarly, one might calculate that a minicomputer installed in one's home could cost something in the luxury car range, with similar running costs.

The purpose of this comparison is to show that a domestic computing service is already within the means of the topmost income groups — by which is meant not merely oil barons, property tycoons and pop stars, but anyone rich enough, say, to employ servants. That they are less in evidence than chauffeur-driven Bentleys must be due to factors other than simply money. And the main reason is not hard to find. Simple ignorance of the possibilities may be a marginal factor, conservatism may be another (after all, the lady of the manor may prefer a butler to a domestic computer just as a business executive prefers a secretary to a dictaphone), but above all, the reason must be that suitable systems are not available. A man may be rich enough to buy his own computer or use bureau services for his domestic affairs, but he is unlikely to have, at one and the same time, the enthusiasm, the knowledge, and the time to develop his own programs for the purpose.

On the other hand, continuing reductions in hardware costs on the lines discussed in Chapter 2, plus the enterprise of a commercial organisation to produce a comprehensive domestic service, could change all this. There is a distinct possibility that in the not-too-distant future it will be possible to offer an attractive system at an attractive price; once such a system became a status symbol among the top income groups, others would doubtless follow and the resulting competition and mass production would in time drive the price down to levels accessible to more and more people.

The kinds of service required from a domestic system for the most part mirror those required from a business system: accounting, stock control, information retrieval. It would keep tabs on bills and on the state of one's bank account, let one know when the last electricity bill was paid, what the amount was, when the next one can be expected, and so on; it would generate suggested shopping lists, including both regular items and slow moving or seasonal items which past records indicate may be due for ordering; it would provide addresses, telephone numbers, reminders to buy family presents; all on a regular basis. Special purpose programs would help with income tax (on the lines described earlier), inform about insurance rates, compare prices, calculate the consequences of hire purchase commitments, and so on. Dial-up services could provide more general information facilities of a less personal nature; while mini-computer systems might not be able to match some such services, like up-to-date prices of consumer goods, they could be given some permanent library facilities by means of cheap exchangeable backing stores, e.g. minicassette tapes, with owners of systems buying databank cassettes on matters of interest to them just as they can buy music recordings today. One further facility not used in the business world, at least officially, would lie in the recreational use of the system, so that when one was alone at home one could, instead of reading a book or watching television, play one's computer at some game. One could even, up to the limit of the computer's capacity in terms of hardware or software, specify the level of skill of one's opponent.

The most successful of such systems would almost certainly be based on a conversational technique, so that the system suggests to the new user what he might use it for, and offers various facilities. At intervals it would ask if the facilities so far used were enough; it would also use a conversational method to extract the information it needed, e.g. by asking such questions from time to time as: "Have you written any cheques recently?"; "Have you received any bills this week?" and so on.

This demonstrates the main weakness of this kind of system: so much depends on the accuracy and completeness of the information supplied by the user. One of the chief problems which the supplier of such systems will have to face is that people who are misled by them because of their failure to use them properly will nevertheless tend to blame the computer; for example, people who run into debt are usually extremely good at finding excuses for themselves, and if the computer tells them they are solvent when they are not they will conveniently forget that this was because they omitted to input various items of expenditure. People tend to look with scepticism at a claim that a motor crash was due to defects in the vehicle rather than the driver only because in that case it is obvious that the driver is the one that makes the decisions; the trouble here is that this is far less obvious in the case of a computer system, and such charges, however unjustified, could therefore gain more credence. A different kind of scepticism was expressed by the wife of one of the editors of this book, who remarked that if the standard of manufacture of domestic computers was the same as that of other domestic equipment, housewives would have to turn themselves into computer engineers to keep the systems going at all.

A number of these problems, if not the last, would not arise in the case of a public utility of the comprehensive nature discussed earlier. In particular, instead of the user having to input each detailed financial transaction, all the necessary records would be available through the network and could be automatically transmitted to his personal accounting system. The range of facilities would also be greatly increased. Bills could be paid by authorisation through one's own terminal, goods ordered, invoiced and paid for, even (given the complete integrated communications network) viewed in a teledisplay before purchase. Recreational facilities would similarly be potentially greater — members of chess and bridge clubs could play without stirring from home, for example, and the network might even supply a human or machine player to make up the game.

But the public utility would have a far more profound effect on everyday life than to make life easier for shoppers, keep people better informed about their financial position, and give greater scope to chess players, and the changes in working patterns described in Chapter 12 would probably be more significant by themselves, even without the utility, than the simple domestic systems described so far. For it is, after all, the patterns of work, education and leisure which, with economic and cultural factors, largely determine the shape of our day-to-day activities. The changes in individual living patterns when a husband becomes unemployed or when children leave full-time education and go to work are familiar to many; and some communities are all too conscious of the changes that can come about when a substantial proportion of the population becomes unemployed.

Broadly speaking, one can expect to see a shift of emphasis away from work towards education, training, leisure and recreation. The central importance in people's lives of finding, keeping and progressing in a job will diminish. Patterns of existence could tend to become more fluid, as periods of retraining and full-time study become more frequent. Families used for forty years and fifty weeks in the year to seeing father leave the house at 8 a.m. for work and return at 6 p.m. will tend to disappear. The housewife's pattern of getting the older members of the family off to work and the younger off to school, and then having a day to herself for housework and peace and quiet on her own (or annoying neighbours with her radio) will increasingly become disturbed by more flexible modes and hours of work and increasing leisure and recreation time.

This trend could become particularly important if, in addition to shorter working hours, there were greater opportunities for working at home, as we have seen could come about through a computing utility. At present people mainly go out to work because this is the only way they can earn enough to live comfortably, but it does also enable them to spend part of their lives in a wider community than the family; in fact, this is sometimes a greater motivation for married women to take a job than the extra income. There is certainly a danger that the resulting patterns of living might impose considerable strains on domestic life. The home, and the family life, of five people will necessarily have to be organised very differently if all are essentially home-based than if all but one or two are out of it for much of the week. The attitude to the home will also change, from a place to which one returns for relaxation and enjoyment, a refuge from the workaday world, to the centre for all one's activities.

Clearly a single terminal would not be sufficient for such a household, when simultaneously two people may be working, one off-duty and wanting entertainment or to communicate with friends, a child at work on a homebased educational project, and the housekeeper wishing to do the shopping through the utility. What such a family would need would be several terminals, probably of differing types, at least one for each member, probably interfaced to the utility through the household's own small computer. The physical organisation of the home would have to be adjusted to cope with needs for working space, with terminals distributed through different rooms.

Other changes in behaviour and organisation of activity would also follow. The term "housekeeper" was used above rather than "housewife" because the traditional role of the wife and mother could well become blurred in such a situation, when much of the family is about much of the time, and the much greater availability of home-based employment could enable her to have a job even when there are small children to be cared for. Each individual's activities would need to take account of the activities of others — a situation possible at present where, on one evening, one person wants to read a book, another to watch television, another to play records, another to complete his homework, and a fifth to get to sleep because he has to be at work at 4 a.m., with all the possibilities of family quarrels which this implies, could extend throughout every waking hour of every day. A side effect of general value could in fact be that more attention is given to the internal and external soundproofing of buildings.

It is probable that, in the event, children will continue to go to school almost as much as at present. Quite apart from questions of educational philosophy, it would be unreasonable to expect parents to take responsibility for ensuring that their offspring were using their teaching terminals properly to any significantly greater extent than they now take responsibility for seeing that homework is done; and, even though in principle it would be possible for a teacher to use the public utility to monitor pupils' use of home terminals, in practice physical supervision would be needed.

We are here, of course, assuming the continuance of the general philosophy that there should be compulsory education for all; it is possible to visualise a computerised society with so little work left for humans to do that it could be left to those few sufficiently motivated to learn voluntarily. This is certainly many more than thirty years ahead, and it may in any case be regarded as a fate for society which we should be anxious to avoid; in any case, if it is regarded as a primary purpose of an education system to teach children to live in society, compulsory education would still exist and with it continuing roles for schools and, of course, for teachers also.

What is much more likely, though, is that in adolescence the homebased part of education would gradually increase, together with gradual involvement in the community at large through part-time experience in a working environment, social work or the like. A gradual detachment from formal education, rather than a sudden departure, is certainly much more in accord with the kind of patterns we are envisaging, and could typically, except for the academically inclined, take place over the ages of 14 to 21.

The risk of generational tension here is obvious enough, especially in the early years, when the parental generation will be used to the idea of "leaving school and going to work". However, this is not specially computer-dependent (in fact, the provision of home teaching terminals might help by making parents see that the child is not simply idling). Much more computer-dependent, and much more serious, is the liability to alienation of homebased workers, such as those mentioned earlier responsible for monitoring computer-controlled machinery, due to a sense of isolation. In such jobs the sense of involvement arising from everyday contacts would to a large extent be missing, and would need to be fostered by such means as frequent meetings to discuss how things are going, what new techniques are coming along which might mean changes, where organisational improvements might be made, and so on. Other kinds of work, though affected, should still retain sufficient human contact for there to be less need for special measures. Managers and designers will probably still continue to go to their offices, though perhaps less often, even given multiway videophone conversations through a communications network; social workers will still have to visit those they are helping. Some service industry jobs (e.g. hairdressing) will be virtually unaffected, as would the work of people like creative artists who are already homebased.

Looking for potential alienation and guarding against it is a management problem and, as we mentioned in Chapter 12, it will be necessary to think not just in terms of occupations but of the several types of work done at different times in his job by each individual. It should also be possible to exploit consciously the increasing need for adaptability throughout a person's career so that if a required mode of working does carry a risk of alienation, at least it will not be worsened by there being no prospect of change. Organisational design will increasingly come to require the inclusion of design of the jobs that the people will do, so that each will have the right mixture of interest, human contact, and variety of task, mode of working, and situation. In time, personnel work would involve modification of systems to suit the individual, rather than trying to find a niche of the right shape, or to fit the individual worker into the shape that exists already.

Finally, we may briefly mention some further, if less striking, effects which might be expected. The general replacement of cash by universal accounting would have some effect on the way people go about their business, but for the most part the changes would be only on the surface. Exceptions to this might be in the kind of work where income at present depends largely on tips, and in some subcultures still heavily oriented towards the passing of hard cash, such as betting and gambling. However, we have already pointed out in Chapter 10 the advantages of cash for small transactions which makes it unlikely that it will have disappeared by the year 2000. A largely cashless society might prove more of a problem for the compulsive spender, who only stops when his supply of cash runs out, although people like this might in fact be aided (voluntarily or otherwise) through universal accounting, by the system only permitting for that account a given rate of expenditure. But, on the whole, people would soon get used to paying for everything by putting a card in a slot. Of course, they might not be happy at the thought that the system (and hence, possibly, authority) would know that they have just left this supermarket, or boarded this pay-as-you-enter vehicle. (In fact, it would be feasible to design vehicle systems to scan account cards on entry and exit and calculate the cost of the journey, so making life difficult for fare-dodgers, but also making it easier to monitor an individual's movements.) But, though such matters crucially affect individuals, they are more properly relevant to the issue of privacy to be discussed later; in themselves such possibilities need not change the ways that people behave in their everyday lives.

More to the point in our present context is that the steady increase in demand for recreational facilities of all kinds, and the growth of participatory and spectator sports, will surely continue. While the facilities of a public utility could, as we have seen, reduce demands on transport systems for commuting purposes, the demand on them for leisure travel would increase, together with the demand for holiday accommodation and facilities of all kinds. However, the demand would be spread out over the day and year more than the rush-hour commuter and seasonal and weekend leisure demands of the present day. An increasing market can be expected for more, and more varied, entertainment facilities, both through the utility and otherwise, and for places of resort and relaxation like clubs, pubs and restaurants. Many people, especially when more homebased, may look to their local community to absorb their energies, through cultural, social and recreational societies, or social work with the less fortunate members of the community. Local groups may flourish where at present, in commuter suburbs and housing estates, they wilt; welfare organisations may no longer have to struggle to find helpers.

At least, this is the hope. In the past, when extra facilities have been provided for such activities, the effect in many cases has been simply to enable the same people to do more, or to do better what they had been doing before, or to have a wider choice. Certainly their appeal seems to be only to a minority, and there is no indication of any certain means of extending this appeal to a majority and being able to sustain it — in today's world too many alternative sources of entertainment exist. This is a tremendous problem, not caused by automation but made more obvious by its effects.

What seems to be lacking in so many cases is a sense of achievement. Those who have jobs which involve responsibility for making decisions, and can make these without stress, derive great satisfaction from their work. There is no doubt, however, that many people whose work has been reasonably satisfying will become dissatisfied when they realise that it could be done as well or better by a machine, and this problem will not be solved by allowing them to continue working as in the past, pretending that it is still valuable. There are already many who can have no sense of achievement in their work, and there will be many more; the difficulty lies in providing this sense of achievement in some other way.

The challenge for the individual in a computer-based society in his daily life will be that he will be far less dependent than at present on force of circumstances and the will of others to shape his activities; he will be thrown more upon his own resources. There are, unfortunately, many responses to such a challenge which are not positive or constructive. One can retreat into the passive absorption of mindless pap from the entertainment media, or take up some activity in which the participation is minimal and largely illusory — one can envisage the public utility being used nightly for nationwide games of bingo with millions of players. However, this is at least relatively harmless emptiness as compared with reacting from boredom into violence, or seeking one's excitement in drugs, or directing one's resentment through extreme political or religious movements against some convenient group of scapegoats. All these are trends in modern society which could be strengthened by the developments described in this book. One challenge for psychologists and educationists is certainly to see that people are equipped to cope with these problems.

And this challenge, at least, is immediate; many of the people who will first have to live in this kind of world are already alive today.

18

Scientific and cultural development

One of the most satisfying of human activities, of course, is creativity, whether scientific or aesthetic, and we can expect that, in whatever ways computers develop, men will continue to solve problems and to create. Indeed, this would be so even if research into artificial intelligence were to lead to the invention of genuinely creative or intelligent machines. Nevertheless the existence of computers will influence the directions that such activity takes. The computer already has a well-established role in research and scholarship, and indeed is itself a creation of it. We shall, therefore, look in this chapter at some of its possible effects in the scientific and cultural fields. "Science" here is used in the more general sense of "knowledge", covering the humanities as well as the natural and social sciences; thus we shall be concerned with research and scholarship of all kinds. In the course of this we shall in effect be bringing together and summarising some of the discussion in earlier chapters where references to the need for research or to the use of the computer as a research tool have been made in particular contexts. It is in research that computers have made and will continue to make their major contribution, so most of the chapter will be devoted to this; however, the impact of computers on artistic expression and creation will not be entirely neglected.

We begin by defining what we mean by the terms "research" and "scholarship". Following Howlett, in his chapter on the subject in "Living with the computer", we take research to mean either (i) the discovery of new facts, by observation, or by the application of established theory to new situations, or by the verification of hypotheses; or (ii) the formulation of new theory to account for or unify existing facts. Unlike the scientific

231

researcher, the scholar is concerned with the appreciation as well as the understanding of the phenomena he studies, and is concerned with the additional activity of critical response and evaluation which usually involves subjective judgments. Nevertheless, research and scholarship both involve two basic activities, processing information to ascertain facts, and building theories. Information, in this context, can be of various forms, for example, music, speech, pictures, text, objects such as archaeological artefacts, and quantitative measurements of physical and behavioural phenomena. This information is collected from various sources, the most important being experiments, surveys and records. In theory building the researcher attempts to formulate statements that sum up our present state of knowledge of the relationship between certain quantities involved in the phenomena or process being studied. This is done by setting up analogues or models, using the symbolic language of mathematics and statistics where the relationships can be precisely specified, and verbal statements where they are less precisely known. In many situations machine analogues (primarily using computers) are useful or necessary. Once the models are built and tested they can be used for prediction and, if the quantities involved can be manipulated, for control.

Research into artificial intelligence could lead to a greater understanding of the intellectual faculties used in research, certainly augment them, and in the long term could even produce creative machines. However, our concern here is rather with the way in which computers act as tools to help men with the solution of intellectual problems and with creative activity, rather than to perform these activities themselves.

The computer already plays an important role as a research tool for these activities — both as an intrument in the processing of information and as an actor in the development of theories. We shall consider each role in turn, in the context of likely technological advances and current experimental work, to try to assess the future impact of the computer on the methodology of research in the three areas of the natural sciences, the human sciences and the humanities. Particular emphasis will be placed upon the computer potential in the human sciences and the humanities, where the impact of the computer has so far been relatively small. There are several reasons for this — the phenomena involved are typically less amenable to quantification and objective treatment than are natural phenomena, and may be relatively difficult to represent in a form suitable for computer processing.

Currently the computer provokes a polarisation of attitudes in these disciplines — either unbridled enthusiasm or curious scepticism. However, technological developments will enable the computer to handle non-numerical information in a much better way than at present and this should stimulate a greater empiricism and quantitive outlook in the human sciences and the humanities. With the increasing availability, ease of use and capabilities of computers and the re-orientation of research methodology that the computer will stimulate, we shall see the computer as a fundamental tool in all disciplines.

We begin, then, with the first basic research activity, the collection and processing of information. The value of the computer in this respect is well established, particularly where large quantities of data are involved. The same techniques, e.g. sorting into categories, are used in processing many different types of data and so converting the data into a form suitable for machine handling allows the researcher to make use of standard programmes to perform these operations. At the present time the conversion of some types of information, for example speech, music and pictures, is difficult and laborious. However, the development of analogue-to-digital convertors which carry out this process automatically will greatly facilitate input and output of all types of information, as well as the interactive, conversational kinds of systems discussed in a number of contexts earlier.

The main impact of these developments will be in the humanities and, to a lesser extent, the human sciences. Currently the humanities researcher has to gain his information from libraries, museums and art galleries; in the future he may be able to access art works, such as musical scores, paintings or literary text, directly from his desk via a computer, have them displayed in front of him, and use computer programs to help him retrieve, organise and analyse them. In contrast, in the pure sciences, computers are already used in complex and sophisticated data collecting experiments, for example, in bubble chamber experiments in nuclear physics, where the paths of particles are automatically recorded, monitored and organised under computer control.

There are two kinds of information that the researcher wishes to process. Firstly he wants to find out about other research in his problem area and about research techniques. Thus he requires ready and easy access to research reports, articles and books so that he can answer specific questions relevant to his problem and keep abreast of developments in his field. Currently a lot of valuable time can be spent searching through the literature of research which is often stored in an inefficient and inconvenient form. Obviously, computer-based information retrieval systems to automate this activity would be of great benefit. Such systems already exist for chemical and medical research (e.g. MEDLARS and SCISEARCH) and similar systems are being devised in other areas. Computer assisted instruction (CAI) as described in Chapter 7 may also be of great benefit to the researcher wishing to learn about new techniques.

The second kind of information required we may call data, i.e. the raw material the researcher uses for his own purposes. It may come from a variety of sources, primarily centralised data banks (including libraries and art galleries) and from investigations that the researcher himself conducts. His task is then to order and arrange this data in a manner convenient to his purposes and perform operations that result in the reductions and summaries required to facilitate his interpretation. There are thus two phases in the information processing activity — (i) collection and organisation and (ii) analysis. We shall now describe two ways in which the computer can help in the collection and organisation phase — computer-based experimentation, and computer-based information banks.

The experiment is an important way of collecting data in the sciences. In essence an experiment is a relatively uniform sequence of decisions and actions with as high a degree of control of extraneous factors as is possible. In the human sciences examples of experiments are interviewing a person with a standard list of questions, and psychophysical studies of human sensory perception. Once a well-defined experimental procedure is developed and the experimenter is ready to collect a large number of observations, the advantages of automation are obvious. There are many examples of experiments in the natural sciences where instruments are interfaced with computers through analogue-digital converters to give automatic control of the experiment. Usually such experiments are only possible with automatic control — they typically collect vast quantities of data, often in continuous form and in real time, which have to be converted automatically from the observed quantities to data relating to properties the experimenter is interested in, and then reduced and analysed. Computer-based control is also necessary where a large number of quantities have to be controlled at a rate incompatible with human response time, and where instantaneous corrective action may be required. Examples of these are most experiments in high energy physics and astronomy. There are also certain kinds of data, for example, human bio-electric signals, that can only be collected by analogue-digital converters. This equipment has unleashed vast quantities of data previously unanalysable and not meaningfully measured.

In the natural sciences an application of the computer which has great potential is in computer-aided experimentation. This involves an interactive use of the computer and is useful where the experimenter must know what is happening at all stages of the experiment. In such experiments the computer is used to monitor the progress of the experiment by processing the data and feeding the results back continuously and intelligibly (probably in graphical form) so that the experimenter can change the course of the experiment if necessary. In this way the computer gives the experimenter extra eyes and hands and faster reflexes.

There is great scope for the automation of experiments in the human sciences. The human subject of the experiment would not then come into contact with the experimenter; this would bring great benefit to the design and conduct of the experiments. It would be quite feasible to have computerised human laboratories which would have a set of computer controlled instruments to provide various stimuli to the human subject, for example oscillographs displaying pictures or questions, typewriter consoles typing out questions or transducers producing acoustic stimuli. The subject would respond to these in various ways, for example by typing an answer to a question, or having a behavioural or physiological reaction, which would be automatically recorded, stored and analysed, and the results displayed for the subject. Such laboratories are already in existence and have been used for administering psychological tests and to investigate the learning behaviour of animals where the reinforcement of the animals has been made automatically contingent on particular aspects of their performance.

The benefits that computer-based experimentation can bring to the human sciences are many. The drudgery of the collecting process is removed and the experiment can be run at any time, day or night, if that is what the experiment requires. Such experiments would be more reliable and accurate, often more sensitive to weak responses, have a greater capacity for handling a large quantity and complexity of response and be able to easily record the time between stimulus and response which is important where time-contingent factors are involved. The computer can monitor the progress of the experiment and check for abnormal responses to which it can respond appropriately. The experimental situation is presented identically to each subject, is free from any biases caused by experimenter-subject interaction and can be replicated precisely. Furthermore, a greater flexibility is allowed because computer control permits revisions of the design to be contingent upon the progress of the experiment. Another benefit is that the computer would facilitate sequential control of the experiment. In contrast to the current procedure where an experimenter takes a fixed number of subjects, automated experiments can easily incorporate a facility to test, after each subject, whether sufficient information has been gathered for the purposes of the experiment (using sequential statistical methods) and stop when this is so. Finally, of course, the results of the experiment can be stored, organised, updated and analysed virtually simultaneously.

In the future, questionnaires and psychological tests and experiments could be administered under computer control, as already discussed in the context of market research in Chapter 14. The subject might go into an experimental laboratory or be contacted in his home via his terminal, and the experiment run as follows. The computer asks him to help and explains the purposes of the experiment or survey. Providing he agrees to co-operate, he is asked for background information, and, on the basis of this, is assigned to one of a number of experiments. He is then instructed in the use of the response equipment, presented with stimuli, and has his various responses recorded. The computer gives hints and repeats instructions when mistakes occur. The subject can get details of his responses on request. The researcher can access the current state of the experiment at any time, for summaries or analyses. Obviously, such developments would have great social implications, particularly on the question of confidentiality.

Turning now to the research use of computer-based information banks, we have already seen that modern computer technology has made possible the creation of large centralised stores of information whose purpose is to make data that has already been collected available on a large-scale basis. Such archives have various functions: the acquisition and maintenance of information, the processing and distribution of data for individual researchers, and the provision of a retrieval service, so that researchers can find out if there is any data in the archive that is relevant to their problem. Currently, archives exist for social science data; examples of the kinds of information held are historical and administrative records, survey data, texts of publications, speeches and reports and census data. As the computers' facility for handling information improves, we should expect to see the establishment of more archives, for all types of data, and this would have profound effects on research and scholarship. Data collection is an expensive activity and archives could save money and effort in making data collected by one investigator available to others who could try out their own hypotheses and theories on it. Archives would allow researchers to widen their data bases, bringing in all relevant data from a variety of sources. Some important types of data, in particular public records, such as census data and governmental statistics, are not easily assembled by individual scholars but could be made generally and conveniently available.

Data archives also encourage the comparability of research both over time and between studies by developing standards for definitions, methods and documentation. Currently many data collecting projects are designed for specific purposes and, because of the high cost involved, are usually one-off investigations. Archives would encourage the collection of integrated and co-ordinated data sets over time, this would be particularly useful in the study of dynamic phenomena or processes.

The archives that currently exist primarily hold numerical and textual information, but developments in the capability of computers to handle artistic information such as pictures, musical scores and poems will stimulate the creation of archives of artistic material. The potential of the computer in this respect is discussed in a report of a conference sponsored by the Metropolitan Museum of Art. Computer-based archives of artistic material would be of great benefit to the scholar who gets most of his information from archival sources.

Much work is required to develop the technical capacity to set up such systems. In particular, problems of the representation and recognition of pictorial information have to be solved — forming digitised pictures and textual and numerical descriptions, perhaps linked with the storage of the work on microfilm, are two possibilities. Undoubtedly such problems will be solved and the scholar will be freed from having to limit his database to within the capacity of hand tabulation or of his memory. It will be possible to scan a collection of art works to detect various definable aspects of the content such as symbols, shapes, concepts and words. This facility could be used for the retrieval and display of art works, satisfying criteria of interest to the scholar. For example, he may wish to examine all the paintings of women by Picasso, or, for a selection of poems, to investigate many stylistic characteristics and their manifold interrelationships. Another useful activity of data archives would be the automatic production of various types of documentary and summary material, for example, bibliographies, catalogues, indexes and concordances. In order to set up successful data archives many financial, organisational, technical and substantive problems have to be solved.

Having collected and organised the data required, the researcher's next task is to analyse the data and hence provide a definitive description of the phenomena of interest. We can distinguish two levels of operation in this activity, the descriptive and the inferential. Descriptive operations usually involve simple arithmetic and logical methods and, for data reduction, possibly complex decision procedures; data reduction is usually necessary both to reduce the dimensionality of the problem and to generate the properties of interest from the quantities observed. Inferential operations commonly require the application of statistical techniques to test hypotheses. Here we consider the analysis of data as a separate stage from the descriptive operations, but the development of data archives and of computer-based experimentation, as previously outlined, would allow the researcher to make the analysis phase an integral part of the collection and organisation stage. The potential of the computer for both kinds of operation has already been exploited to a large degree in some disciplines.

In descriptive operations computers are widely used for trivial but often tedious operations such as counting, selecting subsets of the data, tabulating the co-occurrence of quantities, calculating summary statistics and plotting quantities diagrammatically on maps and graphs. This is a well-established use of the computer in research, and relieves the researcher from much time-consuming low level work.

The future impact of the computer in this role is likely to be in several ways. Firstly, in the social sciences we are likely to see a great expansion in the use of the computer for descriptive operations; advantage will be taken of the computer's speed and facilities so that large quantities of relevant social science data from various sources can be processed. This is of fundamental importance to this discipline which is essentially an empirical science — a position that is forced upon it by the dynamic nature of the phenomena it deals with. The computer should stimulate a greater emphasis on the discovery of facts in the social sciences by providing an efficient, convenient and rapid means of doing this. Secondly, the objective and comprehensive treatment of the content of art works and textual materials will be encouraged. The analysis of content usually involves the identification of content variables such as words, pictorial patterns, or particular sequences of musical notes, counting and then forming frequencies of occurrence and co-occurrence of these quantities. Computer-based content analysis should have great impact on various research activities in the humanities, such as analyses of style, influence, changing values in literature and of disputed authorship. Thirdly, the availability of visual display devices will help all researchers considerably in achieving comprehensive and immediately intelligible descriptions of their data. It is much easier for the human brain to interpret diagrams, pictures, maps and graphs than lists or tables of numbers. Finally, one area of information processing where developments are likely to be of great importance to research is in the solution of the problems involved in recognising patterns, for example, shapes in a picture or structures in a collection of numerical data. Pattern recognition is basic to the fundamental research activity of data reduction, including classification, where the researcher attempts to construct meaningful groupings of the phenomena under study; we have already referred to its importance in the field of artificial intelligence in Chapter 3.

Humans have the ability to discern similarities and differences within and between a group of objects by selecting a subset of all perceived characteristics, but this is something that, so far, has not been done in a general way on a computer. The pattern recognition work done to date has been source-specific, but with the work in progress on digitising pictures, general hardware and software for real-time image processing will be developed. Although pictures can be characterised by various measurable properties such as line, form and texture, recognition problems are still non-trivial once the measurements are made. Developments will be necessary in statistical decision theory and in the design of decision-making devices in order to solve the general problem of pattern recognition.

We turn now to inferential operations, where the computer has helped the application of statistical techniques for the analysis of data in several ways. On one hand it has made possible the easy application of sophisticated techniques to large quantities and various types of data. This role is likely to become more important with the increasing availability of easy-to-use, comprehensive and flexible statistical program packages. We should expect a diminishing degree of involvement in developing software by the data analyst; he will have ready access either to programs that do what he wants or to subprograms that he can combine easily for his purposes. The second way in which computers have aided data analysis is where new statistical techniques based on methods that are only feasible on a computer have been developed. Examples of the types of method that take advantage of the computer's special features are heuristic methods, again already mentioned in Chapter 3, where the computer is used to try many different answers to a problem in some organised way until a solution that satisfies certain criteria is reached, and methods involving the repeated application of a fixed set of rules. These methods have been used for such problems as the reconstruction of fragments of artefacts in archaeology, the verifying of mathematical conjectures, the determination of molecular structures, deciphering ancient scripts and for attempts to perform some of the symbol manipulations of mathematics on a computer.

To illustrate the impact of computer techniques in this sort of work, we shall consider in a little more detail applications of these methods to two problems, both of which are essentially problems of pattern recognition: classification by clustering, and data-dredging. In classification by clustering the researcher aims to group objects into classes according to the similarities or dissimilarities between them. The computer has made possible the development of a number of classification strategies which involve moving towards a solution satisfying some criteria for the adequacy of grouping. Currently many such algorithms exist and much valuable time can be spent in attempts at clustering; in the words of R. M. Cormack, in a review of classification published in the journal of the Royal Statistical Society in 1971, there is a "growing tendency to regard numerical taxonomy as a satisfactory alternative to clear thinking." A more critical use of clustering techniques will bring enormous benefit to research.

Data dredging is a computer-based technique used in the analysis of survey data for searching among the relationships between variables in an attempt to identify subgroups of the whole sample for which different patterns of interrelationships exist, for example the relationship between income and age may well be different for the sexes. This is an essential preparatory activity for model building. J. A. Sonquist and J. N. Morgan, in their monograph "The Detection of Interaction Effects", saw this technique as a way of programming "some of the decisions ordinarily made by the scientist in the course of handling a typical analysis problem, as well as the computations. This required examining decision points, alternative courses of action, and the logic for choosing one rather than the other; then formalising the decisionmaking procedure and programming it, but with the capacity to handle many variables rather than a few!"

We have discussed several examples of the computer's capacity to augment and replace some of the human thought or decision processes used in solving research problems. It is in this role that the computer has probably its greatest potential impact. With developments in artificial intelligence, and ingenuity on the part of researchers, we should expect the computer, perhaps being used interactively, to develop a capacity for solving problems in information processing that we currently think are only solvable by human means.

The disciplines where the computer is likely to have increasing importance as a research tool for performing inferential operations are in the social sciences and the humanities. But first must come the development, with the stimulus of the computer, of mathematical and statistical methods to provide analytical tools for the treatment of the kinds of information they deal with. For example, we may mention some of the problems of social science data analysis for which adequate solutions do not exist at present. The empirical social scientist often has to deal with the difficult problem of relating measured variables to the concepts to which they refer; the measurements may be in categorical form for which many statistical techniques are inappropriate and he may have incomplete data. Undoubtedly, suitable techniques will be developed. The heuristic approach will probably be important in this respect.

Data analysis will also become an exploratory process with the general availability of interactive communication with computers. This will have beneficial effects as the researcher will be able to try a wide range of analytical methods in rapid succession; he will be able to concentrate on solving the problem at hand without having to do large amounts of routine work.

So we see that the overall effect of computers on the research activity of information processing will be to hasten the evolutionary process of science and culture from an impressionistic and speculative to an empirical orientation. Computers will shorten the time necessary to accumulate and synthesise the vast amount of information that is needed for adequate theory to be developed in the sciences and for evaluation and interpretation in the humanities.

We must now consider the other main research activity which we mentioned at the beginning of this chapter, namely the construction of theories which attempt to sum up the relationships between the constituent parts of the system or process under investigation. Most phenomena can be considered as forming part of either systems or processes: examples of systems are "the British economy", "the multinational corporation" or "parliamentary government"; examples of processes are "how people think", "how nuclear reactions take place", or "how people decide to vote as they do". When one characteristic of the system or process is changed, there will be consequential changes elsewhere within it. Provided that the changes can be quantified or the rules governing them specified, these interrelationships can be expressed in the form of models — whether by mathematical equations, computer programs, or actual physical models. Here we shall be concerned with models of the second kind — or, rather, the first and second kinds, since mathematical equations can be expressed in terms of computer programs. For simplicity we shall refer to "systems" in a more general way, meaning "systems or processes" in the senses just employed, and "models" to mean theoretical rather than physical models.

Models, then, are abstractions of the real world in which the relevant relations between the elements of the actual system are replaced by similar relations between mathematical entities or the statements of a computer program. The adequacy of the model is judged by the success with which it can predict the effect of changes in the system which it describes and by whether or not it can account for changes which have occurred in the past. Modelling has two roles in the building of theory, namely aiding the evaluation of theory, where the model is derived from the theory and compared with the system being investigated, and guiding the development of theory, where the model is constructed by direct analogy with the system and abstract ideas are induced. We now discuss the potential contribution that computers can make to the construction of models of two kinds — mathematical and computer simulation models.

A mathematical model is a set of mathematical equations which purports to describe the behaviour of a system; it may be deterministic or stochastic. If the effect of any change in the system can be predicted with certainty the system is said to be deterministic. However, if the system is not fully specified, or random components are involved, there is usually an element of uncertainty about any prediction, which can be accommodated by the introduction of probability distributions and random variables into the model in place of mathematical variables; such a model is described as stochastic.

Deductions can be made from the model by solving the mathematical equations. Very often these equations cannot be solved in general form and numerical methods are required to obtain specific solutions, or the amount of calculation required is so large that the solution is more effectively done on a computer. This particularly applies to complex mathematical models and ones involving quantities which measure rates of change. Computers have been used to perform the vast amount of calculations that are required by these numerical methods — this is the well known computing activity of "number-crunching". The main contribution of computers has been to make possible the investigation of very complex models involving many variables and their interrelationships, something that is usually beyond the capacity of the individual researcher.

Mathematical solutions are particularly intractable in the solution of stochastic models; here there is great scope for the use of computers to provide the means of numerical solution. The development of the ability of computers to do this will be very important in the social sciences, where there has been very little model-building for reasons outlined before. However, as improvements in the measurement of human phenomena are made, we should expect to see a greater use of mathematical models — particularly of stochastic models, as there is an inherent uncertainty about most human activity brought about by the freedom of choice available to the individual.

The second kind of theoretical model, the computer simulation, we have already mentioned as a possible aid to decisionmakers, e.g. in controlling a nation's economy, but it is also a general research tool. Here the researcher attempts to simulate the system under study by writing a computer program that is a scaled-down abstraction of the real system based on his concept of the key elements of the system and of their operation and interaction. The program is then run many times to investigate the relationship between the behaviour of the model and its elements and structure. Computer simulation requires explicit rules for the relations between the elements, but not necessarily the formal apparatus of mathematical models, and the rules themselves need not be numerical. Although many simulation models do have mathematical components and involve quantitative analysis of results, they are different from mathematical models in that they produce results and data which provide systematic information on the nature and structure of the model itself and can be used to investigate the assumptions of the model. There is a sort of model-researcher interaction; by repeating his simulation runs, altering the relationships of the elements, the simulator can learn more about his own assumptions and about the nature of the system leading to further adjustment both in his view of reality and in the structure of the model itself. The discipline imposed on the researcher in specifying the model is one of the great benefits of simulation; the simulator is forced to be precise, to clarify his concepts and definitions. On the other hand the simulation approach has its limitations and dangers, particularly in its high cost and inability to lead to general solutions.

Simulations that have been carried out range from ones involving vague tentative and intuitive models where consequences are being squeezed out of a crude structure put together from suppositions, for example in simulation of decisionmaking processes in international relations, to ones that have solved a specific and precisely defined research problem such as the design of a nuclear reactor.

We shall now consider the potential contribution of computer simulation to our three disciplines.

In the natural sciences computer simulation is an important research technique, particularly in its use to solve specific problems. We are likely to see simulation replacing the traditional means of conducting research by experimentation; laboratories eventually may then only be used to validate the research "done on the computer". Progress in "hybrid" simulation, whereby the computer program model can accept inputs and produce output of physical quantities through analogue-digital converters will be important in this respect.

Computer simulation has several advantages over experimentation — it is usually cheaper and more reliable, and the researcher can choose examples that are more amenable to mathematical analysis than the experiment. Simulation can provide more accurate data and data with a high space or time resolution, such as the position of all particles in a system at a particular moment in time, which are for all practical purposes inaccessible by experiment.

In the human sciences computer simulation has an important role to play as a theory-building and comparing device. Currently there are relatively few social theories in which the relevant elements have been agreed upon and defined in operational terms and in which the relationships among the elements have been defined in relatively unambiguous terms. There are several reasons for this — little empirical work has been done and this has inhibited attempts to derive theories inductively, and, even if there were adequate theories and data, theory testing would be difficult because the human scientist cannot experiment with the real world. However, to a large extent, the computer-based model provides the human scientist with a substitute for the natural scientist's laboratory. It is possible to experiment in the "world" generated by the model, and if this faithfully mirrors reality the results of the experiments will be applicable to the real world. To date the simulations that have been carried out in the human sciences have helped with the initial stages of theory building — for the clarification of concepts and testing of hypotheses — but as the body of knowledge about human matters becomes more coherent and comprehensive we should expect adequate social theories to be developed; computer simulation, as a means of building, testing and comparing the theories will make a vital contribution to this process. This will have important social implications, as for example in the uses by decisionmakers to explore policy alternatives which we have discussed earlier.

In the humanities there have been some attempts at using the computer to produce art works such as musical compositions, films, pictures, poems or choreographic routines. We can view such attempts as computer simulations of how these creative tasks are performed and of the structures of artistic compositions. If we can compose acceptable music on a computer we may, by examining how it is done, learn something about the process by which it is composed. The simulation models used are based on the application of fixed rules with random deviations and components to replace the artist's intuition. For example, one approach to computer music composition is to choose a sequence of notes, according to probabilistic rules of selection, and then apply formal rules of composition, rhythm and dynamics to see if it is an acceptable sequence. Statistical analyses of artistic style may suggest different procedural logics for different styles.

Thus we can view computer art as the equivalent in the humanities to the theory building of the sciences. As theories of artistic processes are developed we must be open, as we said, to the possibility that computers will be used to produce creative things. As I. J. Good has said, "creativity consists of putting ideas together unexpectedly and usefully or beautifully, and there is nothing to prevent a machine from doing this if it has the ability to evaluate the results. It will do the job much faster if it is capable of analogical "thinking", but this ability does not seem to me to be very mysterious. An analogy is a similarity of predicates and would be measurable by a machine that was good at handling descriptions. Thus even creativity will probably be reduced ultimately to a technique."

The computer also offers itself as a public medium for creative activity It can be used by anyone who knows how to program the computer and use its peripherals. The computer program, or its output, is then the work of art. As an artistic medium the computer has certain attractive features that artists may wish to exploit — facilities for the convenient introduction and modification of the elements of an artistic composition using interactive graphical devices in much the same way as they are used for industrial design today, the capacity for reproduction in large quantities, instant destruction and simultaneous display at many points. A further artistic application may be the creation of so-called "cybernetic" environments in which the human receiver interacts with computer-controlled visual and acoustic presentations. We may indeed see the artist in a new role of designing computer-based systems for producing a given sequence of patterns. The artist's imagination would then be used to design the mechanism by which works of art would be produced rather than to make the works with his own hands.

Whatever else, the public utility could possibly offer to the artist the means of getting his work, conventional or otherwise, known to a wider public; a painter, for example, could place the image of his latest work on a publicly accessible file, and not only have the chance of someone buying the original through coming across it browsing through the files — there will still be people who will wish to own works of art and keep them to themselves — but have the chance of a regular income by automatic debiting of a time-related viewing fee whenever the file was accessed.

The computer may thus become a medium for artistic creation, but the main impact of computer-based modelling is likely to be in the human sciences and the humanities, where simulation may well become a fundamental tool in the construction of theories about human and cultural phenomena. In the physical sciences simulation will become increasingly important as a means of experimentation and as an aid to the solution of specific research problems; computers will be necessary for the construction of increasingly complex models of physical phenomena.

To summarise, then, we can say that computers will become, in virtually all fields as they are already in some, fundamental tools for the research and scholastic activities that are basic to the scientific and cultural development of our society. They will be important because of their enormous capacity to handle information of all kinds, because they can be used to do things that could not otherwise be done and because they enable the researcher to spend more time on truly intellectual and creative tasks.

We have considered the computer's potential impact on research in terms of extrapolations of the current state of the art that are more than mere speculation, but there is the further possibility that computers will become intelligent and creative machines. It is conceivable that they could be programmed to make value judgments on results or art works they have themselves produced and to make hypotheses and then verify or reject them. Computers will certainly take over some of the activities of problem-solving and creation that we now consider can only be carried out by the human brain. Whether computers will revolutionise research and scholarship depends not on the developments in computer technology as such, but on the nature of the institutions concerned, their organisation, finances, ability to overcome resistances to innovation and to make meaningful use of the new technology. The projected technological developments will require a large capitalisation in terms of machinery and programming effort which far exceeds the capacity of individual researchers or small research groups. There will need in most nations and disciplines to be changes in the social and financial organisation of research in order to exploit the computer potential effectively and efficiently. The disciplines where the computer is likely to have an important effect on methodology are the humanities and the human sciences where it will encourage a more objective and empirical approach; it is less certain that such an approach will gain ground in the humanities. In the human sciences we may see a computer stimulated change of orientation from empiricism to model building; in the humanities a change from intellectual preoccupations to handling research problems, thus bringing the humanistic and scientific traditions closer together.

Computers will have a great effect on the conduct of research. They will encourage clarity of thought, precision and accuracy and help improve standards. They will increase the pace of research, and possibly also of artistic development. But most of all they will change the patterns of working of individual scholars and artists, and perhaps we should conclude by briefly sketching what the working mode of a member of the intellectual community might be like in thirty years' time. We can expect that most of his work will be done through a working terminal, probably in his home, possibly with special facilities for his needs. Depending on his field and what he is currently engaged on, he will be able to interrogate the system for pertinent literature, and find out if there is any relevant data registered with any of the databanks open to him; or call in a CAI program to instruct him in a new technique; or use standard software to process and analyse information or, if he is a creative artist, generate forms of the kind that he wants; or develop his own programs for similar purposes. He will be able to contact and exchange data or ideas with others; and finally he can deposit his results and reports, or his final created work, in the central files. Journals may still be published, conferences held, papers read, compositions performed, exhibitions held; but it is these central files which would be the main depository of human intellectual and cultural achievement.

19

Computers,
crime and the law

As well as the creative side of the human personality which was the subject of the last chapter, there is unfortunately a destructive side also. It is to this darker facet of the world of individual values that we turn now, and the relationship between computers and crime. Apart from a world-wide morbid interest in computer-based fraud, little has been written on this topic — certainly there has been no broad-based examination of it — and little has been written on possible changes in the pattern of crime over the next thirty years. It is questionable whether the absence of written work is due rather to a lack of constructive ideas than of concrete information on the subject.

Fraudulent exploitation of computers does, of course, capture the imagination, and the sums of money involved could be colossal, but so far the methods employed do not, in general, appear to be of a sophistication beyond detection or prevention by existing skill and facilities; it is possible, in fact, that the evolution of data processing systems will make detection easier and perpetration harder. Misuse of data banks — a topical subject for several years already — has nevertheless not yet attracted its full share of attention, but by its very insidious nature is one of the greatest menaces from the standpoint of criminal (or criminally negligent) exploitation.

To cover the topic adequately, however, we must examine the whole range of peripheral subjects — the social climate over the next thirty years, the causes of crime, detection, treatment — even the preventive aspects of crime which could be developed within the next three decades.

Before embarking on these, however, one point requires emphasis: in the social climate of the 1970s, the nature of crime cannot be classified by "social class" according to traditional sociological standards. Computer operators and programmers (in particular) may by convenient (and tautological) definition be described as middle class, but in this most modern of occupations, social background is totally irrelevant to the work. This may be confusing and frustrating to sociologists, but in the computing world people tend to be virtually classless in outlook, with backgrounds from all points on the social spectrum — a fact unaffected by attempts to fit the phenomenon to traditional sociological theory.

Turning to the social climate and possible changes over the next thirty years, a large number of significant events can be predicted, many of which have been touched upon earlier. The environment will reflect depopulation of rural areas, to large urban conglomerations with still higher population density. The countryside will contain larger, more intensive farms, with (for a long time) largely commuter towns. In these, there will tend to be a reduction in crime, which will probably pass unnoticed in the face of the violent effects of the pressures — social, economic and environmental — generated by the further restricted urban living conditions. Such violence may be manifest as apparently aimless destruction of property or personal attacks, and will to only a limited extent find a common root with other forms of crime, in the pressures generated by "progress."

We have already (in Chapter 17) noted the possibility of increased leisure leading to increased opportunity for boredom and hence to more apparently purposeless violence. In the short term this can certainly be expected; any educational solution would take time, and even if the leisure industry alone could find the answer, which is doubtful, experience suggests that it is likely that a substantial lag would take place between the manifestations of the need for improved leisure facilities and concrete response to this need on the part of the industry.

Economically, three events seem to be on the horizon. First, the improved conditions of the underprivileged sections of the community will be more than matched by the accumulation of still further wealth by the over-privileged. Second, this increased gap in wealth will in turn be even more self-evident, leading to an exponential growth in the *visible* separation between rich and poor. Third, money, as a physical commodity, is likely to diminish in importance, above all to the wealthy; it will be replaced by direct debiting and credit card systems. What is less certain is whether the accumulation of wealth will generally follow the American pattern of conspicuous consumption, or the traditionally British approach of inconspicuous accumulation of durable possessions: the pattern of crime in thirty years' time will be substantially affected by this choice, which is currently uncertain.

In turn, economic aspirations will possibly become less and less attainable; with cash-status symbols becoming less and less worthwhile, it is conceivable that social symbols will assume a value which is measured by other criteria than purely financial wealth. This may be accompanied by a move to the left, politically, which could mean, depending on the political state of the nation concerned, increased state ownership, increased state intervention and control, worker control of industry, the spread of worker militancy and trade unionism to managerial and professional sectors, or similar effects.

Finally, there are the effects of technology itself, which could continue to tend to depersonalise many aspects of life, but to democratise, at least partially, the economy. As the pollution and conservation crises induced by technological advance become more acute this could further strengthen the tendency towards state control of the individual and of industry — for example, a very severe limitation on the private use of motor vehicles could come about for either or both of two reasons: the need to conserve dwindling oil resources, or to limit pollution and congestion. As we said in Chapter 16, there is a hope that computer techniques can solve such problems of the environment, but there is no guarantee, and governments may be forced into very restrictive legislation to cope with them. Also as a result of technological advance, it is likely that, much as the airlines and aircraft manufacturers have been overtaken by the modern hazard of hijacking, that twentieth century analogue of piracy, a whole new range of possible types of crime will evolve which it could be impossible to foresee, and which could be both on a large scale and difficult to prevent, at least initially.

Among such crimes, of course, are those relating specifically to computers, and it is to these that we now turn our attention. Apart from fraud, the most immediately ominous risk is the theft of data, in magnetic tape or disc form, or during transmission: the threat becomes greater as the file of information increases in size or depth of detail. The purposes of such an exercise could be threefold:

(i) to commit fraud (in the future at a fairly sophisticated level);

(ii) for industrial espionage, to obtain details of industrial processes or specialist computer programs: to steal customer or supplier lists, or to discover current or imminent activities of competitors; or

(iii) to commit blackmail or otherwise to exert outside pressure.

The logical extension of data-tapping is, of course, data corruption — with the same broad objectives but perhaps on a more sinister scale. If the social framework changes in the way projected earlier — with a tendency away from tangible possessions, towards social prestige and power — then the objective of damaging personal reputation or corporate image can be added to that of destroying financial credibility or credit-worthiness.

Given the development of a public computing utility, then data tapping and corruption will be taken to the level of the individual — a possibility which is strengthened by the fact that the first private users of such a network are also likely to be lucrative targets. The commission of such crimes will require the active participation of specialists, who will be a corrupt element among computer technologists. These have been the most socially mobile sector of the population, and therefore the criminally inclined among them are likely to be able to adapt to their particular environment more readily than the remainder of the population. Despite the recent trend towards the liberalisation of social behaviour, it appears unlikely that any activities which are today proscribed as criminal (as opposed to socially undesirable) will in the future be accepted, even though still greater social change may yet result from technological advancement, unless there is a total collapse in our social structure.

In the area of non-technological, or at least non-computer-based crime, it is probable that, compared to the amount of change over the last hundred years, the pattern of criminal activity will remain relatively stable, albeit with a change in emphasis. Perhaps the most significant change in crime in the twentieth century has been the shift in industrialised societies away from crimes of necessity towards those induced by social or psychological pressures. Theft, having increased, is no longer generally indulged in in order to survive, but as a regular occupation for gain; crime is often, now, big business, using modern techniques and exploiting modern scientific developments, particularly in urban areas. The pressures of living in large impersonal cities have taken their toll, and if urban areas increase in size or in population, and the density becomes even more oppressive, then an increase in crime — particularly of violence — will ensue, if only because of the mental and environmental strain of living in close proximity to one's fellow beings. At the same time there is no reason to believe that the rate of use of up-to-date techniques will not similarly increase, in theft and fraud for example. It is possible that administrative and statutory changes will reduce the level of some kinds of offence over the next thirty years (the restriction of the use of motor vehicles would, for example, reduce motoring offences) but the increasing complexity of Law will create further pitfalls for the unwary offender, while it will itself need computers for its impartial and effective administration. Technology once again has to provide the solution to the problems it creates, as, indeed, in the case of the use of technology, including computers, to cope with the problems of leisure, as already discussed.

In summary, then, the major non-technical crimes at the turn of the twenty-first century are likely to be caused by one (or more) of the following three factors:

(i) deprivation and relative poverty in a society where the economic gap between poor and rich will have increased still further;

(ii) boredom from increased leisure, without a parallel increase in the development of leisure occupations;

(iii) maladjustment to the stresses and demands of larger, denser urban living and working conditions.

It is particularly towards these areas, then, that computers should be directed in the field of criminological research and the administration of justice — what is to a large extent virgin territory. Computer-based crime prevention can be grouped into two principal areas:

(i) the creation and maintenance of information files, in an extension of existing activities such as the issue of television and motor licence reminders;

(ii) the analysis of available information on criminal activity to determine its causes, with the objective of eliminating it and preventing its spread.

This second method is impossibly huge in scope, and a start has been made, without the use of computers, in eliminating some obvious breeding grounds. It is not always clear, however, whether the effects have been as had been hoped: for example, the belief at one time quite widely held, that the slum environment was a criminal breeding ground, led to the demolition of nineteenth century slums in the UK, only for them to be replaced by housing estates equally arid and drab environmentally, and which are rapidly becoming the slums of the late twentieth century. Quite conceivably, deeper analysis, such as can be made available by means of computers, would identify the true causes of certain types of crime: at the same time, housing areas might perhaps be so designed, as to provide the adventurous leisure activities which are needed to assist in diverting energy away from criminal or near-criminal pursuits.

Such analysis could also contribute to the detection of crime. The keeping of criminal records in a more accessible form is already under way in countries such as the USA and the UK, as are the establishment of ancillary activities such as national registries of motor vehicles, which obviously facilitates the detection of some kinds of offence involving cars, whether directly involved or used for getaway, and which, by reducing the amount of routine work by the police, leave them free for more productive activities.

Such applications can be usefully extended; for example, a system to identify and interpret criminal "trade marks" is one application which, coupled with information on known geographical associates by "trade", would be amenable to on-line interrogation and analysis.

Detection of a crime, in a more practical and immediate sense, within a much reduced time-scale, would contribute greatly to the improvement of the rate of apprehension of the criminals. In the context of computer crime, analysis of the possible methods of checking corrupted information of monitoring the manipulation of files and the prevention of access to the central computer either physically or electronically to remove or erase information, is one which must be left largely to the organisation operating the particular computer system; for a manufacturer to supply a general-purpose security system would lead to concentrated efforts on the part of possible perpetrators to overcome the hazard, with much greater chances of success than in the case of an individually conceived and operated security system, quite independent of the relative complexity of the systems. Foresight will be needed on the part of organisations, therefore, to appreciate the need for this kind of security and for ingenuity in devising it. One can expect to find, growing together, a branch of the computer software industry specialising in security problems, and a criminal profession of computer cracksmen, analogous to safemakers and safebreakers today. The former, if not yet the latter, is already embryonic-ally in existence, e.g. the formation in mid-1972 of a computer security firm in the UK jointly owned by Securicor, a private firm specialising in physical security systems, and Dataskil, the software subsidiary of ICL.

Computer control of its internal systems logically leads to an appraisal of computer-based external control: security systems at the office, factory or home. Computer-controlled security systems already exist, but have yet to prove their long-term reliability, their flexibility in a dynamic environ-ment, and their capacity to cover other functions conventionally delegated to human security guards. It is apparent that in the ultimate, such a system might, for example, be extended to the physical detention of an offender coupled with an emergency call to the police for help (when the system should then also be able to give admittance to secure premises). A household computer of the kind envisaged in Chapter 17 should certainly be able to detect unauthorised entry, alert the inhabitants, and inform the local police through the public network, even if apparently shut down.

Both internal and external security systems might be limited by existing legislation in a particular country, and many states may have to review the relevant laws in consequence. For example, a computer system may detect unauthorised use of files, and possibly even identify the offender, but the contents of those files might not be protected by law. Even if some existing law could be invoked, evidence based on computer detection of the accused might not be admissible in court. An external security system capable of catching an offender might be illegal — for example, in the UK a householder may not install mantraps to catch burglars. So much depends on the legal system of the particular country, and its laws relating to property, personal injury and the liberty of the individual that there is little point in discussing it in too much detail; however, the particular field of individual privacy, in relation to databanks, will be specifically dealt with in the next chapter.

Let us consider now what happens after an offender — however apprehended and for whatever crime — has been charged and brought to trial. Computer systems can aid greatly in the subsequent course of justice. A legal reference system of the kind given as an example in Chapter 9 could be extremely helpful if available at a terminal installed in court, so that points of law and legal precedents could be checked. Other systems could assist on the conviction of the offender and in his subsequent treatment. A major fault in British justice, for example, has been the disparity in treatment between crimes of different levels of gravity, for similar offences, and between different courts. While the final choice of sentence must lie in the hands of the magistrates, particularly in the light of extenuating circumstances, the use of an on-line data-retrieval system would facilitate the fitting of the punishment to the crime, as well as permitting the possible introduction of a more sophisticated sentencing structure.

Extensions of such a system would permit the recording and recall of past and present convictions, would monitor the collection of fines and would allow analysis of the effectiveness of treatment. While we are not here concerned with the economics of such a system, which in real money terms is likely to fall with the passage of time, the importance of the security aspects cannot be overstated: unauthorised access to such a databank would lay it open to quite horrifying abuse.

Having touched on the subject of treatment, let us briefly consider the possible ways in which, over the years to come, computers might be made use of in this field. One way in which they could certainly be used is in research. Records could be analysed in far greater numbers and far greater detail than ever before to gauge the efficacy of different forms of treatment, and methods shown not to have been beneficial either to the offender or to society eliminated. Prolonged confinement, for example, might well prove on close scrutiny to be completely ineffectual, in addition to being costly in both time and money. Similarly, new forms of treatment could be monitored for their effectiveness over a much shorter period of time. More sophisticated uses of computers in this respect would probably depend on advances in the science of penology.

The computer can also become the basis for rehabilitation and training for return to the outside world, and if detention of criminals continues to be demanded by society as a significant form of punishment, it is probable that at least experimental systems for the computer-aided instruction of offenders will become operational. CAI systems could be used here in two ways — to provide offenders with skills to enable them to find a livelihood without resort to crime, or to attempt to instil into into them more socially responsible attitudes and understanding of why they found themselves in conflict with society. The first mode of use is the one most likely to be employed initially, and is unexceptionable, but the second is effectively the same in kind as the brainwashing which we mentioned in a more political context in Chapter 7. There is clearly a moral problem here for penal authorities and reformers; it may be of lesser degree than with the use for similar purposes of drugs or neuro-surgery, but it is of the same kind and for that reason should not be overlooked when the remedial treatment of offenders is discussed.

We shall conclude by summarising the risks and benefits of the administrative use of computers in crime prevention, detection and treatment. Here, one is dealing almost exclusively with the processing of large volumes of data, which would rapidly become — if not so constructed *ab initio* — a series of databases. All the dangers put forward as applicable to databases in general, apply in the area of crime — but multiplied a hundredfold. The effects would be most felt by the innocent and the most vulnerable members of society. Apart from the relatively harmless nuisance value, unauthorised access could lead to blackmail and extortion, exploitation for commercial ends, an increase in the degree of criminal professionalism and perhaps an increase in crime itself. The general availability of the motor vehicle licence records, for example, would not only lead to marketing campaigns on the lines described in Chapter 14, or allow the multiplication of complaints about real or imagined traffic offences, but provide burglars with such information as where there are people who own expensive cars and who hence might be worth visiting, or enable smash-and-grab or similar gangs to match makes, colours and licence numbers with suitable vehicles to cause confusion in pursuit. The possibility should not be overlooked, indeed, of a criminal organisation running its own databank of information about potential victims. In the legal systems, injustice of frightening proportions could arise from inaccurate input or incorrect retrieval programs, for example in the form of misinformed sentencing. Once again the relatively innocent would suffer most, those too poor or weak or ignorant or inarticulate to stand up for themselves properly who would be in the greatest danger.

But, as the public is the biggest potential loser, so is it the greatest potential beneficiary. Properly established and exploited, the databases could have outstanding advantages in making the punishment fit the crime, not merely judicially but by ensuring the best remedial treatment; in identifying as quickly as possible potential or actual malefaction; in enhancing the effectiveness of preventive measures; in improving the success rate in solving committed crimes; in helping to eliminate the conditions which cause criminal activity to develop and thrive. Many of these advantages can be evaluated tangibly, in terms of time and money saved, given research into current costs and the costs of setting up and running a suitable system. It is ironic that the one perhaps most advanced at present (vehicle licences), easily cost-justifiable because of the sheer mass of information, could turn out to be the first to become obsolete because of quite unrelated environmental factors. Nevertheless, similar cost evaluations can be expected in various areas in the years ahead, and systems implemented, perhaps on the lines of, though going far beyond, the American PIN (Police Information Network).

The problem for the ordinary citizen is to weigh the advantages just outlined with the problems of the personal record files — both from potential unauthorised access, and from potential authoritarian use directly by government for political ends, or by the police. An individual picked up for a suspected offence at 11 p.m. may welcome the databanks when his identity can be checked, his fingerprints matched, and his credentials vouched for over the network all in the space of half an hour, when now he might be held overnight or even longer while his innocence was being established; on the other hand, he may the next day be rather worried that quite so much is not only known about him but so easily accessible. The problem for the professionals concerned — lawyers, prison authorities, police authorities, criminologists and penologists — is not just whether and how to use computer methods, but how to use them properly, and how to ensure that it is seen that they are used properly. The disquiet of many, who do not accept the glib response "only those with something to hide have anything to fear" as an adequate answer, shows that they, and the computer professionals who have to advise them, have a great deal to do in this respect.

It is to this issue that we now turn our attention.

20

Privacy

In this chapter we shall examine three things: what is meant by privacy; how privacy can be invaded and how computers can assist in invasion; and how the individual is or could be protected by the law from invasion.

A dictionary might define the term "privacy" in the present context to be the condition of seclusion, withdrawal, or freedom from the interest of others in one's personal and spiritual concerns. Like all definitions of such an elusive concept this one has shortcomings. For example, first, it fails to take account of the relative sensitivity or need for freedom from publication of different facts about an individual: his innermost secrets, the penetration of which would strip him of his individual psychological protection, are different in character from those personal thoughts or aspirations he will share with his wife but with no-one else, and different again from the ideas he will voice to workmates or the public. Some theorists have characterised these variations in an individual's relations with others in terms of a series of concentric circles or "zones" where the "ultimate secrets" are in the innermost circle and will not be shared with anyone; then comes the "intimate secrets" which can be shared, but only with a restricted class of persons; then a series of wider circles concluding in the least sensitive facts. Professor Westin, on the other hand, in his important book "Privacy and Freedom", analyses privacy into four elements: solitude, where the individual is left with the "familiar dialogue with the mind or conscience"; intimacy, in groups such as family or workmates; anonymity, where the individual is one of a crowd and not identified; and reserve, where the individual keeps his distance from others.

Secondly, the definition fails to take account of the variation in the degree of privacy available or sought after from culture to culture, from country to country, from one social class to another, and (for particular facts) from time to time. Margaret Mead, in her book "Coming of Age in Samoa", describes a culture where activities which would in English society be witnessed by limited categories of persons (e.g. birth) are seen by casual observers: "there is no privacy and no sense of shame". The variation from country to country is epitomised by the wonder evinced by foreigners at the train-travelling Englishman who, preferring to bury himself in his newspaper rather than engage in conversation, achieves the privacy of reserve; and by the interest of European family-orientated societies in the Israeli *kibbutzim,* where family intimacy is displaced by group intimacy. The variation from class to class is to be seen in the differing experiences, on the one hand, of the underprivileged and the boarding-school belt, and on the other, of the middle-class day school category. The former are accustomed to living intimately together in cramped and overcrowded surroundings and thus knowing a good deal more about the habits, bodies and personalities of their associates than the latter, many of whom from an early age have a room of their own.

Finally, from time to time an individual may desire different degrees of confidentiality for the same facts; it may be that as he comes more into the public eye he wishes a fact in his past life to be shrouded by the passing of time, or he may be content that with changing circumstances facts he previously did his best to conceal are now much less sensitive to him. The former is obviously the more important in this context — examples would be those of an ex-convict now going straight, or experimentation with drugs as a teenager many years before, or a past flirtation with an extreme political organisation. A stark reminder of what this can mean to an individual was afforded by the American presidential election of 1972, when the original Democratic Party nominee for Vice-President, Senator Thomas Eagleton, was forced to withdraw following disclosure that he had in the past undergone psychiatric treatment.

Lawyers, especially in the United States, have had to consider the concept of privacy in terms of the right of the individual to keep his affairs to himself, as against the right of society in the best interest of all its members to have information. Professor Westin defines privacy as "the claim of individuals, groups, or institutions to determine for themselves when, how and to what extent information about them is communicated to others". Justice Cooley called it "the right to be let alone", while Justice Brandeis said "The makers of (the US) constitution . . . conferred, as against the government, the right to be let alone — the most comprehensive of rights and the right most valued by civilised men". The Privacy Committee of the Society of Conservative Lawyers in the UK have suggested that it might be expressed as "the right of a person to control the flow of information about himself", and this approach is adopted by the Control of Personal Information Bill, examined below. In practice, lawyers and law makers must base their thinking on a definition of privacy which allows for the balancing of the needs of the individual and the community, and a helpful lawyer's definition is contained in a report by Justice, the British section of the International Commission of Jurists, on "Privacy and the Law": " . . . that area of a man's life which, in any given circumstances, a reasonable man with an understanding of the legitimate needs of the community would think it wrong to invade". It is for the community to recognise that, however true it is that in a modern welfare state the authorities must know certain facts about people's circumstances simply in order to plan the provision of such necessities as housing subsidies, social security benefits, clinics, local authority services, and so on, there must be a point at which society recognises that it does not need, or is not entitled, to enquire further into an individual's life; beyond that point enquiry and interference is properly called an 'invasion of privacy', or an infringement of the "right to privacy", and as such is a threat to what we understand to be freedom in a democratic state.

To draw this line between legitimate enquiries and invasions of privacy is the function of public opinion and the legislators of the country concerned; as we have seen, there can be a wide variation in what is socially acceptable even between nations sharing the same basic culture. Nevertheless, it is instructive to examine some of the categories of information which do become available in modern society, and the agencies through which this comes about. For example, the UK has been renowned for its concern for individual privacy and has always resisted identity cards and the compulsory carrying of "papers" which is common in European countries, let alone the kind of general accessibility of personal information which obtains in, say, Sweden. Yet even in the UK much information is available about the private citizen. He is compelled to provide information to central and local government: his income, mortgages, dividends and alimony payments are known to the Inland Revenue; his medical history is known, and his financial circumstances may be enquired into (for example, for supplementary benefit awards) by the Department of Health and Social Security; he may be among selected employees on whom the Department of Trade requires employers to complete a detailed questionnaire on hours of work, overtime, expenses, etc.; the state of his driving record is known to the Department of the Environment; his will is available (posthumously) for inspection for all the world to see his testamentary dispositions; and householders are compelled to complete a regular census form requiring details such as occupation, the number of rooms in the property, and cohabitants. Then on a local level, the town halls contain large amounts of information about public health, rates (and who pays late or by instalments), improvement grants, probation, and so on. And though not central or local government, the police have files of vast quantities of information and not just about criminals.

Next come organisations to which he has to reveal private information, in order to obtain a service. A man wishing to buy life or other insurance must give detailed information about himself, his health, or property; in order to obtain a credit card, credit, or hire purchase he must reveal details of his financial standing; to get a job he will have to reveal personal information, perhaps undergoing aptitude tests or psychological examinations, and in some cases his wife will be "vetted" too; to avail himself of the services of a clearing bank he cannot avoid his financial affairs being open to the scrutiny of the bank manager; to his tailor he must reveal the unpalatable truth which (with his tailor's connivance) he would like to conceal from the world; by having his name inserted in a professional directory he exposes himself to unsolicited junk-mail. In most of these cases the giving of private information or its availability to others is regarded as a necessary element in the commercial relationship: for no-one can blame an insurance company for wanting to know whether its proposer is riddled with disease, or a credit card company for wishing to satisfy itself of an applicant's circumstances. People in turn accept the giving of such information as a necessity.

Thirdly there is information obtained about him without his knowledge, sometimes of recipients' identity or of the type or sources of that information; and without his control or (even notional) consent. In this category are gossip, hearsay "facts" obtained by investigators questioning his associates, information gathered by security services and by wiretapping, or interception of letters, information exchanged between credit agencies or insurance companies (although here proposal forms commonly contain an authorisation to the company to seek medical information about the applicant from any other insurer or from any attending doctor), industrial secrets poached by a competitor, and information derived from "bugging" devices, miniature radio transmitters or receivers, and hidden cameras. These examples are cases of deliberate obtaining of information. We may note also that information can become available by accident: a file is left on a train or unattended in an office; an indiscreet official confides in a friend; a surplus computer printout is left in a waste basket without being shredded or burnt.

Now collection and dissemination of information about individuals, and thus invasions of privacy, have been with us as long as people have been able to communicate. The scope of the inquisitive has been successively widened by the written and printed word, the telephone, radio, and electronic devices in general. It is by no means true that the computer has the monopoly of privacy invasion, although there is no doubt that the introduction of computing techniques will make invasion quicker, more effective, and more comprehensive.

That being so, there is much justified concern about the use of computer databanks. By databank (a word not easy to define in legal terms) is meant a record, wherever stored, of facts about individuals. Before the advent of the computer there were databanks based on ordinary manilla folders and, later, on punched card installations. Indeed there are thousands of such databanks still in use today; perhaps their operators would not use the word databank to describe them. The computerised databank has, however, far greater potential than either the file-based or the punched card-based databank: the computer is an extremely powerful tool which has an unprecedented capacity to sort, analyse, collate, calculate, and compare and reproduce data at very high speeds, and to remember it for ever if so programmed. It can be made to compile dossiers, statistics, or forecasts which by their complexity and size could not hitherto be attempted and such a facility offers unparalleled scope for any user. If a national computer databank were established, all the information the citizen is called upon to provide (sometimes at present several times over because of the present disparate nature of government files) would be asked for once, and would be fed into a single system. The enormously enhanced power and efficiency afforded to the government by such a facility is self-evident. Precisely the same observations apply to private sector computer databanks (such as those operated by credit rating companies) which, as computers become more common, will contain much sensitive information readily accessible not only to the databank owner but also to those (e.g. other credit rating companies) with a contractual agreement with the owner for the interchange of information. Having regard, then, to the geometric increase in the amount of information available and in circulation made possible by the use of computers, it can be asked what the law does to protect individuals, by regulation of databanks or their operators, by restriction of the numbers and categories of those who receive information, and by ensuring that information, when it is given, is correct. The answer may vary from country to country, of course, so to be specific we shall consider for the moment the case of English law. Here, the answer is "not very much" — complex systems are being developed, to quote an editorial in *The Guardian,* "in something of a legal vacuum". We can express the situation by means of the table shown on this page of notional complaints

	Complaint	Remedy
1.	That information is stored at all when the subject is in no relationship with the storer which justifies this.	None
2.	That information is stored without the subject's knowledge.	None
3.	That information stored is wrong.	None
4.	That information stored is passed without the subject's consent to a third party.	Possibly an action for breach of contract, breach of confidence, breach of copyright
5.	That information passed by the databank to a third party is wrong.	Possibly an action for defamation; and see 4
6.	That information passed by the databank to a third party is literally correct but misleading.	Possibly an action for defamation; and see 4
7.	That information obtained from the subject is supplemented by hearsay information or opinion obtained from third parties; and is passed on without distinction being made.	None; but see 4
8.	That the information stored is so old as to be irrelevant and should be deleted.	None
9.	That the databank record has been corrected but this fact has not been passed to recipients of uncorrected information.	None

by an individual against a databank, and the remedies which exist. It
can be seen that only in three of the nine cases is there a possible legal
action which he might bring.

As the law stands at present in England there is no common law
remedy available for invasion of privacy as such, though there is nothing
to stop the courts from developing such a right; after all, much of English
law is common law (that is, judge-made law rather than statute law).
Of recent years, however, there has been a tendency for the courts to
leave the formulation of new law, as distinct from the interpretation of
existing law, to Parliament. For example, some years ago a plaintiff did
in fact try to base part of his case on the invasion of his privacy, but that
particular argument was not accepted by the court.

In the absence of a defined right, the plaintiff must seek to show that
the act he complains of is actionable under some other head of complaint
recognised by the law; the possible heads of claim he will look at will be
in defamation, negligent mis-statement, breach of confidence, breach of
contract, breach of copyright, or trespass; or there may be indirect
protection of his alleged right by specific act of Parliament. Though
invasion of privacy may take many forms, this discussion is confined to
the databank context.

An action in defamation lies where the plaintiff shows that a statement
published about him has lowered his reputation in the eyes of right-
thinking people or has exposed him to hatred, ridicule, or contempt.
Published here means communicated to another person by any means.
This remedy may be appropriate where the damage suffered by the
plaintiff resulted from an inaccurate statement about his creditworthiness by an agency whose business is to sell such information. But if the
agency is a trade association formed to protect its members and not to sell
information it may be able to take advantage of the defence of qualified
privilege in the absence of malice. This is because the defence of qualified
privilege applies where there is a duty to make the communication and
an interest in receiving it. It is possible, but not settled law, that a plaintiff
could rely on the innuendo: that is, that what was said was literally true
but it bore an untrue innuendo. Thus the plaintiff might have his remedy
if the credit rating agency told its client the literal truth but in such a
manner that a defamatory meaning was read into the words by the client
by virtue of his knowing certain extrinsic facts, and that as a consequence
credit was refused to the plaintiff. Although the remedy in defamation
may avail a plaintiff about whom an untrue statement is made it will not,
subject to what has been said about the innuendo, protect someone
about whom the true facts have been revealed in full.

An action for negligent mis-statement is available to a person to whom such a statement is made, provided that he is in some special relationship with the maker that justifies him in relying on the statement's accuracy, and provided that the maker has not expressly disclaimed liability for inaccuracy or its consequences. But this does not avail a third party *about* whom a false statement is negligently made, even though he suffers damage as a result. Thus if X negligently and erroneously makes a statement to Y about Z's creditworthiness which results in Z's failing to get credit from Y, Z appears to have no remedy against X unless the statement was defamatory. There is nothing, however, to prevent the courts developing the law to giving him a remedy in such circumstances.

An action for breach of confidence may lie even where plaintiff and defendant are not in contractual relationship. There is a series of cases which show that if X uses confidential industrial information without the consent of Y he is infringing Y's rights in that information. So far as marital confidences are concerned it now seems that there can be a breach of confidence without any property right of the plaintiff in the document or information concerned, as had hitherto been the case for private confidences. The requirement of such a property right will be a stumbling block for a plaintiff in a databank situation. He will be additionally hampered if the information he is trying to protect is a confidence or communication which in the public interest ought to be disclosed.

An action for breach of copyright may be possible. But in most cases involving databanks the subject does not have copyright, so this remedy is of limited value. The same observation applies to an action for breach of contract. If there is a contractual relationship between subject and databank there may be an express or implied term in the contract that the information supplied by the subject will be kept confidential. If, for example, a credit agency uses computer bureau facilities there will probably, in the absence of an express term relating to confidentiality, be an implied term. COSBA, the British Computer Services and Bureaux Association, in fact recommends its member bureaux to insert a clause in contracts stating that the customer's information is to be kept confidential. The individual, on the other hand, in most cases cannot rely on a contract between him and the databank, even if he is fortunate enough to discover the existence of a record about him.

An action for trespass is available where there has been physical interference with the plaintiff or his property, a useful remedy in privacy invasion cases involving "bugging" or trespass on land, although because action for trespass to land requires the plaintiff to have possession in law of the land, a hotel visitor cannot sue for bugging of his room, whereas a tenant can sue for bugging of premises of which he has exclusive possession during the term of his lease. It is clear that this remedy is of little help in the circumstances we are considering, as there is most unlikely to be a physical interference by a databank, though the enquiry agent who snoops around the plaintiff's property to obtain data to feed into the computer may be a trespasser.

There may be indirect protection of privacy by an Act of Parliament designed to cover a particular case rather than to protect privacy in general. For example, the Post Office (Data Processing Service) Act 1967 imposes an obligation of secrecy on Post Office staff engaged on the provision of data processing services and facilities. The Income Tax Management Act 1964 requires staff of the Inland Revenue to make a declaration not to disclose information received in the execution of their duties. Both these statutes except disclosure "as required by law". This is an extremely wide exception, and the 1967 Act in particular was strongly criticised for that reason by those concerned about privacy in this area. Under the Theft Act 1968 it is an offence to steal property, the definition of which includes "things in action and other intangible property". The difficulty here is that even assuming private information is construed as "intangible property" a prosecution could only succeed on proof that the accused intended permanently to deprive the other of his "intangible property". It would by no means be the case that a databank operator had such an intention. The Unsolicited Goods and Services Act 1971 (Section 2) makes it a criminal offence "in the course of any trade or business and with a view to obtaining any payment" for unsolicited goods, to put or threaten to put any person's name on a list of defaulters or debtors. There are many other statutory provisions which bear on privacy but which are not quoted here because they are irrelevant to the databank context. The fact that the English legal system requires that a claim for invasion of privacy must, in order to succeed, be tacked onto a claim for infringement of another right is certainly unsatisfactory, and it is for this reason that proposals have been made for legislation regarding either privacy generally, or databanks specifically. Three important recent examples (none of which has become law) were Mr. Baker's Data Surveillance Bill in May 1969, Mr. Walden's Right of Privacy Bill in November 1969 and Mr. Huckfield's Control of Personal Information Bill in February 1971, whose broad outlines we shall now describe.

The Data Surveillance Bill was aimed at preventing "the invasion of privacy through the misuse of computer information". It provided for a register of all databanks (defined rather widely as computers which record and store information) kept by government, public corporations, and private operators, including credit and detective agencies and those offering information for sale. The register was to contain details of the owner, the nature and purpose of data stored, and the class of persons entitled to access to the data. The Registrar would have power to order that an item be expunged from the register if its inclusion would inflict undue hardship on a person or would not be in the public interest. With defined exceptions (such as police and security services) the operators were to maintain a record of extractions of data giving details of recipients, nature of data supplied, and the purpose for which it was required. An important clause of the Bill for individuals was clause 4, providing that the operator must supply to any person the subject of a file on his inclusion in the databank, and on request for a fee thereafter, a printout of all data concerning him, together with a statement of the purpose for which the data was to be used, the purposes for which it had in fact been used since last printout, and the names and addresses of recipients of all or any of the data since last printout. The individual could apply to the Registrar for any data on the record to be amended or expunged because it was incorrect, unfair, or outdated, in which case the Registrar could order that any recipient of information be informed of the change and deletion. Criminal sanctions and a right of action in damages were envisaged.

The Right of Privacy Bill was to establish a general right of privacy, and was not confined to the databank. It defined the right of privacy as the right of any person to be protected from intrusion upon himself, his home, his family, his relationships and communications with others, his property and his business affairs, by such means as spying, or unauthorised recordings, copying of documents or use or disclosure of confidential information or of facts calculated to cause him distress, annoyance or embarrassment or to place him in a false light. The court was empowered to award damages, grant an injunction, and to order the defendant to account for profits. In awarding damages the court was to have regard in particular to the effect on the health, welfare, social, business or financial position of the plaintiff, and to any distress, annoyance, or embarrassment suffered. The Bill provided defences — e.g. consent to the infringement, public interest, lack of knowledge or intention that conduct would amount to infringement, or reasonableness or necessity of defendant's acts for protection of his person, property, or lawful business.

The Control of Personal Information Bill was to prevent the misuse of information stored in government or private databanks (defined as stores of information containing details of individuals) and to prevent the

infringement of the right (explicitly created by the Bill) of the individual
to control the collection, storage and use of information about him. To
this end the Bill established a Data Bank Tribunal and an inspectorate of
databanks; it required that any person responsible for the operation or use
of a databank containing details of 100,000 individuals or more must
have a licence granted by the Tribunal. In exercising its power to impose
terms and conditions in licences the Tribunal was to have regard to the
individual's right to control the collection, storage and distribution of
information about him, and in particular was to have the power to decide
whether the licence should require the operator to provide the individual
about whom information was stored, with the information held in the
databank and its sources, and the names of persons to which the information was supplied since previously being given to the individual. If such
a condition was imposed these facts were to be supplied on the individual's
first inclusion in the databank, at any time thereafter on request for a fee,
and at least once every two years. The Tribunal was also empowered to
impose conditions that certain classes of information should not be held
in the databank, or that certain persons or categories of persons should not
be supplied with some or all of the information in the databank. With
regard to the operation of a licensed databank, the Tribunal had power
to order the erasure or correction of any item stored for inaccuracy,
incompleteness or irrelevance to the purpose for which it was stored;
and to order the licence-holder to inform any recipient of information
of such erasures or corrections. The Bill empowered the Tribunal to
order payment of damages to any person to whom loss had been caused,
by the licence-holder's failure to observe conditions laid down by the
Tribunal, by the obtaining of information from a databank by fraud or
without the licence-holder's consent, or by the failure to obtain a licence.
Additionally, stiff criminal sanctions were provided for.

Without necessarily enshrining their suggestions in draft Bills, other
British organisations have made proposals for dealing with the problem
of computers and privacy. Justice recommended in the report mentioned
earlier that there should be a civil remedy for any substantial and unreasonable infringement of any person's privacy, taking into account the
interests of the community and the needs of the press; and that there
should be investigation into the regulation of the acquisition, storage and
communication of personal information by databanks so that the subject
of the information can ensure that it is accurate, and discover to whom
it is given. A sub-committee of the Society of Conservative Lawyers
recommended protection for the individual in the form of printout,
alteration and erasure, and information as to the use to which data is put,

similar to the safeguards in the Data Surveillance Bill, to apply to government or local authority databanks kept for purposes such as the amalgamation of personal data records, the allocation of housing, or the selection
of staff; and to categories of private databanks where "each category
attains a position in which the information contained in the databanks of
the category governs all or virtually all opportunities in a particular field".
The Society of Conservative Lawyers has also recommended that in the
case of any national databank, access by officials to information should be
restricted to that particular department's needs; and they have urged the
creation of a supervisory Databank Authority. The British Computer
Society suggested, in its evidence to the Younger Committee, a Home
Office Committee on Privacy under the Chairmanship of Mr. Kenneth
Younger, set up by the British Labour Government in 1970, and about
which we shall have more to say shortly, that personal information
should be recognised as a property right of the individual, interference
with which should be restricted by law; as a corollary to this recognised
property right the individual should be entitled to examine data on him,
to question its source, to know to whom it is available, and to challenge
its accuracy by way of a reply or explanation to be noted on the file. As
well as recommending a licensing system for owners of banks of "sensitive"
data (which description was not elaborated) the BCS urged that professionals engaged in the construction and operation of databanks
should be licensed, or should at least be governed by professional standards
such as its own Code of Conduct, which would afford protection both to
professionals and to public. As well as this regulation from within, the
computer databanks should be subject to scrutiny by an independent
body with functions analogous to those of the Air Transport Licensing
Board, which has powers to grant licences for air transport services on
certain conditions and in particular to persons it considers competent
and fit and proper to operate the service. The Board may withdraw the
licence if the conditions are no longer satisfied.

The above outlines do no more than highlight the broad principles
proposed in the bills or by the organisations concerned, and many other
points, both additional and consequential, have been examined. For
example, printouts from databanks would not necessarily include medical
information, since the doctor might consider it against the interests of
his patient to tell him certain facts; there may also be good reasons in the
general public interest for exempting police databanks from duties to
disclose; and not even the most optimistic crusader expects complete
printouts from security databanks. On a different level, information in a
databank may not be confidential, but may be available to the individual

in a form or at intervals not strictly within the rules governing printout, so that printout might, in effect, be reduced to the status of a secondary check; an example might be a databank belonging to a vehicle licensing authority, where much of the information held would ordinarily appear on issued documents, and repeating it in the form of a printout would be an unnecessary expense. It seems sensible to suppose also that if printout is required in order that the individual can check what information is held about him, with a view to protecting his right to privacy, there will be cases of databanks (particularly on the basis of the definition in the Data Surveillance Bill) which deal only in relatively non-sensitive information (e.g. name and address) the storage or circulation of which may be of little importance to the subject, and which may have good grounds for exemption from the obligation to supply printout.

There are three main objections to specific proposals on computerised databanks. First, any specific legislation would have to be extremely complicated to be effective in protecting the individual, while at the same time taking account of the other side of the argument; and would probably be riddled with exemptions and exceptions. Secondly, an inescapable consequence of specificity would be that the law would be too inflexible to keep pace with as yet unforeseen developments in technology. Thirdly, it would leave untouched the enormous areas of privacy invasion by devices other than the computer; and that is why it might be more effective to establish the general right of privacy such as proposed in the Right of Privacy Bill and to leave to the courts the task of judging each case on its merits, whether involving computers or not. Here again, there are fundamental problems; first, if you do not know, perhaps from a printout, that a record is kept about you, you will not claim damages for breach of privacy, however serious the invasion may be. Secondly, journalists would quite understandably require written into such legislation safe-guards of their role of bringing facts into the public domain for informed discussion — something which in fact caused the press to attack the Right of Privacy Bill. Thirdly, it is arguable that the establishment of a right of privacy will not *per se* give adequate protection to the individual *vis-a-vis* credit rating agencies, whose activities are potentially the most dangerous invasions of privacy.

Continued expressions of public concern — or, at least concern of some of the informed public — in the late 1960s led to the setting up in 1970 of the Younger Committee mentioned earlier; the fact that technical questions of security were involved as well as legal and ethical problems certainly made it easy to justify further investigation. The terms of reference of the committee were

"to consider whether legislation is needed to give further protection
to the individual citizen and to commercial and industrial interests
against intrusion into privacy by private persons or organisations,
or by companies, and to make recommendations" ...

Informed opinion at once expressed concern at the obvious limitation
of these terms of reference, that they did not include databanks or other
means of privacy invasion operated by government or government agencies,
a concern which the subsequent announcement of a separate enquiry into
such governmental activities did little to dispel, since that enquiry was to be
purely internal. Nevertheless, the findings of the Younger Committee were
awaited with considerable interest and some hope by many people worried
about the potential misuse of computer files of personal information and
the special problems of control of access which these impose.

In the event the recommendations made by Younger have disappointed
many commentators. The Committee recommended the voluntary
adoption by computer users of ten principles to govern their operations;
and the setting up of a Standing Commission to make yet further investigations into the subject of computers and privacy, including any
actual evidence of privacy invasion by computer users, and the possibility
of appointing a "responsible person" charged with ensuring observance
of the ten principles. The commission would also investigate possible
legislation. These recommendations are sound enough, though some have
said that the problem is effectively being shelved by being put to another
committee, while others criticise what they see as complacency in the
Committee; which, however, failed to find any example of invasion of
privacy by computer. Clearly the subject remains a live issue in public
debate in Britain.

We conclude by looking briefly at the situation in three other countries
advanced in computerisation, where the problems of privacy and databanks will first become critical — the United States, France, and West
Germany. In the United States privacy has been a live issue for some time,
as a result of the activities of credit rating agencies, much more important
there because of the extensive use of charge cards as described in Chapter
10, and developments such as PIN (Police Information Network) mentioned in the last chapter. In fact, the American courts have, over the
years, built up a considerable case law on privacy, and it is not pitching
it too high to say that in America there is a common-law right of privacy:
rights not to have one's seclusion intruded upon (e.g. by "bugging" by
the landlord); not to be placed in a false light by publicity (e.g. not to
suffer publicity for a career in crime long after "going straight"); and not

to have one's name used in publicity without consent (e.g. use of name of prominent person for advertisement without consent). But this common law right fell short of giving protection in the computer databank situation so specific situations have had to be dealt with by statute. The Fair Credit Reporting Act 1971, a US Federal Statute, is a most significant development in the field of consumer credit reporting, considered by many to be the greatest risk area for individual privacy in the computer databank situation.

The US Federal Trade Commission, which has primary enforcement authority over the Act, said about it:

> "The new law attempts to balance the need of those who extend credit, insurance or employment to have quick and inexpensive access to the facts necessary to make a sound business decision, and the consumer's right to know of and correct erroneous information being distributed about him. The legislation was drafted to facilitate the free flow of information about the consumer, while at the same time affording the consumer the opportunity to correct any errors causing him unwarranted difficulties. The basic purpose of the law is to protect consumers from inaccurate or obsolete information in a report which is used as a factor in determining an individual's eligibility for credit, insurance, or employment . . ."

This Act does meet some of the notional complaints about a databank given earlier in the table on p. 264. It gives the subject, a potential consumer, the right to be told the name and address of the consumer reporting agency when he is rejected for credit, insurance, or employment. He thus knows of the existence of a record about him and can use his right to correct wrong information on the file. On a rejection, the subject has the right to free access to examine all information on file except medical data and the sources of investigative information. He has the right to be told the non-investigative sources of the information, and who has received reports on him, in the last six months for credit or insurance purposes, and in the last two years for employment purposes. The subject has the right of confidentiality for the data, which may only be reported for credit, insurance, employment, Government licence or benefit, or other legitimate business purpose; and otherwise to have information beyond identification kept from government agencies unless a court orders disclosure. Where there is a dispute as to accuracy the agency must re-investigate, and correct items found to be inaccurate. Any unresolved dispute must be noted on file together with a brief statement of the subject's version of the dispute. Where an agency intends to make investigative reports (those involving interviews with neighbours, etc.) it must inform the subject (a) of its intention, and (b) of his right to request details of the nature and scope of the investigation. The Act imposes duties on agencies to ensure that recipients of reports are authorised to receive them, and that information is accurate and not obsolete, by which is meant over seven years old (and fourteen years in some cases, e.g. for a report of bankruptcy). Wilful non-compliance with the Act entitles the subject to sue for punitive damages without limit; negligent non-compliance gives the right to recover actual damages sustained. It is a defence to an action by a subject for defamation, invasion of privacy, or negligence to show full compliance with the Act, unless information supplied to a user or used is false and furnished with malice or with intent to injure the subject. There are administrative enforcement powers in the Federal Trade Commission and other Federal agencies. The Act, however, does not limit the kind of information that can be gathered, nor does it require the reporting of "relevant" information, and it does not give the subject a right to have a copy of his file, only to examine it.

By concentrating on consumer credit reporting, and by making no distinction as between computer databanks and others, the Act tackles an area of considerable potential abuse while avoiding the pitfall of being too inflexible to meet the advances in technology; on the other hand, the very narrowness of its scope means that it does not succeed in resolving all the difficulties created by databanks. What it does perhaps suggest is that a successful approach to legislation in this field might be to start with an examination of the evils which can arise in a particular area, with the intention of eliminating those, rather than to attempt to legislate on all databanks no matter how harmless their content and purpose. Jurists and others interested in the privacy problem, both inside and outside the United States, will certainly watch with interest to see how effective this Act will be in practice.

Turning now to Europe, we find that in France, as in England, there is no legislation protecting individuals from the specific mischief of privacy invasion by computer databank. However, case-law has created a concept of *"droit de la personnalitè"*, a phrase which does not translate easily into English but means something like an individual's right not to have his private life interfered with. This is supplemented by some specific safeguards; for example, truth cannot be used as a defence in a defamation action where the statement complained of concerned the person's private life. Nevertheless, French law gives better protection than English law to the individual only in that it does, at least in theory, have this idea of a basic right to a private life which could be developed to cover databank abuses. In Western Germany also, case-law has established a right of the personality on which privacy decisions have been based. The cases reveal that, in the absence of consent or of reasonable public interest, it is illegal for a person to publish facts concerning the private or family life of another, and this line of interpretation of the basic privacy right may be extended to cover the databank situation. At the moment there is no reference in specific law to privacy and computers, other than in the state of Hesse, where databank registration was introduced in 1970.

This last example points to the difficulties which could arise in the future in an interstate (in the case of a federal nation) or international context, where laws differ across boundaries. In the European Economic Community, domestic laws such as those governing privacy have to be made uniform, according to Article 100 of the Treaty of Rome, only when the Council of Ministers decides unanimously that they "directly affect the setting up or operation of the common market". However, the obligation of member states to facilitate the free movement of labour within the community may mean the setting up of community databanks carrying personal information about migrant workers. Commercial organisations might well set up similar banks, particularly credit agencies, when the projected monetary union comes about. The growth of international networks accessing such databanks could lead to a situation where a databank might be operated without formality under one legal system while it would be constrained by another. Those responsible for forming regulations in a particular country will need to ensure that access to foreign or off-shore databanks is subject to similar constraints as the operation and use of databanks within the country itself. The ultimate answer, however, is international agreement on laws and standards.

The problems of privacy invasion through computer databanks are in their infancy, as these last remarks show. This is the main reason for the absence of legislation; legal systems to some extent and governments to a large extent are not apt to respond with alacrity to situations which will only arise at some indefinite date in the future. Yet the prospects, discussed in earlier pages, of complete educational and career dossiers, medical records, universal accounting and so on, all in principle accessible through a public utility, are real enough, the impossibility of unauthorised access far from established; the problems may not quite be here, but they are on their way. There is something to be said for hastening slowly; the general principle of keeping law to the necessary minimum, the fact that unnecessary laws tend to be ignored and gain a reputation for being ineffective, and bring the law as a whole into disrepute. The dangers of delay, however, are that undesirable practices can grow which, when the necessity of legislation becomes acute and obvious, have become condoned by usage, so entrenched as to have become ineradicable, or have fallen under the protection of vested interests. Jurists, judiciary authorities, legal departments of state, and so on, not only need to tackle the purely technical questions of law; they need to keep appraised of developments, so that action can be taken in time. Until that time much will depend on the ethical standards not only of databank operators but of the computer professionals who design their systems.

The price of privacy, as of all aspects of liberty, is vigilance; vigilance will certainly be needed if what we have called earlier "decision by default" is to be avoided.

5 Conclusions

21 Politics in a computerised world

Every thing, and every concept, that is of interest to more than a small fraction of any community has a political content, from the position of a new lamp post in a small village at one extreme, to the utilisation of the world's natural resources at the other. This is a definition, not a statement of opinion; it is another way of asserting an observable phenomenon in human society, that when interest in the choice between alternatives reaches a certain threshold, people tend to line up in groups corresponding with conflicting points of view. The groups do not have to be aligned with any existing political party, of course; a question is none the less political even where it does not fit neatly into the rigid patterns of electoral machines which have developed in Western countries over the last century.

In this sense, the whole of the preceding discussion is about politics. The exercise of looking forward to the end of the century is not a mere essay in determinism for any of the contributors; it is an attempt at identification of the choices society has to make over this period, accompanied sometimes by the value judgments of the writers.

It is convenient to classify the material of our study under four headings. First, there are the problems which have given rise already to legislation or administrative action, such as the need felt by many countries to protect their indigenous computer industries from overseas competition. Second, we have a group of questions that are going to need political solutions over the next thirty years, privacy being the most obvious of these. Third, there is a level at which computing is politically neutral, but has the indirect effect of opening up decisions that would otherwise have been impracticable, such as the US and Soviet space programmes. And finally, we must consider the effect of computing on the role of the politician and the structure of political organisations. There is enough material here to extend far beyond the space of a single chapter, and we shall therefore pick out the most important examples in each category. Partly to make the arguments more specific, and partly to utilise further earlier chapters in which we did the same for the same reason, we shall deal principally with the British scene, but we hope it will be possible to transfer the discussions to other countries fairly readily. In many cases similar problems will arise, or will already have arisen.

The observer may at first find it puzzling that practically no references to computing occur in legislation. The only example of any significance in the UK is the Post Office Data Processing Act, which extended the statutory powers of the Post Office to include the operation of a commercial data processing service. But the use of computers by nationalised industries for purposes incidental to their existing statutory functions requires no legislation, and the same applies to local authorities and government departments. The enormous growth of computing in the public sector has been, therefore, almost entirely the result of administrative decisions, and as such has escaped the notice of the public at large. Most of these decisions have been of an *ad hoc* nature, although spasmodic efforts have been made in the direction of co-ordination. For example, every local authority is an autonomous body and tends to design its own computer system with very little regard to what has been done already by others, or to the economies that might be achieved by joint development of software. The Local Authorities Management Services and Computers Committee (LAMSAC) is supposed to act as a forum in which common problems can be solved, but in practice it exercises very little influence on its members.

The fragmentary nature of the decisionmaking process is about the only important feature which is shared by the major components of the public sector: local authorities, nationalised industries, universities, the hospital service, and government departments themselves. Apart from that, each must be treated as a separate market for computing, an essential point not always readily grasped by the private sector, and within each category there is very little co-ordination of policy.

In the next ten years, this situation will change. It has been decided already that in the health service, there will be large regional computers servicing area boards on a bureau-like basis. The Computer Board is exercising a greater influence on the purchases of individual universities;

the gas and electricity boards are becoming subject to greater central direction; and the Civil Service Department, through creation of a more powerful computer organisation to include the Technical Support Unit of the Department of Trade and Industry, will exert a stronger influence on the policy of user departments.

These centralising tendencies have not arisen from the use of computers, which have been confined so far to the automation of current practices; they result from arguments concerned with managerial efficiency and economies of scale. However, the stage has now been reached, in government itself, at which the need to exchange data between separately owned files will begin to affect the organisational structure and the placing of responsibility. In Chapter 4, the establishment of a national data base containing all the information needed by government was foreseen, and the question of how it should be controlled was raised. But long before this ultimate possibility has to be entertained, decisions have to be made for subsets of the national database, to be used by two or more departments or agencies. The system for recording vehicle and driving licences, now under development by the Department of the Environment, will be accessed by the police, for instance. Here there may be no problem since the Department retains control of the system, and the police have no additional powers beyond those which apply to the manual records now kept by local authorities. However, let us consider the advantages of merging social security and income tax records.

The reason for making separate assessments on the individual for entitlement to benefits and liability for personal taxation is the difference in time scale which is sometimes involved. The social security system takes into account short term variations in need arising from circumstances like unemployment or temporary sickness, while personal taxes are assessed on the taxpayer's income for a whole year. Yet there are a very large number of recipients of benefit whose needs do not fluctuate (disregarding the effects of inflation): the elderly, and the chronically sick and disabled. Conversely there is nothing sacrosanct about the period of twelve months as a base for tax assessment and for some taxpayers, whose earnings vary widely from one year to the next, a more flexible approach would lead to greater equity. A combined system of benefits and payments would therefore have theoretical advantages, although it is impracticable with ordinary clerical methods since they would be unable to relate any short term payments to longer-term liabilities. Once this obstacle has been removed by the ability of computers to handle very large files, the Inland Revenue and the social security databases could be merged. Then it would need to be decided whether one department should own the system,

acting as an agent for the other, or the two should be brought together under a single Minister. The former solution would raise problems of ministerial accountability, while the latter would lead ultimately, as the database was extended further, to the breakdown of departmental boundaries. The concept of the functional division of responsibility would be eroded in either case, and it is difficult to imagine what might take its place.

Apart from the effects a large personal database may have on the machinery of government, it may also give rise to the sort of complaints mentioned in the discussion on privacy in Chapter 20. In order to make the problems easier to visualise, let us assume that tax and social security records are merged into a single computer-based file as outlined above. The information is quite properly collected, with the subject's knowledge, and its extent is precisely defined by statute. It cannot be given to third parties except as required by law, and Parliament could restrict the exceptions at any time it is thought expedient to do so. The safeguard against storage of wrong information would continue to be, as at present, the right of appeal to a tribunal. So the main risk, as at present, is unauthorised access to the information by outsiders; the political question is the adequacy of procedures and of technical features in the system for preventing irregular disclosure.

Recent controversies over the census and the credit rating agencies show that security is not a worse headache as a result of computerisation. In the case of the census, the information is not identifiable back to the individual once it gets onto computer tape, and the leakages which occurred were at an earlier stage, when the records were still in written form, or even in the enumerator's head. These possibilities could even be reduced if the householder were enabled to input the information through a terminal subject only to a check by the enumerator, through elimination of the data preparation stage. With the credit rating agencies, alleged to have obtained confidential material from banks, employers and officers of government departments, there was no computer involved; the remedy needed was simply better instructions to the staff concerned on verification of the identity of telephone inquirers.

This is not to say that privacy can be neglected. As we said in Chapter 20, the Younger Committee failed to satisfy critics of the lack of enforceable rights of privacy, and this will continue to be a live issue. But although computers may have helped to focus the public's mind on the problem, because of the ease of collation and speed of access which they provide, this does not mean that there are grounds for applying separate legislation to information kept on discs or tapes rather than in card indexes or ledgers. In fact, the Younger Committee in its report stated "Of all the forms of invasion of privacy which have been cited in evidence to us, that involving the use of computers has been the least supported in concrete terms", though critics of the report do point out that the committee's terms of reference did not include government databanks, and contend that it is better to forestall abuse rather than wait for it to occur.

Further, merely because computers can store and analyse facts faster does not in itself mean that individuals will be required to give more details about themselves. In a free political society such as that in Britain governments and organisations can be made to justify their need for such information, through the action of public opinion, the press, or politicians. Widespread objections were raised to some of the questions in the 1971 UK census, and governments certainly appreciate that, however admirable may be the social aims of collecting additional data, these aims are unlikely to be achieved if substantial errors are introduced as a result of widespread refusal to co-operate. The strongest fears are those not of instant repression but of the gradual erosion of personal liberty, but here again the problem is not one caused by the computers, but has always and will always exist in a democratic state. The computer is just an instrument; the politician must be aware of the instrument and the way it might be misused by a government seeking to extend its control over the individual citizen, but other than that his responsibilities as a guardian of freedom are no different than they have ever been. In any case, the judgments of the political decisionmaker very seldom depend on the availability of data, but rather on the ability to arrange the existing data to give the answers to certain questions. Here the computer will become increasingly important, as we have seen earlier, by allowing a range of assumptions to be made and the consequences evaluated. Indeed, it could be argued that the computer might in the long run reduce rather than increase the need for the collection of data, simply by enabling the data one has to be utilised more effectively.

We have earlier given a number of examples of the use of simulations for government planning, but as a further illustration of the better use of data which already exists we can consider the Registrar General's population projections, which at present give a single set of figures for each of the years covered. If one can alter the model by putting in different sets of age-specific fertility rates, migration assumptions, etc., one can then go on to calculate the differences in public expenditure (other things being equal) that would result from those new values. It can be seen from this that politicians still have to make the decisions. They have to choose one out of an infinite number of sets of assumptions, and they have to fix a level of expenditure on particular services which they consider appropriate for the age distribution resulting from those assumptions.

In general, the computer will never enable society to dispense with politicians any more than it will enable industry to do without managers or armies to do without commanders. In each case, the implications of alternative policies will be made clearer, but (artificial intelligence always excepted) the final choice will always have to be made by human beings. It is a safe bet that in thirty years there will still be pressure groups competing for money on behalf of the elderly, the mentally ill and the disabled, for as the wealth of a society increases the sights of interest groups are raised still higher. The arrangement of priorities between a number of demands for resources cannot be a process of logic; in a democratic society, it should be a reflection of the strength of the need felt by the community as a whole, or that part of it which is directly affected by the choice.

The techniques of market research, discussed in Chapter 14, will lead to improved measurement of public demand, and hence to greater responsiveness by politicians to movements of opinion. Although, as we then noted, computer-based campaigning techniques have started to be used in American Presidential elections, it does not seem likely that in the foreseeable future this will spread to Britain, or indeed most other countries. This is partly because parties tend to be short of money even for their most basic activities, and there is little chance that the value of computer-based techniques, except for a limited amount of information retrieval through a public utility from databanks to obtain or verify propaganda material, will be seen to be worth the expenditure compared with the many other demands on the funds. More important, such techniques might anyway prove not to be worth adopting when almost all the information that parties could in practice exploit effectively would be available from the published results of the independent polling organisations. These organisations, on the other hand, will certainly make greater use of computers, and the increased accuracy and more up-to-date nature of their findings would in turn mean that the parties will pay closer attention to them. This carries with it a risk of populist influences, and politicians confronted by instant referenda will need to remind themselves that in matters of law, disregard of strongly held minority views is just as much a negation of democracy as failure to take proper account of the opinions of the majority.

The social changes resulting from the use of computers are not likely to be reflected in alterations to the structure of political organisations.

Some writers have foreseen the breakdown of parties, which no longer clearly represent homogeneous economic interest groups, but they fail to account for the stability of the political system during an era when all the major parties had already become coalitions. Alvin Toffler suggests in "Future Shock" that we are "rushing towards a fateful breakdown of the entire system of political representation", yet his solution is the reinforcement of the representative principle by means of "social future assemblies" to reconnect the legislator with his popular base. It is not hard to imagine that, if we had assemblies at constituency level discussing long term social goals in Britain, they would mirror the Westminster party set up, and would rapidly equip themselves with the apparatus of leaders, whips and spokesmen.

It is a fair criticism of the parties that they never ask electors what kind of a world they would like to see in ten, twenty or thirty years' time, because there is always a strong temptation to think in terms of the interval between elections or even worse, the remaining time before the next election is due to be held. Unfortunately, the ultimate goals likely to commend themselves may be irreconcilable with immediate popular demands. For instance, while recognising that exponential growth cannot be sustained indefinitely, most people in the developed world have come to expect a steadily increasing real disposable income. Drawing attention to such inconsistencies would not help to win votes, so the parties will leave it to bodies like the Club of Rome to devise and advocate uncomfortable long term policies. The study "Limits to Growth", undertaken at the MIT under the sponsorship of the Club of Rome, was the first attempt to relate population, resources and pollution on a global scale and with a time scale measured in decades, using a computer model. Its findings were attacked on grounds that need not concern us here, but few people doubt that, with improvements to the model, valid conclusions can be drawn. In Chapter 8, a case was made out for the United Nations having control of computing systems of universal importance to all countries, of which disaster prediction and weather forecasting generally was cited as an example. Logically, the work begun by the Club of Rome should be taken up by the UN and we can perhaps expect this to happen, resources permitting, within the next ten years.

If there is a political objection to the expansion of computing power under the control of the UN and its agencies, it is that it might strengthen the hold of American computer firms in world markets. National control of information technology has been, for the last few years, a major preoccupation of industrialised countries other than the United States. Japan, Britain, West Germany and France in particular are determined to have capabilities of their own, and to lessen dependence on the locally based subsidiaries of the US giants. So far this ambition has manifested itself almost entirely as financial support for one or a few mainframe manufacturers, but this can be expected to change as peripherals, tele-communications and software gain increasing shares of the total systems market. With Britain's entry into Europe, there is likely also to be in-creasing emphasis on multilateral co-operation between European firms as a means of countering US competition. It must be admitted that up to now the steps taken in this direction have had no impact whatsoever, and that since the computer industry in Western Europe is in the private sector, governments can do no more than encourage their national companies to get together. In the enlarged EEC, however, there will be greater impetus towards cross-frontier mergers of all kinds, particularly when company law and taxation have been harmonised. Moreover, it is possible that before the end of the century computing will have become such a vital component in the economy of Europe that public ownership of the industry will be seen as essential. By that time also, we may have seen the first takeovers by nationalist governments of locally-based subsidiaries of foreign-owned multinational corporations, as has already occurred e.g. in the oil and chemical industries.

Meanwhile, the scale of assistance to the chosen instruments of purely national computer policies may be expected to grow, both in the form of R and D grants, and preferential buying policies. As we have seen, ICL alone is to receive £14·2 millions from the UK government towards its R and D expenditure in the fifteen-month period ending September 1973, and it is well worth noting that this compares with a *total* sum of £4·5 millions made available to all R and D contractors in the year 1969-70. In addition, most orders for government computers are placed with ICL by single tender, subject to satisfactory price, performance and delivery.

There are some who believe that, in spite of these favourable conditions, European manufacturers of large processors cannot survive indefinitely in the face of IBM's dominance of world markets. IBM already holds about two-thirds of the market in Western Europe other than the UK, and the Europeans hold a negligible share of the market in third countries, excep for Eastern Europe and the Commonwealth. It cannot be denied that, in Britain, users have doubts concerning the future viability of ICL, which may be self-fulfilling if they lead to "playing safe" with IBM.

Whilst there is some recognition of these dangers gradually dawning on British politicians, as we have said before they have yet to face up to them adequately. In the early 1970s the commitment undertaken by the Labour administration when ICL was formed in 1968 was coming to an end, and for the time being there were no plans for continuing support. When it became apparent that further aid was necessary, the plan announced was, as we have seen, only short-term, thus creating the unfortunate impression that at the end of the period the company's future might again be in jeopardy. Nor, when this book went to press, had there been any indication of any real appreciation of the need to encourage the design and manufacture of minicomputer systems, or of the importance of creating a flourishing software industry. By the time this book appears, it is possible that some of these shortcomings will have been removed; but there are still no generally accepted principles for deciding the amounts of public money to be spent, or the objectives to be sought, in computing as a whole.

Yet, as we hope we have shown, the need for politicians well versed in computers and their potential is greater than ever. Quite apart from the politics and economics of the control of the computer industry, many other problems will require informed and balanced judgment in the years to come, in education, in defence, in finance, over law enforcement, over privacy, and many other matters.

Politicians necessarily to some extent have to be jacks-of-all-trades; although there are many other urgent matters to claim their attention, many other major issues calling for their knowledge and judgment, sooner or later they will have to come to terms with computers. The trouble in countries like Britain is that it may be later rather than sooner, so much so that it will be too late for them to exercise any effective influence.

22

The tasks ahead

Of course, when we said in the last chapter that the discussion about the impact of computers on the British political scene could be readily transferred to other countries, this was not to imply that all of the same problems would recur with the same emphasis elsewhere.

As we remarked at the outset, it would certainly be presumptuous and arrogant to suggest that the troubles which Britain has got into as a result of shortsightedness will be repeated elsewhere, and we noted in particular the difference between the interest in computers shown by British Members of Parliament and members of the Japanese Diet. What other countries who are less advanced in computer development may be able to do is learn from the mistakes of others, and by interpreting them in the light of their own circumstances be ready for the problems when they arise, or even avoid them altogether. The nations which can first fully exploit the computer will certainly be at an advantage in the years to come.

Nor will the political issues that will arise be the same in every country. For example, we have seen that the two major current issues in Britain are those of independence of American hardware, and of privacy, and these can be expected to continue to be of importance indefinitely, but this may not be true elsewhere. Politicians in a totalitarian state may not worry themselves much about individual privacy, while those in a small country may recognise that perforce they will be dependent on foreign hardware, and their only choice will be whether this will be from the USA or from some other country. On the other hand, privacy may be a very important issue in the small country, while the totalitarian regime might

289

be very concerned to build up an independent computer industry. In both the question of merging of departmental files could become important, though in the totalitarian state this might well be fought out wholly internally. Nevertheless, politics are still real even if limited to a ruling elite.

Many of the problems we have mentioned in this book will enter the political arena in different countries, to different extents, at different times; some of the reasons for such differences we have already discussed in Chapter 8. Extensive use of computer techniques in defence, education, banking, or similar important and perhaps sensitive areas, or the possible provision of a public utility, are clearly matters which could become politically live given an appropriate set of circumstances. However, there is little point either in going again over the many possible issues which have been discussed earlier, often in some detail, or in trying to visualise all the possible contingencies which might arise. Rather we shall be concerned, in this final chapter, with summing up the kinds of tasks that decisionmakers will have to tackle in the years to come, and the kinds of attitudes that will be required if they are to have any chance of coming to terms with the challenge which the computer represents.

To understand fully what the nature and extent of that challenge is represents the first and perhaps most important responsibility of any decisionmaker. There are two parts to this: recognition of the potential of computers in the area with which the decisionmaker is concerned, and awareness of the new problems which their introduction might create. We have already seen how lack of understanding of the potential of computers effectively determined the present structure of the world computer industry; sheer economics might have meant that in time American firms would dominate, as in so many other fields, but certainly not to the present extent. And there are many who believe that lack of understanding of the problems of databank access will in due course lead to unacceptable levels of privacy invasion, since legislative and technical safeguards will not be introduced in time to prevent it. These are two examples, one actual and one potential, of the decision-by-default situation, one which we have mentioned before we are particularly anxious to see avoided.

To allow a decision to be taken through chance of circumstance, and the co-ordinated or unco-ordinated actions of others, as a result of one's own inaction or lack of awareness is an abrogation of responsibility. It is no defence to be able to say with hindsight that there was nothing one could have done about it anyway; it may be better for a gambler to be lucky than to be knowledgeable about the horses on which he is betting, but in the real world, especially on a matter as important and fundamental as this, the luxury of the attitude "it will turn out all right in the end, somehow" cannot be afforded.

It may be thought that the answer is simply to leave all such decisions to the computer professionals. However, there are a number of reasons why the experts here should be on tap only, and not on top. Computer professionals are as ambitious, as prone to enthusiasms, and as naturally optimistic about the outcome of a project as other people. A good professional will not allow these factors to cloud his judgment, but too much may be involved to take the risk. More important than this, the expert in the field of application should be able to see a wider picture, and perhaps see consequential problems in an area where the computer development is not directly involved, but on which it has repercussions. It is for this reason that his role is the central one.

Nevertheless, the traps into which he can fall are many. He can fail to see the potential of computers, through blissful or wilful ignorance or through overawareness of the problems rather than the opportunities. On the other hand, he may see only the possibilities, and push through a development far faster than he should have done. The two sources of danger in such a situation are that necessary safeguards are left out, through lack of appreciation of their importance, or simply to cut costs, or lack of the requisite techniques; and that, even apart from this, a system may be developed which works much less efficiently or flexibly than it should, but into which too much time, effort and money will have been sunk to be able to change it. It is an important responsibility of the computer professionals involved in such cases to point out the safeguards needed and what the technical possibilities are, but if dangers are going to arise outside the actual development in the way mentioned above it may be quite unreasonable to expect him to be aware of them.

Perhaps the worst kind of trap, worst because it is so difficult to guard against, is where the decisionmaker *thinks* he knows enough about computers: he has read a few articles, attended a one-day appreciation course, visited a computer centre, and is certain that he now knows all he needs to know to make his decisions. It is hard to see what can be done about this, but it does stress the responsibility of the people, particularly the technical journalists, who write the articles, and of those who provide appreciation courses, both to maintain a high professional standard and to stimulate such top administrators and others to think more, rather than believe they are fully equipped.

The same general comments apply to the other classes of non-specialist decisionmakers in a position to influence computer development. Leaders of organisations such as trade unions or professional bodies may have a specially difficult role to play. They will have to determine what are the implications of computer developments for their members; they will have to decide whether the effects are beneficial or detrimental, both in the short and the long terms; they will have to consider whether such developments are actually to the benefit of society as a whole, no matter whether their members suffer or not, and whether they are inevitable or it is possible to stop them, and if so how, or, if they are not inevitable but would in fact be beneficial, how to bring them about. All this will call for a rare integrity and the ability to take a wider view, one not circumscribed by traditional attitudes, concentration on short-term problems and solutions, insistence on traditional but outmoded rights and practices, and disregard of anything other than sectional interests. They may properly and as their duty fight for those interests; but they will need to be able to see beyond them.

But, of course, the main responsibility for taking a wider view will lie with the other main group of non-specialist decisionmakers, the politicians. We have already discussed their role at some length, but it is worth stressing again, especially as very often they will be the ones who will have to decide between the conflicting claims of commercial interests, labour organisations, computer manufacturers, computer professionals, government departments and the public. They, above all, must make themselves aware of all the possible implications of computer development, not just those in a particular area. It is worth reiterating the point made in the last chapter, that in this respect at least they must look beyond the next opinion poll or the next television interview. Even apart from questions of legislation or the expenditure of public funds, the capacity for taking an overall view and for balancing conflicting interests—which is an essential skill of the good politician—is something which will be badly needed during the formative years of the computer-based society, something too valuable to be subordinated to ephemeral party advantage.

Mention of the public is a reminder that the individual citizen too has a role to play, even if his decisionmaking function is minimal or non-existent. Though it would be a pity if the growing disenchantment with computer systems which we have noted earlier were to develop into outright Luddism, it is certainly of value if everyone who suffers from a bad or impersonal computer system complains about it, everyone refuses to accept the excuse, "it's the computer", for inefficient service, everyone whose privacy seems to have been invaded through misuse of a databank tries to seek redress. The best guarantee of the perpetuation of slovenly systems and antisocial activities will be public indifference.

But the greatest influence in the years to come, if in many cases not the ultimate responsibility, will lie with the computing world itself — the specialist industry, and the computer professionals. They, after all, know the capabilities and the limitations of computers; they know what they might be used for, and how they might be misused, even if they may not be able to see all the implications in a particular area. It is the equipment and services which they will provide, the techniques which they will develop, and the advice which they will give, that will largely determine the way that things will develop.

We distinguish between the industry and computer professionals, even though the industry is composed of professionals, for two reasons. One is that some professionals work not for the industry but for customers, educational institutions, the press, and so on; the other is that an aggregation of individuals often has a collective personality very different from what one might expect by considering the separate personalities of its components. In the case of an organisation like a business firm this arises because the individuals modify their behaviour to accord with what is in the best interests of the organisation — i.e., in a commercial case, its profitability and prestige. However, this is not confined to commercial organisations, since in any enterprise, profit-making or not, individual advancement or standing depends on demonstrable willingness to advance what are seen to be the interests of the organisation as a whole.

The problems arise because very often the success of an organisation, whether measured in profitability or otherwise, tends to be inhibited by concern for social responsibility. On the other hand, demonstrable concern for social responsibility can increase prestige. Where there is such a conflict, each organisation evolves its own balance between the two factors. In the case of gun manufacturers, anything which increases the sales of weapons is commercially advantageous, and so one has the notorious "gun lobby" in the United States, perhaps the best-known example of blatant lack of social concern. We have already noted in Chapter 5 existence of some degree of moral responsibility of computer manufacturers involved in defence contracts, but perhaps a better analogy is the case of car manufacturers, in particular their record over car safety. Their attitude, certainly in recent years, has not been one of violent opposition to, e.g. the imposition of stricter speed limits, which is what a gun lobby kind of mentality would have involved; rather it has been one of washing the hands, absolving themselves of a responsibility which they claim lies with governments, to introduce safety legislation which their competitors as well as themselves would have to abide by, or with the consumers, who should demand safety features and make them commercially viable. In some cases they have gone so far as to imply that they wanted to introduce such features but could not afford to do so.

Now, in fact, it is not difficult to believe that the individuals comprising a car firm might, virtually to a man, believe singly that cars should be much safer than they are. Collectively, however, they seem to have found it impossible to introduce many safety features, or even offer them as optional extras and encourage motorists to buy them, or even commit modest sums to the necessary basic research. Further, very commonly, car advertising, styling, and even naming of models has been based on speed, power and aggression to the exclusion of virtually everything else, or to comfort, luxury and superiority; very seldom to safety. It needed a Ralph Nader to force the car manufacturers to begin to take their social responsibilities seriously.

We have described this at some length because we feel it is of particular importance that the computer industry — hardware, or even more especially, software — should not allow itself to get into a state where another Ralph Nader (or the same one) will be needed to force systems to be safe, accurate, reliable, and impossible to corrupt or misuse. We have stressed often enough in the preceding pages the troubles which can arise from poor systems, and inasmuch as the hardware and software industries are providing systems to their customers, they clearly have a duty to provide systems which are as good as they can make them. The danger is that it is so easy to fall into the temptation of undercutting an opponent's price and delivery time, and offering a faster system using less computing power, by cutting corners and eliminating all the fail-safe devices which a good system should have. Of course, the customer should specify that he wants these features, but as systems become more "off the peg" instead of custom-built, as more inexperienced new users of computer methods come on the scene, the more the dangers will grow. It is compounded in this case, as we said in Chapter 2, by the fact that a software product is not in any true sense a physical object; in the case of a car, some at least of the safety features, or their absence, are obvious to all.

If the danger for the software industry is that by 1990 there will be a need for an "Unsafe With Any Input", the danger for the hardware industry is that it may fail to provide what the world really needs. It is possible to fall into habits of competing along given lines, and to condition one's customers into judging on the same criteria. At present, manufacturers make much of processing speeds, memory access time, and storage capacity, whereas it is already true for some users, and will increasingly become the case, that it is the suitability of given kinds of peripheral, and the ease of dealing with such peripherals and with the kinds of software required, which are the really important factors. Computer scientists have been pointing out more and more in recent years that it is no longer sufficient, as in the past, to design the central hardware first and then think about tacking on peripherals and designing the software afterwards; there are signs that the manufacturers have followed this advice, but it is something which could easily get lost in the rush for future orders.

Another possibility in this connection is that hardware manufacturers, especially if dependent on support from prestige-conscious America-fearing governments, might feel it necessary to keep up with the race as far as the enormous, ultrapowerful, number-crunching processors are concerned. Yet, as our earlier discussion of public utilities and other networks showed, it could well come about that the requirement for such machines (though admittedly they would probably be much more powerful than any available today) would be relatively limited, and despite their enormous unit cost the major part of a nation's computer investment would not be in these but in perhaps millions of small processors used as links to and connections between them. It could, quite simply, be better business and a better national investment to concentrate on making these as cheap, efficient and reliable as possible, reckoning to buy one's massive processors from the multinational giants whether American-dominated or not, than in spending vast sums in parallel activities to such firms. The same applies to the myriad of peripherals which will be required. The car industry recognised long ago (at least after Henry Ford) that the real market was in the small family saloon; in this respect at least the computer hardware industry should perhaps, as a whole, follow its example rather than that of the prestige-conscious aircraft industry.

So we come to the computer professional, possibly, if we had to choose one, the key figure in future developments. The reasons for his key position, and the role which he should play, should be quite apparent from what has gone before and does not need to be repeated again in great detail. If he works in the specialist industry, he can help by his actions and by contact with his colleagues to influence it along the directions we have indicated. If he works in an advisory or executive capacity for a customer organisation, he can help to ensure that systems obtained or developed internally are of the highest professional standard.

If he works in a research establishment working on artificial intelligence, he will have a special responsibility. We have already noted in various places throughout this book how crucial the development of genuine artificial intelligence might be. Research workers in the field must be particularly concerned to see that the intellectual excitement of their work, especially when they are nearing a breakthrough, does not blind them to the implications in a wider context of what success could mean. The problems will almost certainly be of the greatest difficulty for those engaged in artificial intelligence research in military establishments; we have already cited the earlier example of the atomic scientists who developed the Hiroshima bomb. The remaining discussion will be concerned with professional ethics generally, but it will be clear that the problems for the specialist in military applications of AI will be particularly acute.

We have already mentioned in Chapter 1 the moves to establish standards of professional ethics and codes of conduct for computer personnel. This is an encouraging sign. If one duty is particularly indicated here, it is that the professional perceives a possible social consequence or potential danger, he should not wait to be asked for his advice before pointing it out, but should draw the attention of those ultimately responsible to its existence. It is very easy to discharge one's professional obligations formally by confining one's advice narrowly to the letter of the questions one is asked but, as we have seen, there are too many places of doubt in current and likely future developments for such luxuries to be afforded. Decisions in these formative years of the computer-based society could be so important that everyone has to ask himself if he has the moral right to opt out.

In this context it is certainly worthy of comment that a leading part in the public raising of the databank privacy issue has been played by computer professionals. Others, not surprisingly, have as a reaction taken a more optimistic line; some, more worryingly, have seemed to regard any suggestion that there might be any cause for concern with complete indignation. Similarly, in the moves towards professional standards that have taken place in the UK, some have apparently seen this less as a means of maintaining high standards as a way to enhance status and to move towards a closed shop. This reminds one that professional organisations do not necessarily exist to raise or hold standards, but can simply serve to propagate the sectional interests of their members. Further, even when high standards of ethics and moral responsibility are laid down and enforced for behaviour at individual level, this by no means guarantees that the profession as a whole has a socially responsible attitude: one can cite the opposition of doctors to national health or medicare services, effectively through being worried about their standards not of professional service but of living, despite the previous problems of their fees being outside the pocket of some of the community; or the high fees and the existence of restrictive practices in the legal profession which tend to rule litigation literally out of court for many. The twin dangers for the professional organisations to avoid are of protectionism and complacency.

And, indeed, if there is one fault which decisionmakers of all kinds who will be able to influence the developments described in this book, it is that of complacency. It is complacency which makes people think they can know all the answers after only a superficial examination of the problems. It is complacency which leads to the attitudes, "it can't happen to me", "it will work out all right somehow", "nobody could possibly make that mistake". It is complacency which leads to decisions by default.

We who have combined to produce this book have not attempted to draw a picture of what the world will be like by the year 2000. We do not claim greater gifts of prophecy than others; whatever mental pictures we may individually have of that year doubtless vary greatly. But of one thing we are certain, and on one thing we are agreed: that world will be very different from the world today. It may be different for one or more of several reasons — because of overpopulation, or environmental disaster, or nuclear holocaust, to mention just three of the most importance. We have only considered how the world may change through the effect of computers; we hope we have been able to show that, if these other major factors give them a chance, computers could be the greatest single cause of the differences between the world of now and the world of the twenty-first century.

We hope also that we have demonstrated that the changes need not come about by chance. There are many, many places in which a conscious choice will be able to be made by those with the power of decision, and the process of computer development is still sufficiently in its infancy, still so much in its formative stage, that the influence of those decisions could be profound. This state of affairs will, however, not continue indefinitely; as time passes, situation after situation in different areas of computer application will pass beyond the stage where major changes will be possible. Systems will become set, the range of options will narrow, wrong decisions will not, for all practical purposes, be reversible. By the year 2000 the pattern for much of the twenty-first century, at least in this respect, may well be determined.

We have before us, then, some thirty years of opportunity — opportunity, hopefully, to move towards a world in which human drudgery will be less and fulfilment more complete, in which computers are used to enrich people's lives and not degrade or enslave them. Opportunities to take decisions of such magnitude are rare and valuable, and should not be wasted, even partially; and there is still time. Let us try to see that our decisions are informed decisions, taken consciously and rationally. Let us, in this respect at least, try to find the future we want, rather than drift on, in the hope that the future we want will come to us.

Appendices

Bibliography

A few points should be noted about this bibliography. Firstly, we have tried to confine ourselves to readily-available material — books, reports or pamphlets — rather than magazine articles, papers in technical journals, etc. Secondly, even of that material we have only made a selection of what exists; to have included everything would virtually have required a second volume. Others would certainly have made a different selection, and we apologise to authors whose titles might validly have been included. Thirdly, some areas are covered better than others in books rather than technical articles, and this is reflected in the selection. Finally, although we have tried to group references under chapters, the groupings are to some extent arbitrary, particularly in the case of those (e.g. under Chapter 15) which cover a general theme.

Part One: The Background

Chapter 1

There are many introductory books on computers, including:

1.1   Davis, G. B.: *An introduction to electronic computers* (McGraw-Hill 1965). A general introduction to the concepts and basic features of electronic computers.

1.2   Hollingdale, S. H. and Toothill, G. C.: *Electronic computers* (Penguin Books, 1970). Explains how computers work, how problems are presented to them, and what sort of jobs they can tackle.

1.3   London, K.: *Introduction to computers* (Faber, 1971). A non-technical, descriptive introduction.

1.4   Pylyshyn, Z. W.: *Perspectives on the computer revolution* (Prentice-Hall, 1970). A reader consisting mainly of collected papers, with commentary, by authors such as Babbage, von Neumann, and Turing; something of relevance to most chapters of this book.

1.5   Rosenberg, J.: *The computer prophets* (Collier-Macmillan, 1969). Biographies of the men who developed what we know today as the computer.

Other books relevant to this chapter are listed under later chapters, particularly the remainder of Part One, and Chapter 13.

Chapter 2

2.1   Fox, L. (ed.): *Advances in programming and non-numerical computation* (Pergamon, 1966). An historical account of the development of programming and a discussion of the theory of communicating with the computer.

2.2   Heath, F.: *Digital computer design* (Oliver and Boyd, 1969). For electronic engineers wishing to learn how to design hardware for digital computers.

2.3   Infotech Ltd.: *"State of the art" reports* (Infotech, 1971). A series of reports on the state of computer technology. Of particular relevance are "The fourth generation", on the computer systems likely to be developed in the 1970s, "Real time", "Computing terminals", "Computing networks" and "Interactive computing".

2.4   Martin, F. F.: *Computer modelling and simulation* (Wiley, 1968). A description of a powerful technique with a wide range of applications.

See also later references, particularly under Chapter 9, and the July 1972 edition (Volume 15, No. 7) of the Communications of the Association for Computing Machinery, which celebrates the first twenty-five years of the ACM and has a large number of articles looking forward to future developments in computing.

Chapter 3

3.1   Andrew, A. M.: *Brains and computers* (Harrap, 1963). Provides a basis for speculation by explaining what computers are and what they can do and by treating brains similarly.

3.2   Carne, E. B.: *Artificial intelligence techniques* (Macmillan, 1965).
       A practical summary of electronic techniques for simulating human
       intelligence.

3.3   George, F. H.: *The brain as a computer* (Pergamon 1961).

3.4   George, F. H.: *Science and the crisis in society* (Wiley, 1970).

3.5   Neumann, J. von: *The computer and the brain* (Yale UP, 1967).

3.6   Nilsson, N. J.: *Learning machines; foundations of trainable pattern-
       classifying systems* (McGraw-Hill, 1965).

3.7   Vorwald and Clarke: *Computers from sand table to electronic brain*
       (Lutterworth, 1968). Traces the history of computers from the
       earliest times, and examines the work done by the digital computer.

There is a discussion of neural nets in reference 6.5; see also 18.7.

Part Two: The World of Government

Chapter 4

4.1   Civil Service Department: *Computers in central government, ten
       years ahead* (HMSO, 1969). An estimate of the likely future
       requirements for computers in the central government of the UK.

4.2   Hearle, E. (ed.): *Automation in government* (American Society for
       Public Administration 1963). A symposium on the application of
       automation to problems of government.

4.3   Rubertson, J. H.: *The design of information-processing systems for
       government* (HMSO, 1967). Discusses problems of cost analysis,
       statistical analysis and, more generally, systems for classifying
       information.

Chapter 5

5.1   Elliott-Automation Ltd.: *About F.A.C.E.; the Field Artillery
       Computer Equipment*.

5.2   Hughes, A. D.: *Multi-computer data processing system for Navy
       command and control system* (Auerbach, 1963). Presented to the
       national convention of military electronics.

5.3   IBM Corporation: *United States Army logistics simulation with the
       IBM RAMAC*. Keeping records, scenario processing and score
       calculating.
       See also 18.7.

Chapter 6

6.1   Elliott Medical Automation Ltd.: *Proceedings of a one-day symposium on progress in medical computing* (1965).

6.2   Enslein and Kinslow: *Data acquisition and processing in biology and medicine* (Pergamon, 1966). Proceedings of the 1964 Rochester conference, Oxford.

6.3   Ledley and Wilson: *Use of computers in biology and medicine* (McGraw-Hill, 1965). Intended to stimulate the use of computers in those fields.

6.4   McLachlan and Stegog: *Computers in the service of medicine* (Oxford UP, 1968). Computers in arrangements for the improvement of patient care.

6.5   Stacy, R. W. and Waxman, B. D. (eds.): *Computers in biomedical research* (Academic Press, 1965, 2 vols.). A collection of papers on computer applications in medical and biological research.

6.6   Taylor, T. R.: *The principles of medical computing* (Blackwell, 1967). Straightforward guide to computers and their potentialities both in clinical and in academic contexts.

Chapter 7

7.1   British Computer Society: *Educational Yearbook* 1971/72. This issue of the yearbook contains a special survey, in a series of articles, of computer-aided instruction.

7.2   Broderick, W. R.: *The computer in school* (Bodley Head, 1968). The relevance of the computer to the teaching of mathematics in school, by the founder and head of the computer department at Royal Liberty School, Romford, UK.

7.3   Centre for educational research and innovation: *Computer sciences in secondary education* (OECD, 1971). Mainly about computing as a subject in the school curriculum, but with some reference to other aspects.

7.4   Grossman and Howe: *Data processing for educators* (Educational methods, 1965). The concept of a school information system presented as an integrated information system which would tie together aspects of the instructional and administrative programme.

7.5   Margolin, J. B. and Misch, M. R.: *Computers in the classroom* (Spartan Books, 1970). An account of the work and findings of a travelling seminar which toured the United States, including some proposals for educational policy.

7.6   National Council for Educational Technology: *Computer-based learning — a programme for action* (1969). A pamphlet containing policy proposals for the development of CAI in the UK.

Chapter 8

8.1   United Nations Department of Economic and Social Affairs: *The application of computer technology for development* (1971). Report prepared for the Secretary-General of the UN on the implications of computer technology, especially for developing nations.

8.2   Vernon, R.: *Sovereignty at bay: the multinational spread of US enterprises* (Longman, 1971). Results of a programme of intensive research into the problems faced by multinational companies undertaken by the Harvard Business School.

Part Three: The World of Industry and Organization

Chapter 9

9.1   Martin, James: *Design of real-time computer systems* (Prentice-Hall, 1967). Emphasises real-time commercial systems, their special problems and dangers.

9.2   Martin, James: *Telecommunications and the computer* (Prentice-Hall, 1969). Discusses the potentialities of the combination of the two technologies.

9.3   Parkhill, D.: *The challenge of the computer utility* (Addison-Wesley, 1966). An extensive summary of the subject discussing the history, technology and economics of the computer utility.

9.4   Phillips, A.: *Computer peripherals and typesetting* (HMSO, 1968). A study of the man-machine interface incorporating a survey of computer peripherals and typographic composing equipment.
See also 2.3, and later references such as 15.4 and 15.8.

Chapter 10

10.1   British Computer Society: *Computing in the city*. Covers difficulties and potentialities, includes both banking and insurance and describes actual applications.

10.2   Data Processing: *Current accounts on a computer*. Reprinted from "Data Processing", July/September, 1960. Banks in general; updating accounts, statistics, statements, balance sheets.

10.3   Institution of Electrical Engineers: *Electronic aids to banking* (1962). Conference report on users' problems, on document handling and on communications aspects.

10.4   Williamson, J. P.: *Investments: new analytic techniques* (Longman, 1971). Quantitive methods using computers for the management of investments.

10.5   Yavitz, B.: *Automation in commercial banking* (Columbia University Free Press, 1967). The introduction of computers into commercial banking presented as a case history of automation.

See also other references, in particular 9.1.

Chapter 11

11.1   Foster, D.: *Modern automation* (Pitman and Rowse Muir, 1963). Intended to explain the possibilities of industrial automation to management in British industry.

11.2   Lockwood, F. B.: *Fundamentals of numerical control* (Machinery Publishing, 1970). Principles and techniques of numerically controlled systems, for engineers.

11.3   Mischke: *An introduction to computer-aided design* (Prentice-Hall, 1968).

11.4   National Computing Centre: *Computer-aided production control* 1967). A brief survey of practical experience in the UK.

11.5   Trusler, J. D. C.: *Production control by computer* (Machinery Publishing, 1970). An explanation for managers of the principles of computerised production control.

Chapter 12

12.1   Anderman, S. D.: *Trade unions and technological change* (Allen and Unwin, 1967). Particular reference to unemployment.

12.2   Chorafas, D. N.: *Selecting the computer system* (Gee, 1967). For executives directly responsible for the choice of data processing equipment and its implementation.

12.3   Hart, B. L. J.: *Dynamic systems design: company control for the computer era* (Business Publications, 1964). On the fundamental problem of change in business.

12.4   International Institute for Labour Studies: *Employment problems of automation and advanced technology* (IILS/Macmillan, 1966). Methods of studying the effects of automation, and the rate and route of advanced technology in the next decade.

12.5   Losty, P. A.: *The effective use of computers in business* (Cassell, 1969).

12.6   McKinsey: *Unlocking the computer's profit potential* (McKinsey, 1968). Research report to management based on thirty-six major companies.

12.7   Mills, A. E.: *The dynamics of management control systems* (Business Publications, 1967). An attempt to integrate theory, techniques, environment and human behaviour.

12.8   National Commission on Technology, Automation and Economic Progress: *Technology and the American economy* (US Govt., 1966).

12.9   National Computing Centre: *Using computers: a guide for the manager* (1971). Non-technical guide to the problems which will be encountered and the consequences which will face any member of the management team wishing to reap the long-term benefits of using computers.

Chapter 13

13.1   Japan Computer Usage Development Institute: *Computer white papers* (annually). Reports on the state of computing in Japan and the activities of the various public bodies involved.

13.2   Moonman, E. (ed.): *British computers and industrial innovation* (Allen & Unwin, 1970). Arose out of the first phase of the Select Committee's work (see 13.5) before the 1970 UK General Election.

13.3   OECD: *Gaps in technology: computers* (1969). Report of an investigation into the technological gap between Europe and America in computing.

13.4   Rodgers, W.: *THINK* (Weidenfeld and Nicholson, 1970, Panther, 1971). A biography of the Watson family and IBM.

13.5   Select Committee on Science and Technology: *The prospects for the United Kingdom computer industry in the* 1970's (HMSO, 1971). The report referred to in Chapters 1, 13 and 21 resulting from an enquiry into the UK computer industry by a House of Commons committee, recommending increased government support. See also 13.2.

13.6   Stsepinsky, I. and Judd, R.: *Report on some aspects of the application of computer science in the USSR* (National Computing Centre, 1967).

Chapter 14

14.1 Alderson, W. and Shapiro, S. J. (eds.): *Marketing and the computer* (Prentice-Hall, 1963). A collection of articles by operations experts designed to explain the application of computers in the field of marketing.

14.2 Amstutz, A. E.: *Computer simulation of competitive market response* (MIT Press, 1967). Presents elements of an organised behavioural theory of market interactivities.

Part Four: The World of Human Values

Chapter 15

The division of books on the social implications of computers between this chapter and Chapter 17 is largely arbitrary.

15.1 Hamming, R. W.: *Computers and society* (McGraw-Hill, 1972).

15.2 Hargreaves, John: *Computers and the changing world* (Hutchinson, 1967). What computers do, and their effects on various sections of the community, particularly on management.

15.3 Hargreaves, John: *Computers in a world of change* (IBM United Kingdom Ltd., 1969). Lecture to the Guardian Business Group, from which some of Chapter 15 is drawn.

15.4 Martin, James and Norman, Adrian: *The computerised society* (Prentice-Hall, 1970). An appraisal of the impact of computers on society over the next fifteen years.

15.5 Matusow, H.: *The beast of business: a record of computer atrocities* (Wolfe, 1968). The misuse of computers, and a do-it-yourself guide for the citizen to fight back.

15.6 Murphy, Brian M.: *The computer in society* (Blond, 1966).

15.7 Murphy, Brian M.: *Computers in your life* (Hutchinson, 1971).

15.8 Sackman, H.: *Mass information utilities and social excellence* Auerbach, 1971).

15.9 Taviss, Irene (ed.): *Computers and society* (Prentice-Hall, 1970).

Chapter 16

16.1 Bray, J.: *The politics of the environment* (Fabian Society, 1972). Includes a critical assessment of "Limits to Growth" (16.8).

16.2   Campion: *Computers in architectural design* (Elsevier, 1968).
        A general introduction to computers followed by a discussion of
        several applications to architectural design.

16.3   Danforth, P. M.: *Transport control — a technology on the move*
        (Aldus Books, 1970). Popular presentation of transport control
        technology and practice in general.

16.4   Felix, F.: *World markets of tomorrow* (Harper and Row, 1972).
        Presents a model of the world, postulating gradually declining rate
        of economic growth; includes a criticism of "Limits to growth"
        (16.8).

16.5   Institute of Civil Engineers: *Area control of road traffic* (1967).
        Proceedings of a symposium held in London in 1967, reviewing
        computer control of traffic lights in urban street networks.

16.6   Institute of Electrical and Electronic Engineers (New York):
        Proceedings Vol. 56 No. 4 (April 1968) is a special issue on applica-
        tions of electronics and computing to transport, and *Transactions
        on Vehicular Technology* Vol. VT19 No. 1 (February 1970) is a
        special issue on automatic vehicle guidance and control.

16.7   Lane, R., Powell, T. J. and Prestwood Smith, P.: *Analytical
        transport planning* (Duckworth 1971). Presents and reviews modern
        land use and transport study methods, with a comprehensive
        and analytic review of past and present techniques.

16.8   Meadows, D. H., Meadows, D. L., Randres, J. and Behrens,
        W. W. III: *The limits to growth* (Earth Island, 1972). Semi-popular
        and widely publicised presentation of the attempt by an MIT
        research team to simulate the behaviour of the world, including
        environmental effects, on a computer, and to indicate how mankind
        can achieve the state of equilibrium necessary to its survival.

16.9   Wren, A.: *Computers in transport planning and operation* (Ian
        Allan, 1971). Refers especially to applications of computers to
        vehicle scheduling.

Chapter 17

17.1   de Ferranti, B.: *Living with the computer* (Oxford UP, 1971).

17.2   Greenberger,   (ed.): *Computers and the world of the future*
        (MIT Press, 1962).

17.3   Tatham, Laura: *Computers in everyday life* (Pelham, 1970).

Chapter 18

18.1 Bisco, R. L. (ed.): *Databases, computers and the social sciences* (Wiley, 1970).

18.2 Bowles, E. A. (ed.): *Computers in humanistic research* (Prentice-Hall, 1967). Papers on subjects such as anthropology, archaeology, history, language, literature, musicology.

18.3 Fernbach, S. and Taub A. H. (eds.): *Computers and their role in the physical sciences* (Gordon and Breach, 1970).

18.4 Franke, H. W.: *Computer graphics — computer art* (Phaidon, 1971). Illustrated text covering aspects of computer art.

18.5 Gretzkow, H. (ed.): *Simulation in social science* (Prentice-Hall, 1962).

18.6 Hiller and Isaacson: *Experimental music* (McGraw-Hill, 1959). Composition with an electronic computer at the School of Music, Illinois University.

18.7 Knight, D. E., Curtis, H. W. and Fogel, L. J. (eds.): *Cybernetics, simulation and conflict resolution* (Spartan Books, 1971).

18.8 Metropolitan Museum of Art: *Computers and their potential applications in museums* (Arno Press, 1968).

18.9 Reichardt, J.: *The computer in art* (Studio Vista, 1971). Comprehensive and well-illustrated text on computer art.

18.10 Sonquist, J. N. and Morgan, J. N.: *The detection of interaction effects* (Institute for Social Research, Michigan University, 1964).

Chapter 19

19.1 Christensen, J. M.: *The use of computers and related systems in US law enforcement* (Stanford Research Institute, 1968). Centralised records as an aid to combating the increasing crime rate.

19.2 IBM Corporation: *Florida law enforcement communications system.* Report on the successful use of modern computer-based law enforcement by the State of Florida.

Chapter 20

20.1 British Computer Society: *Submission of evidence to the Committee on Privacy* (1971) and *Privacy and the computer — steps to practicality* (1972).

20.2 JUSTICE: *Privacy and the law* (Stevens, 1970).

20.3   National Computing Centre: *Privacy, computers and you* (1972). Proceedings of a "workshop on the databank society" organised jointly by the National Council for Civil Liberties and Allen and Unwin Ltd. in November 1970.
See 20.6.

20.4   Rosenberg, J.: *The death of privacy* (Random House, 1969). A general review of the situation in the USA.

20.5   Society of Conservative Lawyers: *The price of privacy* (Conservative Political Centre, 1971). See also *Computers and freedom* (1968).

20.6   Warner, M. and Stone, M.: *The data bank society* (Allen and Unwin, 1970). Describes in detail the technical and social feasibility of constructing integrated databanks to cover all aspects of the lives of whole populations.

20.7   Westin, A.: *Privacy and freedom* (Atheneum, 1967).

20.8   Younger, K. (Chairman): *Report of the Committee on Privacy* (HMSO, 1972).

Glossary

acoustic coupler: a device to enable a teleprinter or similar terminal to transmit and receive data through an ordinary telephone receiver.

algorithm: a set of rules for reaching the solution of a problem after a finite number of steps.

algorithmic method: a method using an algorithm, and so solving a problem by means of a pre-determined procedure; in contrast to *heuristic method.*

analogue computer: a computer in which numbers are represented by physical quantities such as electrical voltages or currents and determined by measuring the magnitudes of these, hence in which the arithmetic is approximate and limited by the accuracy of the representations and measurements and the operations on the quantities; in contrast to *digital computer.* Unless otherwise specified, in modern usage such computers are electronic.

Boolean algebra: a means by which algebraic notation can be used to express logical relationships and deductions; named after George Boole, 1815-64.

central processor: the component of a digital computer which co-ordinates and controls all activities and performs the actual computations; normally consists of a unit to perform arithmetic and other operations, a unit to control the sequence of operations, and an internal memory. Some large modern computers have more than one processor, between which these functions are shared.

code: representation of instructions or data in symbolic form.

communications link: a means such as a telephone line for connecting two computers, or a terminal to a computer.

computer: a machine which can accept data in a prescribed form, process it, and supply the results of the processing in a prescribed form. In modern usage, unless otherwise qualified "computer" means an electronic, digital, stored-program computer.

conversational: an adjective used to denote a mode of operation or method of working wherein a human computer user is in direct communication with the machine (e.g. by direct input of instructions or data through a teleprinter), can obtain an immediate response to his input, and himself respond with further input.

cybernetics: the study of the theory of control systems, in particular the comparisons between machines and the nervous systems of animals and humans.

data: unprocessed information in coded form.

databank: a file or set of files of data stored on a direct access device and used by a number of remote terminals.

database: a file or set of files of data designed for use in a range of applications.

data processing: the operations performed on data by automatic equipment to derive information from it.

delay line: a storage device in which information is coded into sonic signals which are recycled through some material, such as mercury or nickel; now obsolete.

digital computer: a computer in which a number is represented by one of a finite set of specified and distinct states (e.g. patterns of magnetisation or sequences of pulses), and hence in which arithmetic is exact up to the limits determined by the designers of the system and its software; in contrast to *analogue computer.*

direct-access storage device: a storage device which is directly accessible by the central processor, so forming its internal memory; information in other storage devices has to be transferred to the direct-access store before it can otherwise be used by the processor. On modern machines the time taken by the processor to access any item in the direct-access store is constant and independent of its physical location in the store.

disc: see *magnetic disc.*

display: to output a message or selected information for visual inspection.

display screen: a screen like a television screen used to display output; sometimes "display" is used as a noun in this sense.

display unit: an input-output device including a display screen and usually also a keyboard for operator responses.

edit: to arrange, delete, expand or modify information into the form required for processing.

electrostatic storage: a storage device using an electrostatic charge to represent data, e.g. the surface of a cathode ray tube.

facsimile terminal: a terminal capable of reproducing a facsimile of an original, e.g. a photo-recorded document, by conversion of a coded representation transmitted to it.

file: a set of related data items, which may or may not be organised in a special order.

flowchart: a representation in diagrammatic form of a sequence of events, in particular of steps of a computer program.

hardware: the actual physical equipment comprising a computer system; in contrast with *software.*

heuristic method: a method of seeking a solution to a problem by a succession of attempts followed by evaluation of progress made towards the final goal, i.e. a process of trial and error; in contrast to *algorithmic method.*

input: to transfer data or instructions into a computer processor or memory from outside, e.g. from a keyboard or other input device, or a mass storage device; also used as a noun to denote the information actually input.

input device: a device such as a punched card reader used to transfer information into a computer memory.

input-output device: depending on context, either a device capable of both input and output, or (especially in the plural) a device capable of input only, output only, or both.

instruction: a component part of a computer program which specifies what operation is to be performed at the stage in the processing at which it is encounted.

interactive: see *conversational.*

interface: to connect two devices, units or systems for joint operation; also used as a noun to denote the place of connection.

interface routines: routines to enable two linked systems to operate jointly; the software equivalent of a hardware device used to perform the physical interfacing.

keyboard: a device for encoding data by the depression of keys.

light pen: a flexible input device used in conjunction with a display screen; depending on the controlling software, it can, e.g., be used to input a coded representation of a line drawn on a screen, or of the position of a point on a screen, or of an instruction corresponding to a message on the screen, etc.

load: to place data or instructions into a computer memory; sometimes used interchangeably with *input,* or to mean input of a particular kind, e.g. from a mass storage device.

magnetic disc: a mass storage device in which information is stored as patterns of magnetisation on the magnetised surface of a disc.

magnetic tape: a mass storage device in which information is stored as patterns of magnetisation on magnetic tape similar to that used in domestic tape recorders.

mass storage device: an on-line, large capacity storage device, e.g. magnetic tape or disc.

memory: the internal store of a computer.

mercury delay line: see *delay line.*

microsecond: one millionth of a second.

millisecond: one thousandth of a second.

minicassette: a small reel of magnetic tape similar to those used with domestic cassette tape recorders, used for mass storage on a small scale.

nanosecond: one billionth (i.e. one thousand-millionth) of a second.

network: in general, a system which can be represented by a set of points and their interconnections; in particular, a number of computers interconnected by communications links, with their associated terminals.

number-cruncher: a term used for large computers principally designed for fast and massive computation, rather than the ability to handle large data files.

numeric control: the control of machinery, particularly machine tools, by means of numeric instructions.

off-line: disconnected, temporarily or permanently, from the control of a computer processor.

on-line: connected to and under the control of a computer processor.

optimisation: the design of a system or program to achieve maximum efficiency.

output: to transfer information from a computer processor or memory to the outside, e.g. to a printer or some other output device, or a mass storage device; also used as a noun to denote the information actually output.

package: a self-contained program or set of programs designed to be usable without modification by many users; hence, in particular, as independent as possible of a user's data format or organisation.

parameter: a quantity or item of information which can be varied so as to control or modify the actions or results of a computational procedure.

peripheral (or *peripheral device*): an on-line device connected to but not part of a computer processor or its memory, e.g. an input-output device, a mass storage device or a terminal.

plug: a flexible cord with a metal pin at each end used to connect sockets on the control board of early computers in order to control its operation; made redundant by the advent of stored-program computers.

printout: printed output produced by a computer system on a printing device.

processor: see *central processor.*

program: a set of instructions for controlling the operation of a computer to achieve a given result or solve a given problem.

program specification: a description of the purposes of a program, the results required of it, and the procedures to be adopted to achieve these.

programming: the craft/science/art of designing and writing programs.

real time processing: processing designed to take place concurrently with, and within time limitations imposed by, external events related to the purpose of the processing — e.g. analysis of progress of some ongoing activity in time to modify the later stages of that activity, as in an industrial process; a laboratory experiment; or a seat reservation system where a customer is awaiting confirmation at a ticket office.

record: a number of interrelated items of data which together comprise a particular transaction.

remote access: access to a computer system from a distant terminal by means of a communications link.

retrieval: the location of specified data in a file, and its extraction from the file, e.g. by conducting a search for the record with the required characteristics.

satellite computer: a computer interfaced to or part of a large computer system, and partly controlled by it, whose task is to perform processing subsidiary to the main work of the system.

scientific computer: a computer used for, and usually specially designed for, scientific data processing.

scientific data processing: processing in order to solve scientific problems of the kind which require massive amounts of computation but relatively little file handling; in contrast to "business" or "commercial" data processing, where the situation tends to be the reverse.

search: an examination of a file, item by item, in order to locate records which fulfil predetermined conditions. See *retrieval.*

semantics: the study of the relationship between symbols and their meanings.

simulation: the representation of a physical process or system in some other form (in particular, as mathematical relations or a computer program) in such a way that the behaviour of the original system can be deduced from the analysis or observation of the system which simulates it.

software: in general, any program or collection of programs; in particular those used as part of a particular computer system for the benefit of all users, as opposed to their individual programs.

storage capacity: the maximum amount of information which a computer system can store at one time.

storage device: a device which can be used to store information inside a computer system. See *direct access storage device, mass storage device, memory.*

store: to place information in a storage device, and/or to retain information in a storage device; the information is retained until replaced, during which time it can be retrieved when required. Also used as a noun to mean, in various contexts, *storage device, memory,* or the totality of storage facilities in the computer system concerned.

system: in general, any collection of physical and/or conceptual entities arranged or organised in some specific way; in the context of *computer system* it means the collection of hardware and the interconnections between them, usually but not necessarily together with the associated software; in the context of *computerised* or *computer-based system* other activities or operations outside the computer system proper may be included.

systems analysis: the analysis of (usually) a human-based system or physical system, normally as a preliminary to designing an equivalent or associated computer system or computer-based system.

tape: see *magnetic tape.*

teleprinter: a typewriter-like input-output device which can be connected to a computer system either directly as a means of communicating with and instructing it, or via a communications link as a simple terminal.

teleprocessing: processing through the use of terminals and communications link.

terminal: an input-output device connected to a computer system via a communications link.

transducer: a device for converting signals of one medium into a corresponding signal in another medium.

visible record computer: a small computer, usually keyboard-operated, in which a copy of all information input to the computer is automatically printed.

visual display unit: see *display unit.*

Abbreviations

ABM	Anti-ballistic Missile
AI	Artificial Intelligence
CAI	Computer Aided Instruction
CDC	Control Data Corporation
CII	Compagnie Internationale pour l'Informatique
EEC	European Economic Community
IBM	International Business Machines
ICL	International Computers Limited
IFIP	International Federation for Information Processing
MIT	Massachusetts Institute of Technology
MP	Member of Parliament
NATO	North Atlantic Treaty Organisation
NC	Numerical Control
NCC	National Computing Centre
R & D	Research and Development
UN	United Nations
VDU	Visual Display Unit